Lanchester CARS

1895-1956

Compiled by Tony Freeman, Brian Long and Chris Hood
First published in Great Britain in 1990 by Academy Books
Copyright © Academy Books
Introduction Copyright © A C L Freeman 1990
ISBN 1 873361 00 9

Printed by: Academy Print and Design
                22-23 St Mary's Butts
                Reading RG1 2LN

Published by: Academy Management Services Limited   Direct sales enquiries to: Tel: 081 521 7647
                35 Pretoria Avenue   Fax: 081 503 6655
                London E17 7DR

Acknowledgements

We have had much help in preparing this book from a variety of sources, such as the Daimler & Lanchester Owners Club, John Ridley for the loan of certain archive material, Keith Lanchester, Alex Stewart, Ralph Cartwright and the Editorial Team of *The Driving Member*, the Club's monthly magazine.

Roger Clinkscales of the photographic department at Jaguar in Coventry is thanked, also Judith Costantine of Mechanical Engineering Publications Limited.

Lanchester and the Motor Vehicle by M Platt is reproduced from the Proceedings of the Institution of Mechanical Engineers by kind permission of the Council of the Institution.

Thanks are also given to the proprietors of *The Autocar* and *Motor* for permission to use their copyright material.

CONTENTS

INTRODUCTION

By Tony Freeman

Born on 23rd October 1868, Frederick William Lanchester was the son of a London Architect who was looked upon as a "rather dull boy". By his own admission, he was no sportsman (sporting achievements being given more emphasis than intelligence at certain English schools at the time), though his abilities quickly became apparent when he began his technical education. He was soon joined by his brothers, Frank (born 22nd July 1870), and George (born 11th December 1874).

A talented student, who was awarded a scholarship to the Royal College of Science (then the School of Science and School of Mines), Frederick augmented its limited curriculum by attending night classes at the Finsbury Technical School. After working as a hack draughtsman in Birmingham, he was able to obtain an introduction to T B Barker, a manufacturer of gas engines, and was subsequently appointed Works Manager in 1884. He later indentured his brother George, who succeeded him upon his resignation in 1893.

During his time there, Frederick rented a building adjoining the workshop where he set up a small laboratory developing high-speed gas engines. By the end of 1893, he had succeeded in building a vertical single-cylinder "high-speed" engine of around 800 rpm, most gas engines then being designed for speeds of between 150 and 200 rpm.

It was decided to install the engine in a motor boat. The hull was designed by the three brothers in the backyard of the house in St Bernards Road, Olton, and the boat was driven by a stern paddle wheel. It was this work that earned the brothers the title of the "Unholy Trinity" as the work was done on Sundays when all the neighbours were either going to church or coming from it.

Frederick's attentions were beginning to turn towards motor car design. Not impressed by vehicles based on Daimler and Benz's designs, which suffered from the twin problems of noise and vibration, Lanchester, after experiencing a number of these "boneshakers" as he described them, decided to design a motor car from scratch. The drawings were done during 1894, and construction began in 1895. Work progressed slowly, both because Fred was distracted by his aeronautical research, and because of his refusal to compromise and use readily available components, which he considered unsuitable.

The result was a remarkably advanced machine capable of a maximum speed of 15 mph. Some of the features of this first car are incorporated in todays modern vehicles, such as the use of live axles, mechanically-operated inlet valves, low tension ignition and oil filtration. The engine was placed in the middle of the frame, with the single-cylinder air-cooled 5HP engine inclined 30 degrees horizontally in a forward position. Gear-changing was by pedal with the weight of the foot, and speed was regulated by a "knee swell" - an arrangement which resembled the volume control on a church organ. The carburettor, which was integral to the fuel tank, was a hand-operated cotton-wick type, variations of which were used in most Lanchester cars until 1914. The car was tested under cover of darkness sometime in February or March 1896 by Frederick and George Lanchester in defiance of the Red Flag Act, which still required a walking attendant to accompany motor vehicles on the public highways.

It soon became clear that the car was underpowered, and it was later converted to a twin-cylinder 8HP engine and fitted with the first Lanchester worm gear. A syndicate was formed to finance and develop Lanchester's patents, and a more spacious workshop was found at Ladywood Road in Birmingham. Skilled technicians were recruited and time was spent designing and equipping a workshop which would be capable of producing the Lanchester designs.

By the time that the first car was rebuilt in 1897, *The Locomotives on Highways Act* of 1896 was in force permitting speeds of up to 12 mph. In its redesigned form, the car easily made journeys of 100 miles or more, averaging 12mph with a maximum speed of 18mph. This vehicle became the demonstration car with which the brothers canvassed backers in order to commence production. At the same time, a second car (later known as the Gold Medal Phaeton), was built, though this took an inordinately long time. Again, Lanchester returned to first principles, even re-designing nuts and bolts, and evolving a primitive quality control system. The maximum speed of this second car was 30 mph, very fast by the standards of 1898.

By the time the third car was being built in 1898, a production design had been finalised, and the decision was made to form a company and go into the business of selling these motor cars. As a preliminary, the second car was driven to London and entered in the Automobile Club's Reliability Trial and Exhibition of June 1899. Of only two "Special Gold Medals" awarded by the Judges, Lanchester won one for "excellence of design".

The Lanchester reputation was not helped, however, by the performance of its two entrants in the 1000 Miles Trial organised by the Automobile Club of Great Britain and Ireland. Both Lanchester entrants were forced to withdraw with mechanical problems. By contrast, all thirteen of the Daimler entrants completed the course.

The importance of this trial at the time cannot be underestimated. The Automobile Club realised that solid achievement rather than mere spectacle was required if the motor car was ever to become widely accepted by the British public. The very title was a challenge to the motor industry and to the imagination. At that time, a car that ran twenty miles without breakdowns was regarded as something of a curiosity and the covering of a distance of one thousand miles was considered to be an impossibility.

Frederick Lanchester

"When Fred left the Farm House at Cobley Hill, Alvechurch, he came to live at 55 Hagley Road within a few minutes walk of the Experimental Works in Ladywood Road. He brought with him a terrier, born and bred in the country and therefore unaccustomed to town with its traffic. Fred used to take him out to train him to walk to heel, using a short lead.

"One afternoon in Broad Street he was stopped by a middle aged woman member of the R.S.P.C.A. who accused him of cruelty and threatening to take action against him through the Society. Fred feigned being stone deaf and, after the woman had lectured him for nearly ten minutes, he said, "I'm surprised at a woman of your age, and apparent respectability, accosting men in broad daylight". He turned on his heel and walked off, still with the dog on a short lead, leaving the woman purple with rage."

Frank Lanchester

"Frank was one of a party of our Directors who celebrated some event or other at Stratford-upon-Avon. Frank went by road on a 10HP car and on the return journey the following morning, he had a spot of bother with the ignition. It was not amenable to the usual adjustments and was ultimately traced to a fractured wire in the armature winding.

"The car would go for a few yards and then the engine petered out. It was an obscure and uncommon trouble, and was beyond Frank's scope, being untrained in mechanical and electrical matters. Standing by the car and pondering over its intricacies he was heard to remark 'I wish I had Fred's brains and he had my head'."

George Lanchester.

Although *The Autocar*, *The Auto Motor*, and the RAC's own publication gave little space to the Lanchester "Passenger Spirit Phaeton" (hardly surprising really, as *The Autocar* was then edited by Henry Sturmey - a director of the Daimler Motor Co. Limited), a fuller report appeared in *The Times* newspaper;

"A motor carriage has recently been introduced by Mr F W Lanchester of Birmingham, which has distinct improvements over other forms of vehicle of this nature... the motor is a two-cylinder oil engine working on the Otto cycle and occupies a central position well out of sight. The most salient features of novelty occur in this motor, the principal departure from previous practice existing in the means taken to avoid vibration, one of the chief objections to ordinary motor cars driven by oil engines. The result of Mr Lanchester's invention has been to produce an exceptionally easy running carriage equal in fact to one electrically driven, whilst the steering and manoeuvring qualities are quite remarkable. We are informed that the carriage made the journey to London in 6 1/2 hours running time."

It is interesting to note that the time recorded is exactly the time it would have taken if the then national speed limit of 12 mph had been the average speed! Lanchester returned to Birmingham, but never again took part in any competitive events.

In the meantime, Frank Lanchester continued in his efforts to raise capital for the formation of the company. On the 27th of October, the formation was announced in *The Motor Car Journal* of *The Lanchester Engine Company Limited*, which was finally incorporated in December, 1899. Frederick Lanchester was appointed manager of the Company and Frank Lanchester appointed Company Secretary. Frederick Lanchester was by nature a perfectionist and was not prepared to commence production until he could do so on the basis of precision-made interchangeable parts. As there was no technology which could be drawn on in 1900, most tasks had to be reduced to first principles. The directors frequently exhorted Lanchester to commence production of anything so at least they had something to sell!

Finally, the company went ahead with production,

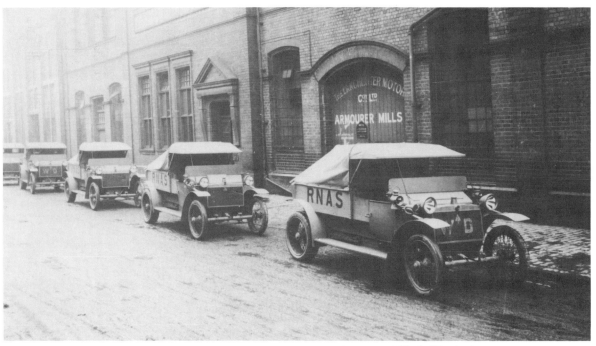

War-time Lanchesters: 1915 Lanchester 38HP lorries leaving the Armourer Mills in Birmingham.

and by August 1901 the Lanchester 10HP air-cooled production cars were on the road. The 10HP model proved to be a modest success and in 1902, a water-cooled 12HP model was introduced. Capable of up to 40mph, three to four hundred were produced and priced at £525-£550. 16HP and 18HP models followed in 1903 and a four-cylinder 20HP model, capable of 50mph, was introduced in 1904.

A 16HP air-cooled model, driven by C W Dixon and Archie Millership (the firm's chief tester and demonstrator) completed a trial of 500 miles in 1903, averaging 22mph at 19.8 miles per gallon. Ten years later, when Dixon repeated the run in the same car (this time with water cooling), the average speed rose to 24mph and fuel consumption improved to 28.3 miles per gallon.

Other achievements included the winning of the Gorcot Hill Climb in 1902 and providing a course car for the Gordon Bennett Trials. Thanks to Archie Millership's efforts in trials at Brooklands, the firm also won one of the first War Office contracts for the supply of automobiles, with orders being placed for six 10HP air-cooled tourers.

Despite making healthy profits of £8,669 in 1903, the Company was suffering from the effects of overtrading. Although business was brisk, profits were insufficient to attract new investors. An attempt to raise a further £24,000 by public subscription failed, not least because some of the directors had insufficient faith to take up any of the offered shares themselves.

Nevertheless, the Lanchester Company prospered, ironically after being placed in the hands of A H Gibson as Receiver on March 4th 1904. However, this was at some personal cost to Lanchester himself, who had to relinquish the post of General Manager and had his salary reduced from £350 per annum to £250 per annum. He also found himself a scapegoat for his directors' lack of foresight in failing to adequately finance the business. Lanchester's involvement in the management of the business diminished, though he himself regarded it as an

opportunity to pursue other interests in aerodynamics and aviation and he later became attached to the Daimler Company as Consultant and Technical Advisor. The Institute of Automobile Engineers was formed and in the first instance he took a prominent part, being elected President for the years 1910-1911.

Following the receivership production of a cheap light car was suggested but the Company did not develop the idea, preferring to take on the Birmingham selling agency for the American-built Oldsmobile, which was probably intended to assist cash-flow in this difficult period. By the 1909 season, the tiller steering which characterised Lanchester cars was replaced with the more conventional steering wheel, although the tiller remained an option for those that preferred it until 1911, when Lanchester began to adopt more conventional technology.

The operation of the early Lanchester cars was idiosyncratic, which goes some way to explaining the initial customer resistance to them. However, compared with their contemporary competitors they were better engineered, quieter and smoother in their operation. Whilst the modern arrangement for accelerator pedal, brake and clutch was coming into use elsewhere, on Lanchesters only the left foot was engaged on the throttle. The right foot was idle, the right hand was for control of the "side steering lever" (tiller), and the left hand dealt with the rest. A trigger operated the three gears, which could be pre-selected to "low" or "intermediate", which engaged indirect forward gears and reverse as well as acting as an auxiliary brake. The third selected the "high" gears and the transmission brake. Additional levers served the hand petrol pump, the two governors and the vapour regulator for the wick carburettor.

From 1895 to 1909 Frederick Lanchester had been solely responsible for every aspect of the Lanchester car's design, down to the smallest detail, with brother George acting as right-hand man in the execution of these designs. In 1910-11 the roles began to reverse with the introduction of the 25HP and 38HP cars, which

1916: Lanchester 38HP Armoured Car chassis prior to leaving the works.

conformed to more conventional motoring design practice, utilising a steering wheel rather than a tiller and a foot operated clutch for the first time. By 1913, George Lanchester realised that despite a number of technical advantages in the unorthodox Lanchester designs, there was need to design a car of conventional appearance utilising a conventional side-valve engine. In this he was influenced by the non-technical Board of Directors. The result, the Lanchester "Sporting Forty" was a moderate success with motoring journalists, but disliked by the designer.

The commencement of the First World War effectively stopped the manufacture of motor vehicles for some time. The War Office, demonstrating that astonishing lack of foresight and common sense so prevelant in government bureaucracies, ordered the Lanchester Company to produce three-inch shrapnel shells, previously found to be effective during the Boer War. It took some time for the military mind to discover that these were all but useless in trench warfare, so the War Office then ordered the production of 4.5 inch high-explosive shells! In 1916, the powers that be finally relented and placed orders for 42 Armoured Cars, one which the Armourer Mills was far better suited to fulfill. This was followed by additional orders for high-speed searchlight tenders, field kitchens and lumber wagons carrying winches for observation balloons, all based on the 38HP vehicle chassis.

Lanchester Armoured Cars were built from 1915-1917 using the 38HP chassis, engine and transmission, but with reinforced suspension. Capable of 50mph, they compared very favorably with the more common Peerless vehicles, which had a maximum speed of 16mph. Thirty-six of the Lanchesters saw service on the Russian front, the remaining six being sunk en-route to Saudi Arabia, where they were to have supplemented the Rolls-Royce vehicles.

Work on a new 40HP Lanchester began early in 1919. A prototype was tested in August and production commenced shortly afterwards. The new "Forty" had an overhead camshaft engine clearly influenced by aircraft designs. An advanced design by 1919 standards, it remained in production until 1929. The 1919 Show model was an unusual saloon, adorned with marquetry panelling to doors and roof, and was the most expensive car at the Motor Show. The fittings were so extravagant that George V was moved to remark:

"very fine Mr Lanchester, but more suited to a prostitute than a prince, don't you think?".

The Forty was a direct rival of the Rolls-Royce Silver Ghost and was actively marketed as such. Press reports were encouraging and customers included Sir John Killerman (said to have been the richest man in England), the Duke of York (later George VI), and the Maharajah of Alwar. In 1921, prices were reduced from £2,200 to £1,800 to be £50 cheaper than the Ghost. In 1925 the Forty was first fitted with four-wheel brakes, a direct response to rumours in 1924 that the next season's Ghost would be fitted with the same.

In 1921 Lanchester racing cars made their first appearance at Brooklands. T Hann's "Softly-Catch-Monkey", a modified 1911 38HP car, won it's third event and continued to race for a further four years. Lord Ridley's 1913 38HP achieved 90 mph beating the more modern racers such as Bentleys and Vauxhalls. A Lanchester Forty appeared in 1922, a standard chassis fitted with a two-seater racing body. Another Forty was prepared by George Lanchester and A W Bird for Lionel Rapson to test his company's tyres to destruction. Driven by J G Parry-Thomas, the car broke 30 records in 15 hours and achieved an average of 104 mph for the last 100 miles.

In 1922, George Lanchester designed a new Armoured Car. Based on the 40HP engine and gearbox, the chassis was of armour-plated girders allowing protection of the mechanical parts. A six-wheeled vehicle with four-wheel drive, the car had an exceptionally flexible suspension which allowed it to traverse rough terrain. Designed specifically as a fighting vehicle, the Armoured Car was accepted by the Mechanised Warfare

One of the most elaborate Lanchesters. This 1924 Lanchester 40HP was built for the Maharajah of Nawanagar. The coachwork was in Royal Blue and the interior trimmed in blue silk.

Department, equipping the 11th Hussars and the 12th Lancers with twelve cars in 1931 after trials in 1922 and 1930. The 12th Lancers used the cars in Saar in 1934 and they later saw service in the early part of the Second World War.

1923 saw the development of the 21HP six-cylinder Lanchester, described as a "pup" off the Forty. Designed for the owner-driver, this car once again directly rivalled Rolls-Royce's 20HP "Gutless Wonder". Sales of both the Forty and the 21HP did well during 1923-26, though the Forty lost ground to Rolls-Royce, who had meanwhile introduced a new model. Demand for "Gentlemen's Carriages" had begun to decline and Lanchester was particularly vulnerable to a fluctuating market, being a low volume manufacturer with only two current models, both in the luxury car class.

During the 1920s a growing middle class were providing a market for small cheap cars. These were provided by the likes of Henry Ford, William Morris and Herbert Austin. Well aware that this new market was there, George and Frank Lanchester submitted designs to the Board for four years. In *Lanchester Motor Cars*, George Lanchester said:

"This design I revised from year to year in the light of development of current practice and re-submitted it, but the Directors could not see the need for it - or would not provide the necessary financial support to launch such a venture."

A further Lanchester was developed in the 1920s, the 1928 30HP Straight-Eight, which received favourable press reports and was subsequently sold to an enviable list of distinguished customers.

The financial crisis of 1930-31 had its origins in the loss of market confidence which followed the Wall Street Crash of October 1929. This had profound repercussions on both the Daimler and Lanchester concerns. The BSA Group (which owned Daimler), had already undertaken an enforced economy drive, which included the termination of Frederick Lanchester's consultancy in 1929 and the closing of Lanchester Laboratories Limited,

a company set up with the object of developing Frederick Lanchester's inventions and carrying out research and development work.

The Lanchester Company got into serious trouble. Constrained by a range of cars which catered for the carriage trade and only the richest of owner-drivers, the Company was one of the first to be hit by the belt-tightening that followed the 1929 crash. Chronic under-capitalisation had resulted in dependence on an overdraft for day-to-day financing. This hard core of short-term finance fluctuated between £40,000 and £50,000, the equivilant of 30 cars on the road. The Company's bankers, losing their nerve, called in the overdraft at short notice. In a market where financiers and investors had lost heavily, the Company was unable to raise the necessary finance and faced closure in a matter of weeks.

The BSA Group on hearing of these difficulties, put in a successful bid to acquire the business, paying £26,000 for Lanchester, a small price for a prestige car manufacturer, even in 1931. By any standards the speed of the take-over was quite remarkable. Writing in *Dudley Docker*, R T P Davenport-Hines speculated that *"there*

Lanchester 21HP drophead coupé.

The 1930's Lanchesters were popular with coachbuilders. This 1934 example was bodied by Avon and is now on display at the National Motor Museum at Beaulieu.

Winning entrant of the 1932 RAC Rally, Colonel A H Loughborough (right) with his Daimler-built Lanchester 15/18 saloon, which featured preselect gearbox and fluid coupling. The runner-up in J Mercer's Daimler was Daimler apprentice "Lofty" England, later Chairman of Jaguar.

must be a suspicion that the extensive influence of the BSA directors was behind the bank's decision to recall the loan and trigger the Lanchester cash crisis..."

The take-over of Lanchester was fortuitously timed, since Daimler desperately needed access to the smaller car market but was conscious that the use of the Daimler name alone would compromise the firm's reputation with customers for its luxury vehicles. Take-over provided the opportunity to remove a competitor from the latter market and utilise that competitor's reputation for build quality and innovation to break into a volume market. It almost certainly prevented the premature demise of both marques and, according to director Percy Martin, rescued the Daimler Company from total collapse during the exceptionally grim period of 1931-32.

The last purely "Lanchester" design was the 15/18 which set the style for the Daimlers of the 1930s. Powered by a 2.5 litre six-cylinder engine with overhead

poppet-valves, the design suited the owner-driver admirably, featuring the Wilson preselect gearbox with fluid-flywheel transmission, which would be fitted to most Daimlers and Lanchesters until the late 1950s. Although George Lanchester worked with Lawrence Pomeroy during the early thirties, Lanchester cars were soon to be wholly designed by Daimler. Though of undoubtedly sound design, economies of scale meant that they did not really bear comparison with the earlier "strict" Lanchesters in terms of performance or refinement. There was considerable goodwill attached to the name, and both before and after the Second World War, some of the larger Daimlers were "badge-engineered" as Lanchesters, the most prominent customer being the Duke of York, later King George VI.

Lanchesters were supplied to the British Royal Family for many years. This 1938 Lanchester Landaulette was in fact a "badge-engineered" Daimler, modified at the request of George VI.

Indeed, this practice continued until the late 1940s, with a particularly fine example being built on a Daimler DE27 chassis for the Royal House of Nawanagar, who had been buying Lanchesters since the 1920s. This particular car was bought for the use of "Ranji", the famous Indian cricketer.

The Lanchester LD10 was conceived prior to the war, but production commenced in 1946. Originally with a Briggs all-steel body, it was replaced in 1951 by a coachbuilt Barker-bodied car. The Lanchester 14 was introduced in 1950, and in 1953, there was an attempt to move the Lanchester up-market with the Hooper-bodied 2.4 litre Dauphins, although this project was abandoned after testing only two prototypes. This, together with a convertible coupé of the Lanchester 14, represented several attempts to revive the Lanchester name, which failed because of a poor pricing policy, dealer resistance and a poor reception by the motoring public.

Daimler made one final attempt to resurrect the Lanchester in 1954. The two-litre Lanchester Leda had been a heavy, underpowered car, and it was decided to try and improve on the original concept. Increasing the power to 2.5 litres eventually led to the introduction of the Daimler Conquest range of cars. In addition, a second, more radical approach to the problem was taken.

In the early 1950s Panhard & Levassor produced a sleek aluminium-bodied car, the Dyna 850. Capable of over 75mph and returning approximately 40 miles per gallon, a small light car of this type would have fitted nicely into the Daimler/Lanchester range, by providing a small economic entry model. The original intention had been to assemble the Dyna 850 in England, but the Government precluded that particular option by preventing the import of ready-made body panels into the UK.

BSA, in spite of its size and resources, did not have the capacity to produce its own panels. The only solution was to design a completely new Lanchester which incorporated the features of the French car. A new fully automatic gearbox was to be provided, and the work was entrusted to *Hobbs Transmissions Limited*.

The car, code-named LM150, made its debut at the 1954 Motor Show as the Lanchester Sprite. The phase one Sprite was priced at £760 plus tax and although five chassis numbers were allocated only three cars were ever built. None of the cars were registered and all have been lost.

Development of the model continued. Three phase two prototypes were built and one was used for handling and fuel consumption tests whilst the other two cars were sent to the MIRA test track. The customary 1,000 mile tests had to be done in stages, as the cars shed parts everywhere and suffered from gearbox and torsional rigidity problems.

In contrast to the phase one Sprites, which had resembled the contemporary Singers, the phase two Sprites bore a distinct family resemblance to the Daimler Conquest, utilising a number of common panels, the front and rear windscreens and a number of suspension components. Front bench seats were fitted to make the car a full six-seater and in 1955 two Sprites were displayed at the Motor Show. Deliveries were scheduled to commence in mid-1956 at a price of £1,230 including tax. Including the original three phase one prototypes, only thirteen of the cars were ever built.

Tentative plans were made for the introduction of more powerful engines and even convertibles were envisaged at one stage. A number of cost-cutting measures were implemented; steel replaced aluminium

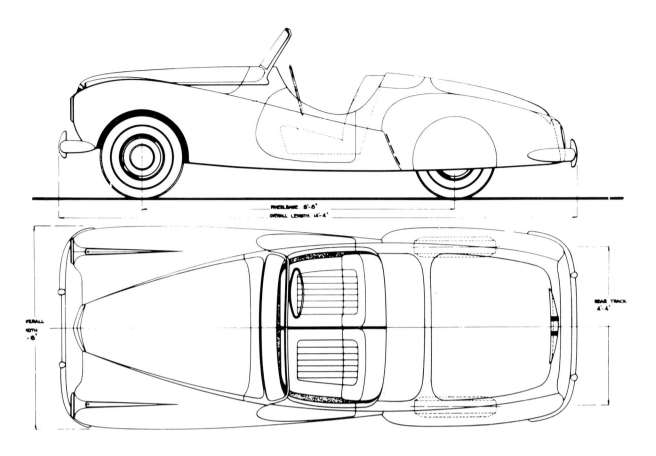

A design drawing of a Lanchester Roadster, dated April 1953. Overall length would have been 6" shorter than the Daimler version.

The new drophead coupé by Lanchester never went into production. The few cars that were made were later re-badged and sold as Daimlers.

The only surviving Lanchester phase two Sprite.

panels, plastic trim replaced leather and the chrome trim on the vehicle was virtually eliminated.

By 1956 a number of potential customers were already awaiting delivery. However, on 30 May 1956, the driving force behind the Sprite range, Sir Bernard Docker, resigned. The initial start-up and production costs of approximately £500,000 were cited as the reason for dropping the model, but it was clear that the new Board was attempting to distance itself from the former chairman's projects as quickly as possible. It continued with the production of the Conquest range, which was the best-selling model by Daimler during the 1950s. Ironically, the Lanchester Sprite would have cost 20% less to produce to roughly the same specification. In fact, the price of the Daimler was reduced to below that anticipated for the Sprite, which undoubtedly contributed to the poor financial performance of the Daimler Company in the late 1950s.

Frederick Lanchester suffered badly from the closure of Lanchester Laboratories, but continued with his experimental activities, seriously hampered in the mid-1930s by the onset of Parkinson's disease and cataracts in both eyes. He continued to publish papers on a variety of subjects until 1942, when his achievements in aeronautical and motor engineering, as well as in other fields, were finally formally recognised. Awarded the James Watt Medal in 1945 by the Institution of Mechanical Engineers, he was too ill to collect the award personally and died on 8 March 1946 at the age of 77. *The Autocar*, on reviewing thirty-six modern characteristics of the modern car, attributed at least eighteen of them directly to Lanchester's theories and designs.

George Lanchester remained with Daimler until 1936, when he moved to Alvis to take up a position as Fighting Vehicle Development Engineer through the Second World War and was retained by the Sterling Armament Company as Consulting Engineer. In 1961, he retired at the age of 87. His retirement was spent writing articles, taking an active part in motoring organisations and even a little inventing. An active patron of the Daimler & Lanchester Owners Club and the Lanchester Register, his death on 13 February 1970 was sudden and unexpected.

Frank Lanchester, though overshadowed by the engineering parts of the Unholy Trinity, was the businessman who built up the early Lanchester Company on good faith and attention to detail (he never let a letter go unanswered), which enabled him to sell the cars against stiff opposition whilst with Lanchester, and subsequently as the Sales Director of the Lanchester division of Daimler. He died on 28th March 1960.

The Company lingers on as a dormant, whose only outward manifestation is a small brass plate in the reception at Jaguar's Browns Lane factory in Coventry. Whether the name will ever be revived is a question of increasing uncertainty. A marketing exercise was carried out in the early 1980s, but the public memory had faded and associations with Lancaster bombers and Burt Lancaster made the relaunch of the marque a difficult proposition.

Lanchester's demise can be attributed to a number of factors. Some are rooted in the character of Frederick Lanchester. Dr Fred was no doubt a pioneer scientist and engineer whose influence is still apparent in modern motor vehicle design practice. He was capable of original thought, which often conflicted with so-called "truths" taken as gospel by his contemporaries. Throughout his

14

career he steadfastly refused to be influenced by others, which while resulting in some remarkable innovations, must have made him very difficult to work with.

Lord Montagu described the Lanchester as the "car of too many firsts". This probably sums up the inherent problem of the early Lanchester, where innovation and technical excellence took precedence over commercial realities. Frederick Lanchester was frequently pressed by the directors of the Lanchester Engine Company to produce something for sale. George Lanchester later commented that the brothers were extravagant in research and development and this no doubt contributed to the deterioration of relations between Frederick Lanchester and his directors.

Further evidence of Dr Fred's difficulties with commercial concerns is found in his relations with fellow engineers and the operation of Lanchester Laboratories Limited, a subsidiary of Daimler, where he was engaged as a consultant after leaving the Lanchester Company. For example, Lawrence Pomeroy, who joined Daimler as Chief Engineer in 1925 had been recruited on Fred's recommendation. In many respects Pomeroy was Lanchester's equal, something readily acknowledged by Lanchester when writing to Daimler's Percy Martin in 1919:

"If I had any shares in Vauxhall I would sell them quick. It was as near a one-man show as anything in the country!"

However, Lanchester's dealings with Pomeroy as a colleague were punctuated by frequent and resounding rows during Lanchester's tenure at Daimler!

When Frederick Lanchester's association with

George Lanchester, pictured in 1964.

Daimler finally ended in 1929 with the enforced closure of Lanchester Laboratories Limited, this was not without some acrimony, with the accusation that too much money had been spent on irrelevancies. There may have been some truth in this, since his interest in science and discovery had contributed to the delay of the first production Lanchester car some thirty years before.

However, The Lanchester Engine Company Limited (reconstructed as the Lanchester Motor Company Limited), was never a one-man band and the directors and managers had plenty of time to rectify the shortcomings of its founder after his departure in 1909. One thing was apparent throughout the entire history of Lanchester as an independent concern, and that was its lack of working capital. The appointment of A H Gibson as Receiver in 1904, revealed not a loss-making operation on the verge of liquidation, but a profitable concern which suffered from appalling cash-flow, partly because of the inability of the directors to adequately fund the business. Further evidence is given by George Lanchester, who aware of the Company's over-dependence on the carriage trade in the 1920s, advanced plans for a small cheap car, which were turned down on at least four occasions, but the direction of the business was limited by concentration on a shrinking, highly competitive market for luxury motor cars.

This was hardly helped by a lack of confidence on the part of the Company's bankers, who were financing the concern in 1931 with short-term borrowings, which allowed BSA to snap up a competitor at a bargain price. By this time Lanchester vehicles were highly advanced in their design, something which benefitted Daimler tremendously in the difficult early 1930s, since they had invested barely £70,000 in capital expenditure in the 1920s, preferring to rely on the outdated sleeve-valve engines designed by Charles Knight.

Attempts from then on to market the Lanchester as a cheap luxury saloon were hampered by Daimler's pricing policy, which made them anything but cheap! Nor were the Daimler-Lanchesters particularly good value. Many were underpowered, the post-war Lanchester Fourteen is one example and many were obviously cheapened versions of Daimler designs. This policy may have been very wide of the mark. The Lanchester reputation was built on large, well-appointed cars which were owned by Royalty and the Nobility. Daimler's mistake may have been in removing the Lanchester from this market as this provided customers for their competitors at Crewe. The attempt to produce a small, light car in 1956 was probably ill-timed, as the unprofitable Daimler Company was hardly in a position to compete on the same terms with the likes of Austin, Ford and Vauxhall.

In this volume we have assembled a collection of material which includes the recollections of Frederick and George Lanchester as well as the memorial lectures delivered by Maurice Platt at the Institute of Mechanical Engineers. Road tests and technical data are provided as well as some manufacturers brochures and material on models which never went into production.

In *Lanchester Motor Cars* in 1964, Anthony Bird and Francis Hutton-Stott said that *"one name which has not been given the attention it deserves is that of Lanchester."* This volume tells the story of the Lanchester Company through the words of its founders and those who knew them and provides performance data and road tests on many cars of the marque.

LANCHESTER MEMOIRS

By Frederick Lanchester

From about the year 1890 when I associated myself with the Gas-Engine business, entering the service of T Birkett Barker, trading under the style of T B Barker & Co., as Works Assistant and subsequently as Designer and Works Manager, I had great faith in the future of the internal combustion engine for locomotive purposes, and as early as 1891 I was giving serious attention to the problems of road traction and aerial flight. The aeroplane or flying machine was then little more than an impracticable dream, and to have put forward any suggestion in that direction would have branded one as a maniac. Apart from this it was evident that the time was not yet ripe. The aero-engine was not yet, its evolution depended upon finding some kindred commercial purpose as a nursery for its development. A movement in this direction was already on foot on the Continent, where the motor vehicle, or automobile, as an engineering problem was already attracting serious attention.

I believe the first indication of this appeared in the Paris Exhibition of 1889, which I visited; I have a hazy recollection of seeing a vehicle of German origin (probably a Daimler), rather having the appearance of two bicycles coupled side by side, a body with a motor and transmission mechanism bridging between them.

During 1890 and 1891 I spent two or three months abroad in Paris making enquiries and sizing up the position and possibilities. At that time very little had been done, I think I am right in saying that Panhard and Levassor had just produced their first car driven by a Daimler engine. I am not sure whether, when I saw this, it had actually been on the road. From this time onwards I visited Paris on more than one occasion to keep in touch with progress. On my return from one of these visits in 1892 or 1893 in order to get on with the job I built and engined a light-draught stern-wheeled river launch driven by petrol motor, and with this several demonstration runs were made on the River Thames.

This very modest beginning enabled me to interest a few friends who joined me in financing, first the construction of an experimental road vehicle, and afterwards a developmental campaign which led ultimately to the formation of the Lanchester Company.

THE SYNDICATE STAGE

The first step in advance was when in 1894 Messrs. James and Allen Whitfield introduced by Tom Birkett Barker (whose firm I had served as Works Manager for some few years), agreed to put up the money estimated by me necessary to build a trial car. This followed a demonstration on the Thames of the motor stern-wheeler to which reference has already been made. In the Syndicate as originally formed Tom Barker had a small holding. The amount of the estimate as agreed was £700, out of which I had agreed to allow a commission to Barker for the introduction, the net amount remaining being £600.

Actually the cost to me by the time the car was on the road and ready for demonstration was over £1000, not allowing anything for my own time.

Having made the contract the difference had to come out of my own pocket; I did not even mention it to my fellow members.

The first Lanchester car, as originally built in 1895-96

With the body removed, the mechanical arrangements with the engine amidships, can be clearly seen.

After some preliminary road trials in the summer of 1896, it became apparent that a certain amount of reconstruction was necessary, so I decided to fit an entirely new motor of twice the power and to substitute a direct worm drive for the chain-drive originally fitted. For this more money had to be found. The Whitfields were willing but Barker not so. In discussing the situation it transpired that Barker besides receiving a commission from me, had also taken commission from the Messrs. Whitfield. On that becoming known, Barker was dropped; on what terms he was disposed of I do not know; he faded out and the Whitfields and I carried on without him.

About this time (1897), I rented a piece of land at Ladywood Road, Birmingham, purchasing a galvanized building as it stood, and equipped this with the necessary plant with which to carry on the work and removed the scene of operations from Barker's Works at Saltley where the first construction had been carried out. I had already relinquished my post of Works Manager in favour of my younger brother George Lanchester. This change was an advantage in many ways, not the least of which was that it prevented over charges being made, which it was otherwise difficult to avoid. The cost of this establishment amounted in all to between £1300 and £1400, for which I made myself personally responsible. The number of men engaged amounted to eight in regular work with an occasional extra, the wage bill amounted to approximately £10 a week, and I still remember the names of my employees and the wage rates at which they were engaged; these were as follows:—

Hopton, all-round mechanic and tool maker	34/—
Chapman, lathe hand	30/—
Chapman (junior)	26/—
Richard Cliff, turner	32/—
Trickett, lathe and capston	20/—
Hayward, smith and handy-man	20/—
Labourer	18/—
Albert Lee, apprentice	5/—
Total:	185/—
	= £9. 5s. 0d.

Shortly after setting up this establishment my brother George gave up his post at Barker's and joined me in the capacity best described as right-hand man, otherwise second in command, at a salary of £3.0.0. a week, making the total weekly wage bill about £13 or, £650 per annum. No exact records remain, but the total outgoings including materials and work done out, amounted to between £1000 and £1200 per annum, and this expenditure continued with fair regularity from the autumn of 1897 up till the date the Company was formed in December 1899. This represents a total of about £3000.

From this expenditure we reconstructed the original vehicle including an entirely new engine, and built two further vehicles, namely the 'Gold Medal' three-seat Phaeton and a Mail Phaeton, a duplicate of the three-seater so far as concerned the chassis and motor and transmission mechanism. This work had taken us from the middle of 1897 to the end of 1899, two and a half

The second Lanchester car. Built in 1897, it was awarded the Gold Medal at the Richmond Park Trials in 1899. Frederick Lanchester is driving with George Lanchester as passenger.

17

The Richmond Trials were held at the Old Deer Park, Richmond, by the Automobile Club in June 1899. The Lanchester is seen here on Petersham Hill during the hill-climbing test.

years in all, during which time I also designed a river launch for Mr James Whitfield, the hull of which was built in Bathurst's Yard in Tewkesbury and fitted with a water-cooled balanced engine and propeller mechanism of my own design. This launch is still running on the River Severn after a lapse of forty years.

The following is a rough schedule of the expenditure as incurred:—

| SUBJECT | DISBURSED BY | |
	F W Lanchester	Messrs. Whitfield
Thames stern wheel punt including engine, etc.	£300	—
First Lanchester car.	£600	£600
Reconstruction and two later cars including experimental work and sundry alterations.	—	(say) £2800
Building and Plant at Ladywood Road.	£1400	—
Five years work without remuneration, say—	£1500	—
	£3800	£3400

The above makes it clear that I contributed more money, or value, than the financial members of the Syndicate. On the other hand the building and plant expenditure was finally taken over by the Company on its formation, in return for which I received the equivalent in fully paid shares. With due allowance for this the amended totals are:—

Lanchester £2400   Whitfields £3400

So that in view of the terms of the original agreement (half shares or 50/50), my contribution as a patentee, which included not only the original patents but all improvements related to motor vehicles, was represented by a modest £1000 vis-a-vis of the other members of the Syndicate. That is to say, representing the position in the form of an account, we have:—

Lanchester (cash)	£2400	Property of Syndicate		
Lanchester (patents)	£1000	at cost		£6800
Whitfields (cash)	£3400			
	£6800			£6800

On the formation of the Company this expenditure was represented by 16,000 fully paid £1 shares in the Company, which were fully alloted. My impression is that a block of these shares was reserved and alloted to members of the Pugh group, who joined us to form an enlarged Syndicate shortly before the actual flotation. This was termed "coming in on the ground floor".

The Company was formed in December 1899 being registered under the name of The Lanchester Engine Company Limited. The first Directors were, Charles Vernon Pugh (Chairman), John V Pugh, Hamilton Barnsley, J Taylor and James Whitfield; Messrs. Gibson and Ashford were appointed Auditors. The Solicitors to the Company were Messrs. Pinsent & Co.

18

At the first Meeting of the Directors, held on the 19th day of December 1899, Mr Frank Lanchester was appointed Secretary at a salary of £200 per annum, to start on the 1st January, 1900,-"he giving his whole time and services to the Company". At the same meeting I was appointed Manager of the Company at a salary to start at £350 per annum, at the same time a formal agreement was entered into by which the Company took over the rights to inventions previously vested in the original Syndicate. Also at cost, plant and tools, etc., from my experimental establishment at Ladywood Road.

We entered into possession of works at Montgomery Street, Small Heath, in January 1900. As General Manager my duties included incidentally those of designer and, for the time being Works Manager also. This continued for a period of twelve months, during which the building known as The Armourer Mills was completed and enclosed, and the plant of all descriptions fixed and put to work.

In January 1901, Max Lawrence was engaged as Works Manager at a salary of £3 per week. He had no previous experience in that capacity, but the salary having been fixed by the Board, the applications I received were none too numerous. When Max Lawrence took charge a great deal of production material was already well forward, and a start was being made on group assembly. The first cars were on the road in August of that year, that is, within eighteen months of the date at which the works came into our possession. Thus, in eighteen months the works had been completed, machinery and plant installed, designs carried to completion, patterns, jigs, and gauges made, and the first of the production cars were ready for the road.

The production was organised on an interchangeable system, with tolerences and gauge limits specified. Actually the components and units of the production cars turned out were strictly interchangable. This, at that date, was a remarkable performance. Nothing like it had previously been done in this country in the production

1904 Lanchester four-cylinder car.

of any machine of so great a complexity or consisting of so many parts. We were the originators of what is now known as the 'unilateral' system.

The finance from the first was insufficient, the amount subscribed in cash being £25,000. No ready-made components were available at that date, we had to make everything except the rims, the tyres, and the lamps.

From the second report, July 1902, the subscribed capital had been increased and the total liabilities, including issued capital, loan on debentures, and sundry creditors, amounted to £77,900. Of this £16,000 stood for patents and goodwill, shares to that value having been issued to the vendors (developmental syndicate). The third report, July 1903, showed a profit of £8,669, the turnover for that year being between £70,000 and £80,000.

Before the report could be prepared and issued for

1904 18HP Lanchester.

THE LANCHESTER.

MIDLAND HILL CLIMB.

"The honours of the afternoon rested with the Lanchester Cars." *The Globe, August 5, 1903,*

SIX

LANCHESTER

CARS IN THE

FIRST TWELVE

CARS UP

STRONG ON

HILLS.

LUXURIOUS IN

RUNNING.

THE

IDEAL CAR

FOR DIFFICULT

COUNTRY.

FOR STOCK STANDARD FINISH CARS.

Agents :—LONDON GOY & Co., 4, Praed Street, Paddington.
MANCHESTER R. RAMSBOTTOM, 81, Market Street.
GLASGOW NORTH BRITISH MACHINE Co., Carlton Place.

LANCHESTER ENGINE Co., Ld., Sparkbrook, BIRMINGHAM.

Although Frederick Lanchester took no interest in competition after the 1000 Miles Trial in 1899, Lanchester cars continued to enjoy repeated success in this field.

the year ended July 1904, the Company was placed in the hands of A H Gibson as Receiver. Profits were made during the receivership, and ultimately the Company was reconstituted under the name of the Lanchester Motor Company Limited, the Board being strengthened by the inclusion of A H Gibson, formerly receiver (prior to that the Company's Accountant), and by Allan Whitfield, one of the original syndicate.

On the formation of the Company some question arose as to the position in the management that I should occupy. After discussing the matter with our Chairman (C Vernon Pugh), I decided to accept the position of General Manager, under the Board. If I had pressed for it I have no doubt that I could have been appointed Managing Director but I took the lesser position by choice. I well knew that the finance would not prove sufficient for the undertaking; as Managing Director I should have had to take the responsibility or share the responsibility, for the provision of further money, which I did not consider my job; whereas as General Manager having obtained the sanction of the Board for a programme, my responsibility was limited to carrying it out. All I need add is that I found my decision coincided with the wishes of the Chairman.

So far as the internal work was concerned my authority was practically the same as though I had been in the position of Managing Director, but my presence was only called for at board meetings to present and discuss my reports and to receive instructions from time to time. A nod from the Chairman signified my release. I considered my position protected so long as I obtained the sanction of the Board for the programme and policy and for all other decisions of serious importance.

My anticipations as to the insufficiency of the subscribed capital proved to be well founded. Although the profit shown by the Balance Sheet in the year ended July 1903 was substantial, it was not sufficient under the conditions then prevailing to attract investors, and we were definitely short of money. In 1904 the Directors attempted to raise further funds and a prospectus was drawn up for that purpose, but the scheme fell through and on March 4th of the year Mr A H Gibson of the firm of Accountants, Gibson and Ashford, was appointed Receiver; the liability to creditors then amounted to about £20,000. Gibson after running the business for a couple of months found that he was making steady profits, and I do not believe that at any time during the receivership did the Company cease to make profits.

Although it often happens that when a Receiver is appointed drastic alterations take place in the management, in our case the business was carried on under the receivership without any change in the personnel, and I continued to serve the Company as before.

Early in the receivership I found myself in a little trouble owing to my having taken instructions from the Chairman in a matter that involved a small expenditure which came to the Receiver's notice. I was immediately "carpeted" by him and told in a most emphatic manner that I was to take my instructions from him and from no-one else. I took the rebuke in good part, but suggested that it would be less likely to disturb harmonious relations if he would signify his wishes to the Chairman direct. I will say that he at once appreciated my point and from that time we were the best of friends. Gibson was a fine man, but to earn his respect you had to stand up to him and be direct of speech.

A 1912 Lanchester 38HP.

On reconstruction I was retired from the management (incidentally being mulcted to the extent of 2,000 fully paid shares), and remained with the Company as Designer and Consultant, which position I held for many years, finally relinquishing my position with the Company in 1914.

The fourth report (after the reconstruction), is dated September 30th 1908. Accumulated profits amounted to £23,763 and were devoted to writing off the amount standing to patents and goodwill, which then stood as before at £16,000 plus £3,365, the total being £19,365.

Profits for the years up to the War were as follows:—

1905	£2,204	
1906	£11,996	
1907	£3,253	
1908	£6,308	
1909	£14,261	....50% (paid in the form of Pref. shares)
1910	£28,570	....50% (paid in the form of Pref. shares)
1911	£30,000	....25% on Ordinary (paid in cash)
1912	£27,056	....25% on Ordinary (paid in cash)
1913	£22,915	....25% on Ordinary (paid in cash)
1914	£ 5,031	....10% on Ordinary (paid in cash)
1915	£12,214	....20% on Ordinary (paid in cash)

From which date no accounts were made up or report issued till 1917 and no acounts were presented till after 1922. Dividends were paid out of money received in post-war settlement, the amount of which was about £180,000 based on pre-war profits.

When a reconstruction of the Company took place, and the receivership was terminated, the creditors accepted preference shares in the new Company and additional shares were taken up by the members of the Board. As I had already invested my all in the Company I was unable to subscribe further, and the Chairman demanded that I should surrender a block of shares to be distributed amongst those (mainly the directors themselves), who subscribed the new capital. My reply was simple, I said that whatever conditions were

necessary to the continuation of the business I would accept. I did, however through the kind offices of Gibson (who was now joining the Board), secure certain concessions that were clearly just.

I had been informed by the Chairman that my services as General Manager would be terminated, and that under the new regime a Managing Director would be appointed (Hamilton Barnsley), under whom I should serve as Designer and Technical Consultant, with a considerable reduction in my pay, namely £250 per annum instead of £350. The most important of the concessions which I obtained were - (1) that the clause in the agreement making over any further inventions or improvements to the Company should be abrogated; and (2) that nothing in the new agreement should be deemed to affect my right to associate myself as Consultant or otherwise with other firms. These conditions were agreed. For the period 1907 to 1914 I retained this position and all cars manufactured and sold up to that date were of my design.

In accepting the new conditions I suggested that, if in the future the Company should become so successful as to demonstrate that the sacrifice on my part was not justified, the shares surrendered, or their equivalent should be returned (I have a copy of this letter still in my possession). When, some years later, about 1912, I raised this with the Chairman he, with something of a sneer, replied, "Well, you didn't expect it did you?", to which no answer was possible.

I felt keenly at the time that scant justice was being done to me but I allowed myself to be guided largely by Mr Gibson whose manner to me was almost fatherly. He told me that undoubtedly the receivership had been a great blunder, and the Chairman and directors had to "save face" otherwise they would have been the laughing stock of Birmingham for not supporting a prosperous business. Without putting it in so many words I was led to understand that I had been made a "scapegoat". By putting in the new Managing Director and retiring me from my position they were able to keep up appearances. He, Gibson, said definitely that I was not strong enough (which meant financially strong enough), to deal with the Pugh crowd and that I should be much happier in the new position offered me, and this was certainly true.

The change in my position was in many ways to my advantage, the work I was called upon to do did not average more than a quarter of that I had been doing previously - about ten to twelve hours a day - so that, in measure of time, £250 per annum was, relatively speaking, a princely salary. I found myself at liberty to resume my work on aerodynamics and aviation which had been suspended for four years. This done and published in 1907-8, I became attached to the Daimler Company as Consultant and Technical Adviser, a far more important position than would have been open to me at the Lanchester and a trifle more remunerative. About this period the Institute of Automobile Engineers was formed and from the first I took a prominent part, contributing many papers of permanent value. I was elected President for the years 1910 - 1911.

There is no doubt that Pugh and the other Rudge-Whitworth contingent had no conception of the future of the industry in the early days when the Lanchester Company was in difficulties. That Pugh was genuinely discouraged I do know definitely, for on one occasion shortly before the receivership he offered me his holding at half a crown per one pound share, I had not the means with which to accept that offer and Pugh's reputation was so great, owing to his then recent commercial success in the cycle industry, that the mere fact of his wish to sell out, if it had become known, would have been disastrous in its effect. I think Messrs. Pugh in supporting the venture were inspired by a get-rich-quick policy and they were not prepared to face realities.

Shortly after the outbreak of War (in the autumn of 1914), I gave up my regular connection with the Lanchester Company; since that date I have been two or three times called in to advise on new designs, or to help them out with difficulties. Up to that date every car sold by the Company was of my design and the profits of the Company were all derived from the manufacture and sale of those cars, as was also the very large sum obtained from the Government in the post-war settlement. I believe from that time onward, although dividends were paid out of accumulated profits, no further profits accrued. A few years later the whole of the liquid resources of the Company had disappeared and there was an overdraft at the Bank of some £50,000.

Although the matter which led finally to my resignation (in 1914), was serious enough, I had previously had so many troubles and differences in my relations with the directors that it was certain my association with the Company could not last. Although my position as Designer was well supported for a time and, as shown elsewhere, contributed to a period of great prosperity, I experienced many petty interferences which certainly were not conductive to the welfare of the Company. The following are a few incidents which made the most impression on me in this matter.

The standard width of door in horse-drawn vehicles, such as broughams and the like, was 19 inches, and there seemed no reason to perpetuate this. I therefore designed a body with doors having a width of 28 inches Six of these were put in hand, three went ahead. The Chairman saw one of these partly finished in the works, and as the saying is "went up in smoke" . After telling me, in no uncertain terms, what he thought of it, he himself gave

orders that the others should be altered to the pre-existing standard. Actually when the public saw the wider doors it became a feature of all orders received, and the three which the Chairman had had altered had to be altered back again. All new bodies put in hand after that date had the wide doors and this feature, in the adoption of which we were the leaders, has since become almost universal.

Members of the Board took the view that all Lanchester features were a disadvantage and prevented the Company obtaining a larger share in the industry. After a board meeting I was sent for and had a meeting with Mr John Pugh who said that the Board had decided to give up the worm drive in favour of the more popular bevel, and that was to form part of the specification of the new design then under consideration, this was about 1912 or 1913. I did not directly question the decision but asked for further instructions namely whether the floor level was to be raised (a matter of 6 inches), or whether the rear body was to have a "tunnel", or whether a compromise was to be effected, the rear suspension being made stiffer, or limited by buffers, and the floor raised to a lesser extent. I learned that this had not been considered, and after that interview I heard nothing further - the proposal was dropped.

The directors also talked of abandoning the epicyclic gear but better counsels prevailed. Later however, in the 20HP Lanchester, designed by my brother after the war, under the instructions of the Managing Director, an ordinary gearbox took the place of the epicyclic. My brother designed and wished to adopt an epicyclic box giving four speed ratios instead of three (as on the earlier Lanchester cars), but this did not satisfy the Managing Director whose one idea, which he ventilated several times in my presence, was that "Lanchester features were holding the business back."

Earlier in the history of the Company we had to abandon some of the Lanchester features on perfectly good grounds. About 1906-08 we finally abandoned our system of tiller steering in favour of the wheel. A few years later in 1914, owing to the inferior quality of the motor spirit available, we gave up the surface carburettor which had served us in good stead for a period of nearly 20 years. In one case, namely, the introduction of water-cooling, I know that I was regarded as out of sympathy with the change, but that is not altogether true. In the original design I had provided for the alternative of water-cooling, the drawings of the cylinder with water jacket formed part of the original design; the patterns had been made and actually a few castings were in stock. The difficulty was one well known to any production engineer, namely, that of the introducing of a change without interfering with his programme.

A GREAT MOTOR CAR PROCESSION.

We believe we are right in saying that on Saturday last, at Birmingham, in the Chamberlain birthday

A view of a part of the line of ninety cars waiting outside the Council House, Birmingham.

celebration, the motor car was used for the first time in a great public function and to the entire exclusion of the horse-drawn vehicle. On this occasion the Lanchester Motor Co. placed seven of their landaus at the disposal of Mr. and Mrs. Chamberlain and the Highbury house party. These vehicles were used to convey the hero of the hour and his relatives and friends from one point to another in Birmingham during the celebration. The function was of rather a unique character, including a tour of practically the whole of Birmingham, with stops at a number of pre-arranged points, at which Mr. Chamberlain was presented with addresses. The seven Lanchester cars lined up outside the Council House at the head of a rank of some ninety cars, which were taking part in the procession. They started at four, made a tour of the parks, and finally landed at Highbury at 7 p.m. At 9.15 p.m. the cars were used to take the party to witness the fireworks. On Monday the festivities were continued, and it was in the torchlight procession that the Lanchester cars surpassed themselves, as they were used by Mr. Chamberlain and his friends to accompany the torchlight procession, and for one hour and twenty minutes they never exceeded two and a half miles an hour, and yet never stopped for a single second. In fact, they ran like clockwork throughout the entire proceedings, and more than justified the exclusion of the horse. The circuit made on Saturday was somewhere about twenty miles, and although the cars left the Council House half an hour late, they finished on time.

Mr. Austin Chamberlain and his *fiancée* in the second car, with Mr. Fred. Lanchester, its designer, at the helm.

Mr. Chamberlain in Mr. Hamilton Barnsley's Lanchester car, about to accept an address at one of the Birmingham parks.

THE PROCESSION OF MOTOR CARS IN BIRMINGHAM. Mr. Chamberlain about to leave the Council House in the Lanchester car to make his tour of the Birmingham Parks after the reception of the civic authorities. Mr. Chamberlain is to be seen about to enter the car, and conspicuous on the pavement are the eight Birmingham bluejackets from H.M.'s *Good Hope*, who insisted upon taking a prominent part in the proceedings. This is the first great procession in which motor cars have been exclusively used, over ninety taking part in it.

HISTORY OF THE LANCHESTER MOTOR COMPANY

By George Lanchester

In telling the story of the three Lanchester brothers, or the Unholy Trinity as they came to be known, one naturally commences with brother Fred, since his was the original brain that conceived and evolved all the early Lanchester cars.

Few people know that F W Lanchester was working on the theory of aerial flight some two years before he designed the first Lanchester car, and but for the advice of a close friend of his, the late Sir Dugold Clerk, who had been associated with him in the development of gas engines and gas engine starters, automobile engineering might have been deprived of the benefit of his genius.

Having advanced some considerable distance in the theories governing the science of aerial flight in 1893, he was forced to the conviction that flight could only be successfully accomplished if some form of prime mover could be designed and made, much lighter than any kind of motor then existing.

He consulted Dugold Clerk as to the prospect of raising money for the development of an aero-engine. Clerk's advice was terse; "If you were to seriously propose making an engine for a flying machine, you would be regarded as a crazy inventor, and your reputation as a sane engineer would be ruined."

Resulting from this advice, Fred turned towards the light road motor, a new development which had commenced some five or six years previously on the Continent, but in this country remained untouched except for a few experimental cars or cycles such as Butler's three-wheel car of 1884, and J H Knight's car, originally a three-wheeler, later modified to four-wheel, Colonel Holden's motor bicycle, and experiments in mechanical transport vehicles by Colonel Crompton, to name a few. All of which for one reason or another failed to develop beyond the experimental stage.

Being already an authority on internal combustion engines, Fred naturally sought a solution in developing the light liquid fuel engine. In 1893, he designed and built a single-cylinder engine, running on Benzoline, with hot tube ignition. This was a preliminary try out. The engine ran at 800 revolutions per minute, a phenomenally high speed at that time. It developed about 3HP, and was installed in a flat-bottomed river craft which was used on the Thames for some ten years. The hull was designed by Fred and built by the three of us in the "Back Yard" of Fred's house in St Bernard's Road, Olton, and the boat was driven by a stern paddle wheel. It was this work that earned us the title of the Unholy Trinity, as the work was done mainly on Sunday's, when all the neighbours were going to church, or coming from it. I believe this was the first British-built motor boat.

Fred's next task was the design and construction of the first Lanchester car in 1895. In this he studied, first hand, designs that were current in France and Germany,

and after absorbing all that was being done on the Continent, he came to the conclusion that they were all crude adaptions of cycles or coach engineering, and decided to start "de nove", working from first principles.

The result was a completely novel conception of what a motor car should be, and although external appearance has changed vastly, many features employed in his first car exist in accepted designs of the present day. For instance, the torsionally rigid chassis frame, live axles, mechanically-operated inlet valves, low tension magneto ignition, and air filtration to mention a few. *The Autocar* once stated that of thirty-six primary features in the modern motor car, Fred Lanchester was responsible for eighteen.

At first, the car had a single-cylinder 5HP air-cooled engine placed amidship, with a chain drive on to an epicyclic gear mounted on the rear axle.

In this state the car, a five-seater, was under-powered, and had to be assisted up quite moderate hills by pushing, so later in 1897, the 5HP engine was replaced by a two-cylinder 8HP flat-twin, air-cooled and carried at the rear on an outrig frame. Concurrently with this alteration the car was fitted with the first Lanchester worm gear.

It was at this stage that I became Fred's assistant, and shared with him the pleasures of successful experiments and trials, as well as the disappointment of failures. The disappointments were tempered by the fact that there was always something learned - whether theory or practice was at fault and how or where we had misjudged unknown factors. This sounds comic today when one can almost design a car from text book data, but it should be borne in mind that half a century ago, we had no accumulated data and many problems connected with road locomotion - the effect of bad road surface coupled with what was then high speed - were imperfectly understood and in spite of careful application of scientific principles and theory, much had to be deduced from trial and error.

Following the conversion of the first car to a two-cylinder 8HP, the second car was built, an 8HP two-seat Phaeton; this was completed and took to the road in 1898. The chassis frame and body were entirely tubular and as cars of the period were, it was a fast and silent one.

I well remember the joy of our first non-stop run of sixty-eight miles. Fred and I had been testing the car round and round a block of houses in Edgbaston, and were so fed up with just sitting, we set off, regardless of the fact that we were hatless and coatless, to Pershore, Evesham, and back to the works without stoppage or mishap and we averaged 28 miles an hour.

In the same year as this car was built, a third 8HP motor was made, identical with the car motor in every respect except that it was water-cooled. This was made for a water boat put in hand by Mr James Whitfield (one

In the formative years of the Lanchester Engine Company, advertising was George Lanchester's responsibility. This example, from 1902, shows a Lanchester 12HP with George Lanchester (left) and Archie Millership as passengers.

of Fred's financial backers). The hull was built by Bathurst of Tewkesbury to Fred's design and was equipped with a reversible propeller of a type that was unique at that time, and bore a remarkable resemblance to one of the most modern reversible propellers, exhibited at the Engineering and Marine Exhibition in 1947.

About twenty-five years ago, the boat was fitted with a modern four-cylinder in-line engine, but up to the 1939 World War, the boat was still in commission on the Avon at Evesham and retained the original propeller.

Reference to the motor journals of the period reveals little if any information about Lanchester cars, and excepting an article in an obscure journal called "Our City" published in Birmingham, and long since defunct, I cannot recall any press publicity until 1899 when the two-seat Phaeton of 1898 was entered and driven by Fred in the Richmond Show and Motor Trials, and was awarded a Gold Medal for its design and performance. The Gold Medal Phaeton as it was henceforth called, is now in the safe keeping of the Science Museum, South Kensington.

Hitherto, our cars were but little known outside the Birmingham locality, though in Birmingham they were a constant source of anxiety to the Police and annoyance to the horse loving magistrates.

We never sought publicity for the good reason that we were not yet manufacturing cars for sale.

It was at this time the opportunity arose for Frank to take a hand and join the partnership. His first contribution was in the realm of propaganda, and consisted of convincing skeptics of the great possibilities of the new form of locomotion, and spreading the gospel of motoring amongst his many friends and acquaintances,

not an easy job in those days when most people of means were horse owners or horse minded. Frank was ideally cast for this role, for he had a ready facility for making friends.

He entered into the business enthusiastically and played his part with consummate skill; it was to him more than any of us that credit is due for the formation of the Lanchester Engine Company late in 1899, when a factory was acquired for the manufacture of the 10HP air-cooled Lanchester, familiar to you all, by its frequent appearances in the Veteran Car Club events. An important innovation in the 10HP was the cantilever

This 1903 Lanchester 12HP was a water-cooled experimental car. In contrast to accepted motor engineering practise at that time, many of the early production Lanchesters were powered by air-cooled engines.

suspension, which was outstandingly ahead of its time.

The factory was the Armourer Mills in Montgomery Street, Sparkbrook, originally built as a rolling mill and tube drawing factory, and after we took it over, it remained the main production shop of a succession of Lanchester cars until 1931.

Fred had commenced the design of the 10HP in 1898, and the prototype was built in our experimental works in Ladywood Road, Birmingham.

On the formation of the Company, six 10HP cars were put in hand, these were in the nature of a trial trip. The cars were for the use of our Directors and for demonstration. The year 1900 was for all three of us, a year of intense activity. Alongside of the initial production, for which we had to rely to a considerable extent on the resources of our experimental shop; Fred had to organise and equip the new factory and, assisted by Frank and myself, get together the executive team.

The organisation of the commercial, sales and publicity devolved upon Frank, and my province lay in assisting Fred in the shop layouts, design and supervision of jigs, tools and gauges, and the many problems incidental to such work. One could not buy then, ready made gauges, and all these special kinds of equipment were made in our own tool room.

Such was our confidence in the design of the 10HP air-cooled car, that we made these jigs, tools and gauges, on the assumption that the car would remain unaltered for five or six years.

Naturally, the men we had trained in the experimental shop formed the nucleus of our works personnel, in fact every one of them became foremen, each in his own sphere, and most of them remained with us for many years.

It was characteristic of Fred that he not only insisted on a high standard of interchangeability in the engine and chassis components, but also in the bodywork, for all our coachwork was built on jigs and could be exchanged from one chassis to another. Bodies could be assembled to their chassis in fifteen or twenty minutes, and dismantled in less time. It is also a fact that some twenty years later we were able to supply replacement parts that required no fitting when assembling, and I can confidently say that at that time, no other car manufacturer in the world could make that boast.

Looking back, our policy may be criticised as extravagant, but had we failed to adopt the ideal of production accuracy, I do not believe our cars would have achieved the reputation for quality which they earned, and which has been fully justified.

In the years before and indeed after 1900, little was known of the technique of driving; motorists would discuss problems such as the best way of manoeuvring out of some awkward situation. They were painfully aware of the effect of skidding, but few understood the cause or the means of correcting a skid. This was in the days of smooth tread tyres, neither studded nor ribbed tread tyres had been invented. For the enlightenment of our customers, Fred wrote and published a treatise on the art of driving, illustrated with diagrams showing how to manoeuvre; and most useful, how to correct a skid or even make use of it in an emergency.

I cannot pass over this period of progress, both technical and commercial, without references to Archie Millership. He was a wizard driver and an artist at skidding.

The Lanchester London Showrooms at 95, New Bond Street, circa 1910. The car in the foreground is a 28HP six-cylinder landaulette.

He came to us in 1897 as an amateur motorist owning in succession a variety of foreign cars. A Bollee tricycle, an 8HP Mors dog-cart, a Petit Duc Mors two-seater, and lastly a Locomobile steamer, most of which in turn he used to bring to us for maintenance adjustments or overhaul. In our works he received a brief mechanical training and when the Company was formed he doubled as the tester of parts and sales demonstrator, and later joined Frank's staff in the latter capacity.

Ultimately, when Frank opened our London depot, Archie became Sales Manager for the Midlands area.

During the years 1900 to 1905, the 10HP design stood the test of time fairly well; no major changes were found necessary, but contrary to our optimistic anticipation, some modifications had to be made. Sales demand caused us to increase the width of the tonneau to make the rear seat more commodious for three passengers. Side doors were added to the front seats; these were pivoted to the front wings and opened and closed when the leather covered dashboard was raised or lowered, but the major modification was in adopting water-cooling in place of air-cooling. Air-cooling admittedly had a very narrow margin of cooling efficiency, and the centrifugal cooling fans were liable to get noisy. This was to be tolerated whilst water-cooling gave trouble, as it did in the early days, but as design and construction of radiators and water pumps improved, we decided to adopt water-cooling with a gain of two or three horsepower - that was the amount of power lost driving the fans, hence the 10HP became a 12HP.

Whilst the production of 10 and 12HP cars was active, Fred had kept himself informed on Continental development where the growing trend was towards multi-cylindered engines. From the commencement our transmission system showed itself superior to that of Continental cars, the vast majority of which had adopted chain-drive from a cross shaft integral with, or adjacent to, the gearbox on to sprockets on the rear wheels mounted on a "dead" axle.

But, with the advent of multi-cylinder in-line engines, it became evident that the days of our flat-twin balanced engine were numbered, and Fred designed two new types to supersede the 10 and 12. In 1905, the 20HP four-cylinder was introduced, and the 28HP six-cylinder followed in 1906. In their original form, both of these cars were tiller steered, but the 28HP proved too heavy for tiller steering, and in 1907 wheel steering was adopted. Due to the growing popularity of the closed body, tiller steering became impossible, and the wheel was adopted on both models.

A feature of both these cars was that they had pre-selector gear change on all gears, whereas the 10 and 12 only had pre-selector between the low and second gears.

The 20 and 28HP cars had other features many years in advance of their time. The chassis frames were constructed of box tube member 6" x 2" pressed from $^{1}/_{16}$" steel plate, which closely resembled some chassis frame members that came into vogue about 1937, and are used in some present day cars. As originally produced, they had cast aluminium rear axle casings. The worm gear box, axle casing and suspension brackets being integral. The engines had overhead valves; a characteristic feature of all subsequent Lanchester cars. High pressure lubrication was employed for the first time - today, it is practically universal. However, I will refrain from wearying you with these mechanical details.

When Frank migrated to London, he quickly made his influence felt in automobile circles, both as a member of the Council of the Society of Motor Manufacturers and Traders (of which he was later President), and as a member of the RAC. His flair for making friendships brought both social and commercial distinction to the Company, enhancing the already high reputation accorded to Fred's original and scientific achievement on the engineering side.

In 1909, Fred became consultant to the Daimler Company, and made a substantial contribution to the successful development of the Silent Knight engine (the Daimler sleeve-valve). This, and his work on aeronautical science, occupied much of his time, and the responsibility of Lanchester designs was transferred to my shoulders.

It was in the next phase of development that I first collaborated with Fred; on equal terms in 1911, we designed the 25HP four-cylinder and 38HP six-cylinder cars.

In general layout these followed the lines of the 20 and 28HP, but considerations of designing to facilitate production took a more prominent place than in the past. Chassis frame design was simplified by adopting pressed steel channels, a comparatively new art. It is difficult to believe that up to this time and even after the First World War, some cars were still made with chassis frames of ash with steel flitch plates and gussets. We still retained many of the previous Lanchester features, giving particular adherence to torsional rigidity of the chassis.

From this time onwards, Fred became too fully occupied with consulting work on aircraft engineering and advisory committees on aeronautics to devote time to our Company, and I became responsible for all the

The bonnetless body styling of the early Lanchesters distinguished them from their contemporaries. In fact, this unorthodox styling often concealed performance and build quality which was very advanced. This 38HP Lanchester is powered by a six-cylinder engine and dates from 1911.

A 38HP Lanchester six-cylinder touring car, pictured here at the 1913 Swedish Winter Trial. Lanchesters were awarded two bronze plaques in this event.

Lanchester technical activities, and found immense satisfaction in maintaining the high traditions which he had established.

The First World War put paid to our production of motor vehicles for a time. Frank made it his duty to maintain close touch with the Services, and after much persistence on his part, the Ministries discovered that our greatest contribution to the War effort lay in our own trade - motor vehicles and aero-engines - and not in ruining our plant by producing shells! Frank's efforts were rewarded with contracts for Armoured Cars and RAF 1a aero-engines; subsequently, we made many other instruments of war, including paravanes (mine sweepers), and kite balloon mobile winches. Latterly, I was largely responsible for co-ordinating the design of the 200HP Sunbeam Arab engine. On conclusion of the war, we had to re-establish our private car trade, and in 1918 when the Armistice was signed, we were caught without a line on paper towards a new design, and our pre-war designs were obsolescent.

Realising that during the war, aero-engine design had exercised an educational influence on the motoring public, I set to work on the design of a 40HP six-cylinder car, adopting many very advanced features borrowed from aero-engine practice, combined with a number of well established Lanchester features incorporated in an orthodox tout ensemble. The prototype made its first run in August 1919, and was in production from 1920 until 1929.

In 1922, I designed an experimental armoured car of a new type, based on the 40HP engine and gearbox; the chassis frame was constructed of deep armour plate girders giving a substantial measure of protection to the vital organs. It was a six-wheeled vehicle, four-wheel drive car with exceptional flexibility of suspension for traversing rough terrain. This was the first example of an armoured car specially designed as a fighting vehicle, and not merely adapted from a private car or commercial vehicle chassis.

By 1924 the car had got through its teething troubles and was accepted by the Mechanised Warfare Department, and the first two Cavalry Regiments to be mechanised, the 11th Hussars and the 12th Lancers, were equipped with these Armoured Cars.

My next design, in 1923, was the 21HP six-cylinder Lanchester, which has been aptly described as a pup off the 40. The main departure from Lanchester practice being the adoption of sliding gears in place of the more expensive and heavier epicyclic gear. This change was dictated by economic policy.

Most followers of motoring history are familiar with Lanchester designs from this date. In 1924 the 21 became the 23HP, the cylinder diameter being increased from from 3" to 3.1", and shortly after that date came the 30 Straight-Eight, a natural evolution from the 23, having identical major components and dimensions, excepting for the increased length due to the two extra cylinders. The Straight-Eight had an outstanding performance, its speed was little short of present day practice, and for acceleration it was quite equal to modern American standards.

Based on the 40HP chassis of 1922, this Lanchester Armoured Car had six gears and saw service in many theatres of war.

This 1921 "Brooklands" Lanchester 40HP was named "Winni Praps Praps" an onomatopoeic name derived from the exhaust note on over-run.

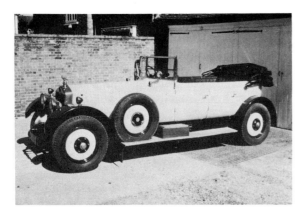

A more conventional Lanchester 40HP.

Lanchester 21HP Drophead Coupé.

Archie Millership, the Lanchester Company's Chief Demonstrator and Tester, shown here at the wheel of a Lanchester 21HP.

In January 1931, the Lanchester Motor Company was acquired by the noted BSA Company, Birmingham, to enable them to increase the capacity of the Daimler Company by the production of smaller models. The Lanchester brothers, Frank (then Managing Director), and myself (then Chief Engineer & Designer), transferred our services to the BSA Group to assist our old company under the new regime in Coventry, which brought out the Lanchester 18HP car, the 10HP, shortly followed by the 14HP, which were warmly welcomed by the public (carrying as they did, the quality and prestige of the noted larger Lanchester cars), and which we sold successfully in considerable quantities up to the War in 1939.

(Extracted from a paper read by Mr George H Lanchester, before the Veteran Car Club, on 21st February 1948.)

29

LANCHESTER AND THE MOTOR VEHICLE

By M Platt, M.Eng., C.Eng., F I Mech E.

Introduction

The major achievements of Dr Frederick William Lanchester in the field of automobile engineering were compressed into a period of about 20 years which ended during the First World War. His brilliant intellectual gifts, creative genius and remarkable engineering talent are reflected in the striking originality of the early Lanchester cars and in the many outstanding papers he wrote for the engineering institutions and journals. these two sources, the cars and the papers, have been the main foundation for this attempt to present a centenary tribute to the man and his work. I am also deeply in indebted to the many friends and acquaintances who have furnished me with valuable information. References and other information are given in Appendix 1.

A very great man is something of an enigma, even to his contemporaries , and an interval of about 60 years now seperates us from the period when his most creative work was done. As L P Hartley once observed, " The past is a foreign country. They do things differently there ."

In his character and career Lanchester seems to me to bridge two eras; he was a nineteenth century individualist with the vision, resourcefulness and inventiveness engineering genius of a Stephenson or a Maudslay, but also he had a great talent for the more scientific and analytical approach which is typical of twentieth century engineering. It is significant that he became impatient with academic teaching during his four years as a student at the Normal School of Science and School of Mines (now the Royal College of Science), and felt such an intense need for practical instruction that he concurrently attended evening classes in workshop practice and toolmaking in Finsbury, entirely on his own initiative.

Like many other pioneers of modern car development, Lanchester started his engineering career with industrial gas engines. The Thomas Hawkesley Lecture which he gave to the institution in 1937 provides a most interesting account of this experience. He records his indebtedness, as a student, to Professor Goodeve who was responsible for arousing his interest in gas engines and he says that the professor's personality " *.....counted for much in the days before academic engineering had become a branch of mathematics"*. He also remarks that at that time an engine in which only one stroke in four was a working stroke was regarded with mistrust by the steam engine men.

In 1889 Lanchester joined Mr T B Barker who made the Forward gas engine in a small Birmingham factory. He was given the job of assistant works manager after striking out a clause in the contract of employment which would have assigned to the company any improvements that he might make. It was a gesture typical of his bold self confidence. Quite soon the company was paying him royalties on a pendulum governor and by 1890 he had invented a simple and ingenious device which removed all the danger and difficulties in starting gas engines. This lead to an association and a firm friendship with Dugold

Henry Jones Lanchester with his wife Octavia, seated in an early Lanchester, and their nephew George in the back seat.

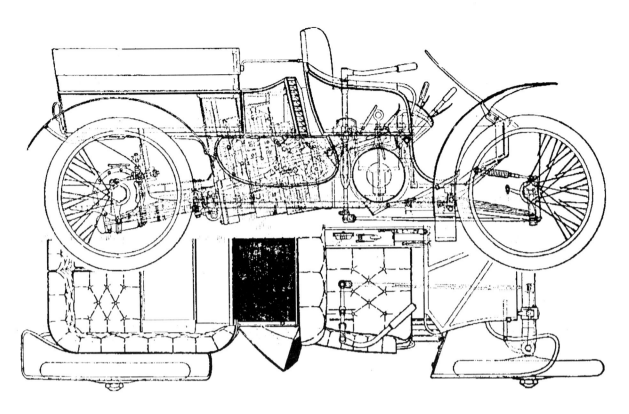

Drawings of the first 10HP Lanchester production model of 1900 – 1901.

Clerk. In 1892 he made a visit to the United States on gas engine business. Soon after his return he left the company to work on his own, financed in part by friends and also by the handsome return that he had obtained from the assignment of his starter patent to the Crossley Brothers. His brother George, who had just completed an apprenticeship with the Forward Company, succeeded him as works manager. Lanchester's involvement with petrol engines and motor cars had begun.

THE LANCHESTER CARS

The first experimental Lanchester car was started in 1895 and tried the road shortly before the repeal of the Red Flag Act in the following year. Lanchester had previously studied contemporary Continental vehicles but decided to design a car, from first principles, that would avoid the defects of the Horseless Carriages of the day. He was particularly critical of the noise, vibration, discomfort and unsafe handling that were the common faults of those machines and saw no point in copying them. His first car had an air-cooled engine but was soon rebuilt with a more powerful two-cylinder engine. During 1897 a similar engine was used in a much more advanced machine with an epicyclic transmission, worm-driven rear axle and two-seater phaeton coachwork. It secured a gold medal at the Richmond Trials of 1899 and is preserved at the Science Museum in South Kensington. Here the superior design can be compared with the crudities of contemporary vehicles. Later in 1899 the Lanchester Engine Company was formed and serious preparations for car manufacture started.

The First Production Model

The best account of the first production car that I have come across was written by Lanchester himself for one of the series of manuals which the Company issued to the owners of Lanchester cars. The Montagu Museun library possesses a number of these publications and the one to which I refer was probably written in 1902. Particularly interesting are the author's comments on what he calls "System of Manufacture". He explains that this is devised to ensure interchangability, *"each part being viewed and passed to limit gauges. The gauge limits are in some cases finer than are employed in the gun trade, which has hitherto been considered the acme of high-class workmanship. The organisation and completion of our manufacturing and gauging system delayed the commercial debut of the Lanchester car for some twelve months longer than would have been the case had we been building cars in the ordinary way. The result, however, has proved of the greatest possible benefit to the users of our cars ..... We have not sold any experimental machines to the public at all, and in all important respects the machines we are manufacturing are interchangably the same as the first batch we turned out."*

Those of us who have had some experience of the commercial pressures applied to design engineers and production engineers when a planned production date is in jeopardy can appreciate the grim determination with which Lanchester must have pursued his chosen course for that extra twelve months (following five years of experimental development) in the face of acute shortages of manpower, manufacturing equipment and capital.

He devised a unilateral system of fits and tolerances, and then had to make all the gauging equipment. Whitworth threads were too course, so a Lanchester fine thread series was designs which anticipated B.S.F. standards by about 10 years. Every single part of the car had to be designed and made, including a carburettor and a complete ignition system. Men had to be trained in new workshop skills and methods.

The first 10HP production car has been described many times. It had a two-cylinder engine amidships, a three-speed epicyclic gearbox and a worm-driven back axle; I propose to clarify the design objectives by quoting further passages from Lanchester's descriptive manual. He starts by making it clear that the frame is very stiff in torsion and that *"....the whole of the elasticity required to go over the roughest roads, or to surmount any chance obstacle...is supplied by our patented suspension"*. In actual fact the fabricated side members of the frame were girders in which an aluminium web plate (18 inches deep) was riveted to a steel angle along the top and a steel channel along the bottom. The main cross-member was a 12 inches steel tube which also formed the petrol tank. Cantilever leaf springs were used at the front and back (supplemented by radius links above and below), and the end of each was slidably connected to the axle. This parallel motion was aligned to the front with the longitudinal drag link of the steering gear. Spring rates were exceptionally low, corresponding to a frequency of about 80 cycles per minute at normal load.

A unique feature of the steering gear was that the side lever, or tiller, by which it was controlled was reversed so that it pointed forwards from the pivot located under the driver's right shoulder. Lanchester seems to have been the only man of his time to realise that the dangerous instability of the bath-chair type of tiller could be corrected by this reversal. Writing in his manual nearly 70 years ago he remarks *"...to oversteer is almost a physical impossibility owing to the centrifugal force acting on the driver's body tending always to moderate his steering effort."* I would guess that is the first recorded use of the term "oversteer". Later on he discovered that stability could be improved by adding a few pounds of lead to the operating end of the tiller; a provision that also made the steering virtually irreversible if a front wheel struck an obstacle at high speeds. The steering was in fact so safe and sensitive that the Company retained it after all competitors had adopted steering wheels, but to the public a tiller was a tiller, whichever way it pointed, and was regarded as out of date.

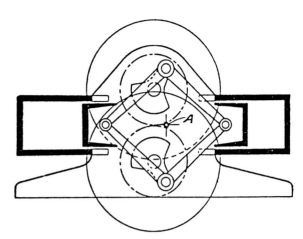

Diagram showing principles of the two-cylinder Lanchester engine

A Fully Balanced Engine

Lanchester's fully balanced two-cylinder horizontally opposed engine, requiring two geared crankshafts, two flywheels and six connecting rods, was a complicated and expensive piece of mechanism and demanded high standards of accuracy in manufacture. The geometry was such that the pistons and connecting rods always formed a symmetrical figure about a point which moved to and fro along the centre line. In this end Lanchester used the principle of contra-rotating flywheels and balance weights that he had first applied to his experimental single-cylinder engine of 1895, as described later in this lecture. The reciprocating masses were balanced by the horizontal components of the rotating masses and in the vertical plane these (latter) masses balanced one another. There were no rocking couples.

Another most important virtue of this design was the absence of fluctuating torque reactions of the kind which caused such unpleasant low-speed vibrations in all other cars at a time when flexible engine mountings were unknown. In a classic paper on engine balance, Lanchester explains that the early engine designers used heavy flywheels to minimize torque and speed fluctuations in the crankshaft and drive, but paid little or no attention to what he called 'recoil'. He also explains

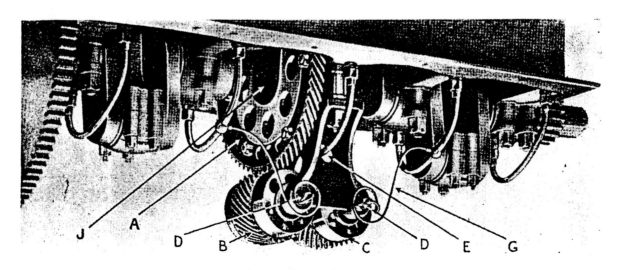

Lanchester harmonic balancer as applied to the 23/60HP Vauxhall. (A, gear wheel; B and C weighted drums; D, Spindles; E, mounting brackets; G, oil feed pipes; J, crankshaft web).

that with his contra-rotating flywheels *'the storage of energy does not involve a change of angular momentum of the system'* and points out that because of the absence of recoil, the unequal firing intervals of his two-cylinder engine were of no consequence.

This seems a convenient point at which to mention the application of contra-rotating weights to four-cylinder in-line engines which Lanchester patented in 1911 and which were used by Vauxhall for their 23/60 model in the early 1920s. Driven by gearing at twice crankshaft speed, the weights provided a fluctuating vertical resultant force to balance the secondaries set up by the reciprocating masses- and were self-balancing in the horizontal plane. The geared drive was not subjected to any fluctuations of torque. It was a most ingenious device but added length, complication and cost to an engine so that it never became widely used. Soft engine mountings eventually provided a simpler and less expensive solution.

Returning to 1900, the reason for using six connecting rods in a four-link system was simply to avoid any twisting couples at the gudgeon pins. There is an interesting survival of this mechanism in the so-called rhombic drive used in the Stirling engine as developed experimentally by Philips of Eindhoven and by General Motors Corporation. Apart from balance, one of the advantages gained from this arrangement is an absence of side loads on the piston-rod seals.

Alternative Cooling Systems

As initially produced, in 10HP form, the engine was air-cooled by fans, shrouds and cylinder fins. In 1902 a water-cooled version (designated 12HP) became available as an additional model, circulation being maintained by a gear pump driven from the crankshaft. To quote the manual: *'The choice of cooling system rests with the purchaser'*, and to aid him in his decision some notes on the pros and cons of each system were appended. However, the writer was in no doubt as to the merits of his wick carburettor, which was conveniently located in the fuel tank and was *'. . .not liable to accidental disturbance or stoppage of any fine apertures'*. Neither was it disturbed by a little water in the fuel. This carburettor was, in fact, retained up to (and into) the First World War and finished a long career in Lanchester Armoured Cars. The story goes that during the Archangel expedition they were the only vehicles to run without complaint on Russian petrol.

Epicyclic Transmission

One of Lanchester's early inventions, which has since been used in innumerable automatic transmissions, was to employ a compounded sequence of simple epicyclic trains. In a patent specification dating from 1900 he explains the limitations of a simple train with regard to choice of gear ratio and the mechanical problems involved in the alternative use of double planet gears of differing diameters. He describes his invention as *'...providing an epicyclic gear of suitable ratio and in compounding with it one or more sets of epicyclic gear trains, the outer element of the first and of each succeeding train being capable of receiving motion from the intermediate element of its adjacent train, thereby enabling the first to be rendered operative alone or through one or more of its compounded gears'*. This is illustrated in the specification by a three-train

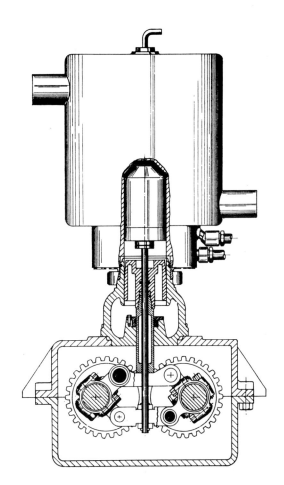

Diagrammatic view of the Stirling engine, showing the rhombic connecting-rod linkage (courtesy General Motors Corporation).

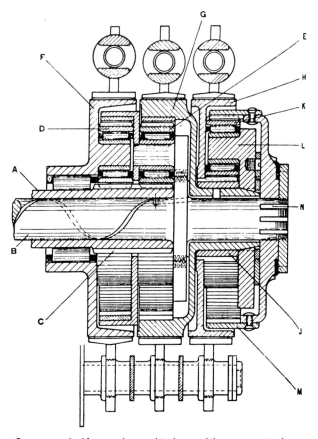

Compounded forward speed trains and the reverse train of the Lanchester epicyclic transmission of 1900.

33

Lanchester chassis layout, as introduced in 1905, illustrated by a later 38HP model (courtesy 'Motor')

transmission giving two alternative forward speed ratios (one simple and one compounded) and a reverse speed. As applied to the first two-cylinder Lanchester production car this transmission, was driven from the lower of the two crankshafts and was supplemented by a direct-drive cone clutch, so providing three forward speeds in total. Although rearranged and improved in many ways the compounded epicyclic three-speed transmission survived, in principle, in all the later Lanchester cars. Lanchester was pleased with the convenience of assembly which resulted from using simple epicyclic trains and once quoted a visitor to the works as having remarked that *'everything went together like piling muffins and was secured by one final nut'*.

It is a remarkable tribute to Lanchester's inventive talent that he should have hit upon the idea of compounding simple trains within four years of building his first experimental motor car and his flair for mechanical detail is apparent from his use of long, caged rollers for the planetary gear bearings and his invention of splines to secure the rotating elements to their shafts in place of keys. He had used plain planet bearings for the two-speed transmission of his second experimental car in 1897, but trouble with seizure convinced him that roller bearings were essential. To complete the picture one must also remember that he had to find ways of making rollers and of cutting splines. To solve the former problem he invented centreless grinding.

Lanchester's compounding principle was used in a similar way in the Wilson epicyclic transmission of the nineteen-twenties with an additional train to provide a fourth forward speed. I am indebted to Mr T C Stott for calling my attention to the following tribute paid by Major W G Wilson (1), when he wrote:

'The earliest effort was a most far-sighted and ingenious compound epicyclic patented by Dr F W Lanchester. . . It is of special interest as it was the first, and one of the only designs of true compound epicyclic gears, and consisted of using the annulus of the first speed as the planet carrier of the second, and vice versa. It had a great many most important features, noticeably the low speeds of revolution of the planets. It demonstrated clearly that the running gear of the true
epicyclic possessed such a degree of silence and length of life as to make it a practicable proposition.'

The Worm-Driven Rear Axle

While it is not surprising that Lanchester should have abandoned a chain drive in favour of a live rear axle in rebuilding his first experimental car in 1897, the choice of a worm drive is less easy to understand. Bevel gears at that time were certainly noisy and an underslung worm made possible a low drive line as well as being quiet. On the other hand worm drives were generally regarded as an inefficient means for transmitting power.

Another important decision was to use the Hindley type of hollow worm in place of the better-known parallel worm. Lanchester devised a design procedure and then invented and built an ingenious hobbing machine with which to make his worm and worm wheel which he patented in 1897. It remained in production use until 1907 and is exhibited at the Birmingham City Museum.

Just to complete this brief account of the first production car, I must mention that the service brake was derived from the inner member of the cone clutch and so took effect through the final drive. It was applied by retracting the cone beyond the normal position of disengagement whereupon it made contact with a fixed backing ring of cast iron. Drivers were permitted to use the indirect forward gears (or even reverse) as auxiliary means for slowing the car. There is a Lanchester patent for a disc brake, dating from 1902, which closely resembles modern practice but for the fact that it was designed for mechanical operation, but apparently this was never used.

Four and Six-Cylinder Models

The business vicissitudes of the Lanchester Company are beyond the scope of this short paper but the crisis of 1904 must be mentioned in the context of car development. The unhappy combination of a towering engineering genius (of a forceful disposition) with a group of Birmingham businessmen used to small ventures and a quick return on investments: resulted in capital resources that were totally inadequate in relation to what we would nowadays call the product programme. It proved impossible to raise additional funds and a Receiver had to be appointed. For a year or so Lanchester worked for the Receiver instead of the Board but in spite of all these difficulties and anxieties he designed and developed an entirely new four-cylinder car. Known as the 'Twenty', it was every bit as original and outstanding as the two-cylinder model. Production started when the Company was reconstructed in 1905 and at that time Lanchester ceased to be General Manager and accepted the position of Consulting Engineer and Designer.

The most unusual feature of the remarkable Twenty was the location of the vertical engine between the driver and the front-seat passenger. Lanchester preferred to say that the engine was in a *normal* position and that '. . .the improvement consists of carrying the leg spaces of the front seats forward on each side of the engine (which) thus appears to be swallowed up'. He gained the advantage of wide side entrance doors without pushing the engine over the front axle and his layout has, of course, become widely used for forward-control trucks and coaches. The later six-cylinder car illustrated shows the conception very clearly.

I well remember, as a boy in London 60 years ago, the distinction and grace of these Lanchester cars in contrast with the general run of bonneted vehicles. Examining a survivor recently, one was reminded of the success with which Lanchester designed an engine narrow enough to permit him to place it between the seats, although admittedly he had to adopt the unusually wide track dimension of 58 inches. He enclosed the engine with a well-fitted detachable housing with inner and outer skins of sheet aluminium between which slag wool was packed to suppress heat and noise. The bore and stroke were respectively 4 inches and 3 inches (a most unusual 'over-square' ratio for those days) and these proportions, in association with the underslung worm drive, enabled the engine to be placed low in the car. The sloping drive line will also be noticed in the illustration.

I am indebted to another 'Descriptive Manual' from th Montagu collection for the cross-sectional engine view shown. This actually represents a later 4 inches x 4 inches version of the engine, but the unusual disposition of the valves and combustion chamber is identical with that of the Twenty, and was no doubt derived from Lanchester's gas engine experience. Flat blades returned the valves to their seatings, in place of coil springs. The lubrication system was remarkably advanced for the times, oil from

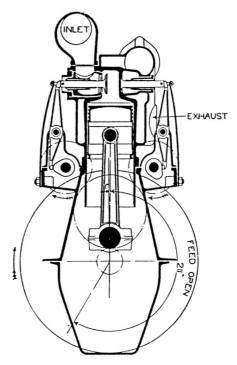

Cross-section of the 4" x 4" Lanchester engine, showing valve gear (courtesy Montagu Motor Museum)

the pump being delivered to the main bearings and thence, through diagonal drillings, to the crankpins and on through the connecting rods to the gudgeon pins. It is interesting to note that an additional piston ring, for oil control, was fitted near to the open end of each piston. Water circulation was by thermo-siphon, the radiator being favourably located relative to the engine.

Transmission and Brakes

Engine and transmission were built as a unit (which was not common in 1905), and light alloys were used for the crankcase, sump and transmission case. The three-speed epicyclic transmission was located immediately behind the engine, followed by a direct-drive multi-disc clutch and a multi-disc *brake;* the flywheel was carried at the front end of the crankshaft. Oil was circulated, by pump, through the transmission, clutch and brake discs. Internal expanding 'reserve brakes' (so named in the manual), were provided on the back axle.

In wishing to retain the same kind of three-speed epicyclic transmission as in the earlier car, Lanchester was confronted with the problem of where to place a direct-drive clutch. His solution is shown here, the epicyclic trains A being placed between the crankshaft and the multi-disc clutch B1 and B2; the latter was operated by plungers C and a ball thrust D. More important, however, was a new control system in which a lever was used for selection and a pedal for the actual change from one gear to another. A powerful spring applied a brake to the preselected epicyclic train. With various improvements this transmission was used in many later models.

Cantilever road springs (with radius rods) and a torsionally stiff frame were retained in the new Twenty. A steering wheel was offered as an option and thereafter the reversed tiller system suffered a decline in popularity until it was finally abandoned two years later. A typically original touch was to attach the steering wheel by a hinge

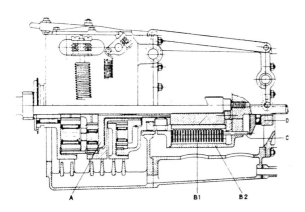

Epicyclic transmission and multi-disc clutch of the 20HP Lanchester of 1905.

so that it could be flipped up, out of the way, when entering or leaving the driver's seat.

The Twenty was followed closely by the introduction of a sister car, with a six-cylinder engine having the same bore and stroke, which the makers called their 28HP model. Both cars were obtainable with alternative wheelbase dimensions which were 113 inches and 125 inches for the four-cylinder version and 125 inches and 137 inches for the 'six'. Cars of this size could accommodate large and heavy coachwork and the excessive weight and poor design of the 'custom' bodies of the period caused Lanchester to engineer and build bodies on his own account. As early as 1905 he was building touring and landaulette bodies with aluminium panelling and interchangeable structural parts. Like so much of his work they were notable for sound design and an attractive appearance.

The Torsional Vibration Damper

However, in the manner which has so often been repeated in the motor industry, more power was eventually demanded and by 1910 the 28HP six-cylinder engine was extensively re-designed; the stroke was increased from 3 inches to 4 inches, leaving the bore unchanged at 4 inches. One of the recognized merits of the short-stroke engine had been the torsional rigidity of the crankshaft, but as a result of studying similar problems for the Daimler Co., (to which he had been appointed Engineering Consultant in 1909,) Lanchester had invented and patented a torsional vibration damper which had saved the day for an almost unsaleable Daimler six-cylinder model. Vibration periods at certain speeds had, in fact, caused trouble in six-cylinder engines ever since they were first made popular (by Napier) in 1905 but the causes were not understood. In one of his papers Lanchester delightfully refers to these engine resonance periods as *'Changes of voice at certain speeds'*. His patent specification describes *'. . . a rotary frictional or fluid frictional dashpot by which any tendency to irregular rotary motion is destroyed and so synchronous vibration is prevented'*. Various possible designs are illustrated, including an assembly of discs driving a heavy drum, and the device is shown mounted at one end of a six-throw crankshaft which carries a flywheel at the other end.

Soon after the over-stroking of the six-cylinder Lanchester engine the same change was made in the four-cylinder model which thereafter became known as the 'Twenty-Five'. The Lanchester Company continued to build these two cars (25HP and 38HP) up to the start of the First World War, with various improvements, of which the most notable was the introduction of an elaborate Delco lighting and starting set in 1913. At one stage some technical writers believed that the Lanchester chassis layout would be widely copied, instead of which it remained the odd man out in a generation of bonneted motor cars. Shortly before the war the Company announced a new 40HP model with a conventional relationship between engine and body locations and a suitably imposing bonnet. The decision to abandon the unconventional layout, used since 1905, had become commercially inevitable. Timing and fashion have always had a great influence upon the products of the motor industry and in American phrase 'you can't buck the trend'. Even by 1905 the bonneted car had become too well established to be challenged by the Lanchester chassis layout.

Lanchester's Engineer Brother

During the years covered by this review, the part played by Mr George Lanchester had become increasingly important. He joined his brother's Company in 1897 and gave him invaluable support both in matters of design and in problems of manufacture. His responsibilities increased when Fred Lanchester accepted the role of Consultant in 1905 and this was officially recognized when George Lanchester was appointed Chief Engineer to the Company in 1909. The unique personality and exceptional engineering abilities of George Lanchester enabled him to make an indispensable contribution to the achievements of his distinguished brother and the strong bond of affection that existed between them survived circumstances that might have caused a rift between two lesser men. It is not possible to make more than a brief tribute to 'Mr George' on this occasion.

The finest record of Lanchester's engineering philosophy, reasoning and early experience in the motor car field is contained in the eight papers that he presented at meetings of the Institution of Automobile Engineers between 1906 and 1916, one of which was his Address as President of that body. He wrote them in a vigorous and direct manner and often hit upon a word or phrase that makes a statement vivid and memorable. Fortunately, the early I.A.E. Proceedings also record the discussions which followed Lanchester's papers which give ample evidence of the high opinion in which his work was held by many famous contemporaries and which also confirm his formidable skill in debate.

The extent to which these papers and meetings influenced contemporary designers is very difficult to assess. Although expressed with great clarity and precision, some of Lanchester's analytical studies must have been above the heads of many engineers who by training, experience, or commercial necessity were more inclined to seek to improve the reliability and behaviour of their machines by empirical methods than by making a fresh start from first principles. On the other hand, Lanchester's views on the the engineering problems of the day must surely have been an inspiration to the younger generation of automobile engineers which was growing up with the new and expanding motor industry.

All the pre-1917 papers are listed in Appendix 2 together with the titles of ten additional papers, written after 1921, which in many cases provide a valuable record of much earlier events but are otherwise beyond the scope of this lecture.

Horsepower, Bore and Stroke

Lanchester's very first I.A.E. paper, written in 1906, was his famous study of horsepower in relation to bore, stroke, weight and other variable factors in engine design, brilliantly developed from an initial statement of the dimensional theory, and can be read today with undiminished admiration and respect. He showed that piston area was an inadequate basis for the comparison of power ratings when the geometrical proportions of engines differed seriously and proposed the alternative basis of (bore)n(stroke)2-n with the suggestion that the index should be either 1·5 or 1·6. He also wrote: '... *any rating rule whatever is an addition to the conditions of the problem of automobile design and as such must*

36

A fine example in the pre-1914 Lanchester tradition, a 20 hp 4-cylinder 5 seat Rotund Phaeton.

result in distortion; all that we can secure by intelligent forethought is that the rating rule is of such a nature that the distortion is of a beneficial kind, or at least that it shall be harmless.'

In the discussion that followed the author's work was highly praised by Professor Callendar and Dr Hele-Shaw —but what was the outcome? The R.A.C. horsepower formula (based solely on the square of the bore) became the legal basis for car taxation, the I.A.E. set up a committee on horsepower rating which tested one hundred engines and came to somewhat different conclusions and the Lanchester engine continued to be the only important example of 'over-square' proportions. Even when the government asked the British motor industry to recommend a new basis for car taxation, soon after World War II, the choice fell on engine displacement and I recall no reference to Lanchester's earlier findings. They were eventually and admirably "re-discovered" by Mr F R B King writing in 1963.

A special meeting of the I.A.E. took place in 1910 to discuss the report of the horsepower formula committee. Lanchester was President at the time, but in order to attack the report more freely he handed over the chair to Mr L A Legros and then personally opened the discussion. He criticized the corrections to the R.A.C. formula that the committee had so tardily recommended, reminded the audience that he had resigned from the committee at an early stage and condemned the policy of basing conclusions upon testing a large number of engines in uncompromising terms. He said: *'I have repeatedly expressed the opinion that little is to be gained from the statistical examination of quantities of motors. The present Report is a monument to the futility of any such course, though the fact remains (not without its humorous side), that the committee themselves appear to be blindly unconscious of that fact.'*

Some Design Problems of 1908
Returning to a chronological sequence, Lanchester gave an I.A.E. paper in 1908 in which he explained many of the design problems of the day and how they had been solved in his own cars. At that time (he writes) there were about 1,000 Lanchesters with tiller steering on the road and he remarks that by reversing the tiller *' . . . the dynamic forces, previously a source of danger, became immediately a source of security'*. He remarks that his

cantilever springs and radius arms provide a parallel motion for controlling axle movements and a low side location for the chassis is mentioned as another advantage. He gives excellent advice on the design of laminated springs and recommends that the thickness of the leaves should be graduated. The Lanchester suspension was much 'softer' than was usual in those days and discusses the problems of a compromise between roll and riding comfort.

Tractive effort was the subject of Lanchester's next I.A.E. paper (in 1909), in which he describes a pendulum accelerometer which he had designed and made in 1889 and also a later and improved model made in 1904. He explains how the instrument had been used in trains and in cars for measuring acceleration, braking and even lateral acceleration on curves. He remarks prophetically that the maximum acceleration that people can stand is probably much higher than is generally supposed and points out that it is the rate of change of acceleration that is important to passenger comfort, especially in braking.

The Presidential Address
Lanchester's Presidential Address was delivered to the I.A.E. on 12th October 1910 in the Lecture Hall of the Institution of Mechanical Engineers. Unexpectedly, he starts with the statement that *'...engineering, as a profession or calling, is of essentially military origin. The greatest efforts of man in the earlier stages of his civilization were largely devoted to thwarting and destroying his fellows'*, and he goes on to forecast the military importance of aircraft.

The Address, in the main, is a far-ranging review of contemporary practice in automobile design with a digression concerned with road building which he called *'the question of the hour'*, and one of special importance to the future of commercial vehicles. He comments upon public preferences as having a conservative influence upon automobile design and forsees a period in which improvements would occur through the process of development rather than by fundamental changes. He considers that the sliding-change gearbox is a weak element and that epicyclics provide a superior but more costly solution. The most promising alternatives, he believes, were *'hydraulic or electrical transmissions that can go directly from the motor to the road wheels'* - remember that he was speaking 58 years ago.

Efficiency of Worm Gears
Worm gears were the subject of Lanchester's next I.A.E. paper, given in 1913, and in reading it one is reminded of the difficulties that he experienced in proving that a worm drive could be highly efficient and, further, that his version of the Hindley hollow worm was more efficient than the parallel worm. In 1912, the Lanchester worm drive was used in the back axles of Lanchester, Daimler, Siddeley-Deasy and Sheffield-Simplex cars and was made under licence by the Warner Gear Co. of Indiana. However, the parallel worm was an increasingly strong commercial competitor.

Why Lanchester became so completely convinced of the superiority of the Hindley type of worm I have not been able to discover, but he seemed certain that the shape and relative motion of the contacting surfaces were conducive to self-sustaining film lubrication to a degree not possible with the parallel worm. Consequently the Hindley-Lanchester worm drive had a higher efficiency

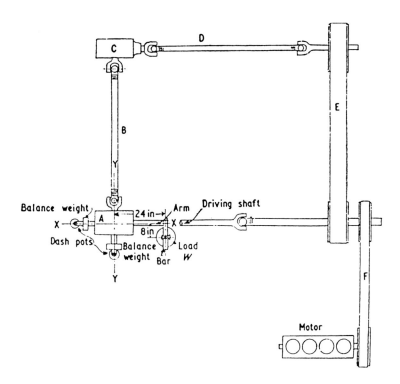

Efficiency test rig for worm gears as illustrated in Lanchester's I.A.E. paper of 1912.

and a greater load capacity for a given centre distance. These claims were not, of course, accepted by his competitors—notably F J Bostock, the talented designer of Messrs. David Brown.

An interesting outcome of the contest was typical of Lanchester's determination and inventive genius. He realized that the established method of trying to determine the efficiency of a drive by measuring input and output torques was insufficiently accurate, so he designed and built a test :- in which the *losses* were measured.

Dr Hele-Shaw called it one of the most ingenious testing machines he had ever seen. Referring to the diagram, the worm gear under test A is free to turn on ball bearings about the axes XX and YY and is driven from any suitable motor by a belt F. In the bevel box C the gear ratio is a little greater numerically than that of the worm gear, so that the return belt E tries to turn the input driving shaft somewhat faster than is desired by the first belt F. The torque load applied to the worm and wheel under test A can be adjusted by varying the tension of the return belt E and the motor has only to overcome the power losses in the circuit.

Output torque is first measured by adding a weight W to an arm on the XX axis at a radius of 24 inches. This weight is then moved along an arm set at right angles to the first arm until, at a distance S, the input torque is also counterbalanced. It is easy to show that the mechanical efficiency is simply $24/RS$, where R is the speed ratio of the worm and worm wheel under test. Lanchester called in observers from the National Physical Laboratory to confirm that his machine was sensitive to differences of 0.2 per cent in mechanical efficiency and later on the machine was transferred from the Daimler Works to the Laboratory.

Engine Balancing

Lanchester's important paper on engine balancing was presented early in 1914. He began by describing how he used and patented two contra-rotating flywheels for the single-cylinder engine of his first experimental car in 1895, and how this idea was developed for his two-cylinder engine of 1896. The rest of the paper provides a wonderfully clear account of many aspects of balance and vibration in multi-cylinder engines with graphical illustrations and a minimum of mathematical abstractions. He also deals with the vibrations that result from lack of rigidity such as resonances in a crankshaft or a crankcase. I believe he was the first to use the descriptive phrase 'looking-glass symmetry'. The whole work occupies 64 pages of the Proceedings and (to quote L. H. Pomeroy) it is a model of lucidity. I remember very well my excitement in reading it for the first time in the early nineteen twenties.

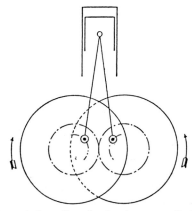

Contra-rotation of two flywheels, as used in Lanchester's single-cylinder engine of 1895.

It was my interest in engine balancing that gave me my one opportunity to talk with Lanchester in person. This occurred after a meeting of the I.A.E., in London, in March 1924, at which H S Rowell (4) presented a highly theoretical paper on the subject. In those days the graduates made a practice of selecting a representative to take part in senior discussions. The choice fell to me on that memorable evening and my remarks were somewhat cynical and disrespectful. Lanchester liked my comments sufficiently to seek me out after the meeting. As a young engineer I was surprised and delighted by the friendly interest of this great man who was my senior by 30 years. I mention this as one of very many instances of the encouragement that he enjoyed giving to younger people.

The Importance of Weight Saving

Another I.A.E. paper in the first series, which was concerned with cooling, was read in 1915. It is partly historical and provides an interesting account of the early development of radiators for motor cars. However, one of the most interesting passages is concerned not with cooling *per se,* but with the more general subject of scientific weight saving. Lanchester once said that this problem alone was important enough to justify the formation of an Institution of Automobile Engineers and the comment that he made in 1915 is quoted below to complete my sketchy selection from his published work:

'It is not so generally recognized and accepted as should be the case that almost every problem concerning the automobile, whether it be on land, air or water, is essentially a problem of scientific weight saving. Under the stress of competition it is inevitable that as the years go by a given achievement must be performed with less and less weight of material, and, if the weight saving is not effected by scientific means, it has to be effected by weight cutting pure and simple with its attendant disadvantages and its invitation to disaster. It is for this reason that every problem, however old it may be in other branches of engineering, however completely it may have been worked out in its other applications, takes on a new colour and a new interest immediately its application to automobile practice is in question.'

In Conclusion

By limiting this lecture to a period of 20 years I have been able to focus attention upon Lanchester's major achievements in automobile engineering but with the penalty of describing only a part of his long and many-sided career. I also feel very conscious of other defects and omissions. His magnificent work in aerodynamics is the subject of the companion lecture but in the context of these pages it may be remarked that he began to write his two great books on aerial flight immediately after completing, in 1905, his most creative and intensive years as an automobile engineer.

After the First World War, Lanchester must have felt a disenchantment with the motor industry. Although he continued to act as a Consultant for Daimler, Lanchester and other companies, he was no longer in the main stream of motor car development. The papers which he continued to write on automobile subjects often reflect an anxiety to remind a heedless generation of the many things that he had originated in the early years and which had later become accepted practice. A list of these innovations is given in Appendix 3 and makes impressive

reading. The scope of his inventive talent is also illustrated by the fact that he took out no fewer than 405 British patents between 1888 and 1939. I am greatly indebted to Mr John L Walls for compiling from Patent Office records the list given in Appendix 4.

In his later years Lanchester's restless intelligence and inventive talent found interests in many other fields, of which the mechanical reproduction of sound was one of the most important. He published a remarkable monograph on the musical scale and also wrote books on relativity and the theory of dimensions.

Recognition of Lanchester's genius took many forms. The earliest were the LL.D. conferred by Birmingham University in 1919, his election as a Fellow of the Royal Society in 1922 (sponsored by Sir Dugold Clerk), and the creation of an Institution Medal, by the I.A.E., which carried his name and has since been combined with the Crompton Medal. He was awarded the Ewing Medal of the Institution of Civil Engineers in 1941 and (the one he most prized) the Institution's James Watt International Medal in 1945 when his distinguished friend and admirer, Sir Harry Ricardo, was in the Presidential chair. Amongst some of the high awards to Lanchester that can be seen in a collection at the University of Southampton, it was touching to come upon a bronze medal which he received in 1887 from the Normal School of Science in South Kensington, for proficiency in 'practical plane and solid geometry'. Southampton University has its Lanchester House, there is a Lanchester Hall at Cranfield, the Institution has a Lanchester Room and by the happy inspiration of Dr A J Richmond the new College of Technology at Coventry was named after him.

The words which follow were written by Sir Harry Ricardo for the Royal Society after Lanchester's death in March, 1946:

'In Lanchester we had one of the very rare combinations of a great scientist, a great engineer, a mathematician, an inventor and a true artist in mechanical design. He was a man, too, of remarkable versatility, for his interests and his inventions ranged over a very wide field, including musical instruments (for he was a great lover of music) and all forms of sound reproduction. He was also a poet and a philosopher. His mind worked so quickly and so directly through the intermediate stages of thought that few could keep pace with it and this rendered him rather intolerant of their slower processes; for this reason he was a difficult man to help and nearly all the work he achieved, he achieved single-handed.

'Whatever problem he tackled, he tackled always from first principles, for he refused to be influenced by fashion or by the beliefs of others, unless they accorded with his own experience or common sense.'

Acknowledgements

The author acknowledges with gratitude the help he has received from a large number of people including the longsuffering staff of the Institution library. He would like to mention particularly the exchange of views which he has enjoyed with Mr George Lanchester, Sir Harry Ricardo, Sir Roy Fedden, Mr Maurice Olley, Dr H E Merritt, Dr A J Richmond, Dr John Weaving, Mr Ray Bent, Mr Frank Shaw, Mr B B Overy, Mr Francis Hutton-Stott, Mr Anthony Bird, Mr St John Nixon, Mr H A Dean, Mr T C F Stott, Mr Philip L Sumner, Mr N W Bertenshaw and Professor A V Stephens.

APPENDIX 1

REFERENCES
(1) WILSON, W G 'Epicyclic gearing', *Proc. Instn Auto. Engrs,* Vol. XXVI, 217, 1931-32.
(2) KING, F R B 'Engine specific output', *Automobile Engineer,* April 1963.
(3) The Rating of Petrol Engines: discussion on the report of the horsepower formula committee, *Proc. Instn Auto. Engrs,* Vol. V, 168, 1910-11.
(4) ROWELL, H S 'Balancing of automobile engines', *Proc. Instn Auto. Engrs, Vol.* XVIII, 502, 1923-24.

THE MOTOR VEHICLE

BIBLIOGRAPHY

GEORGE H LANCHESTER. 'F. W. Lanchester, LL.D., F.R.S.: His Life and Work', *Proc. Newcomen Society,* March 1957.
F W LANCHESTER. 'Concise History of my Career', typescript filed with other collected papers, Museum of Science and Industry, Birmingham.
SIR HARRY RICARDO. 'Frederick William Lanchester, 1868— 1946', *Proc. Royal Society,* 1948.
SIR CLAUDE GIBB, SIR MELVILLE JONES and MR PERCY KIDNER. Citations on the presentation of the James Watt International Medal, *Proc. Instn mech. Engrs,* 1945.
P W KINGSFORD. 'F. W. Lanchester: a life of an engineer', Edward Marshall (Publishers) Ltd., 1960. Also 'The Great Masters' series, *Chartered Mechanical Engineer,* January 1966.
ANTHONY BIRD and FRANCIS HUTTON-STOTT. 'Lanchester Motor Cars', 1965 (Cassell).
KENT KARSLAKE and LAURENCE POMEROY. 'From Veteran to Vintage', 1956 (Temple Press Ltd).
L T C ROLT. 'Horseless Carriages', 1950 (Constable).
H O DUNCAN. 'The World on Wheels', 1928.
F W LANCHESTER *et al.* 'Lanchester Descriptive Manuals' issued to owners by the Lanchester Company, Montagu Motor Museum Library.
F W LANCHESTER. 'The Lanchesters', *Autocar,* Vol. LXXIX, Pt 2, 269, 1937.
ST JOHN C NIXON. 'Lives of the Great Designers', Motor, Vol. 81, 266, 1942.
Collected Papers, University of Southampton, Lanchester College of Technology and Museum of Science and Industry, Birmingham.
Early Lanchester Cars exhibited by the Science Museum, South Kensington, the Montagu Motor Museum, Beaulieu, the Museum of Science and Industry, Birmingham and the Motor Museum, Brighton.

APPENDIX 2

SOME PAPERS BY DR F W LANCHESTER READ BEFORE ENGINEERING INSITUTIONS

Institution of Automobile Engineers—First Series

1906 The Horse Power of the Petrol Motor in its Relation to Bore, Stroke and Weight; 1, 155.
1908 Some Problems Peculiar to the Design of the Automobile; 2, 187.
1909 Tractive Effort and Acceleration of Automobile Vehicles on Land, Air and Water; 4, 123.
1910 Factors which have contributed to the Advance of Automobile Engineering and which control the Development of the Self-propelled Vehicle (Presidential Address); 5, 8.
1913 Worm Gear; 7, 215.
1914 Engine Balancing; 8, 195.
1915 Cylinder Cooling of Internal Combustion Engines; 10, 59.
1916 Worm Gear and Worm Gear Mounting; 11, 79.

Institution of Automobile Engineers—Second Series

1922 An Investigation of Certain Aspects of the Two-stroke Engine for Automobile Vehicles (with R. H. Pearsall); 16, Pt 2, 3.
1928 India-rubber as an Auxiliary to Suspension; 22, 575.
1928 Automobile Steering Gear—Problems and Mechanism; 22, 726.
1929 Coil Ignition; 23, 214.
1935 Motor Car Suspension and Independent Springing; 30, 668.
1937 Units and Dimensions—the treatment of problems in engineering by dimensional analysis; 31, 45.
1938 Independent Springing (with G H Lanchester); 32, 412.
1924 Epicyclic Gears (with G H Lanchester); 107, 605.
1937 The Gas Engine and After (Thomas Hawksley Lecture); 136, 195.
1939 The Energy Balance Sheet of the Internal Combustion Engine; 141, 289.

APPENDIX 3

SOME AUTOMOBILE DESIGN FEATURES WHICH ORIGINATED WITH LANCHESTER

Balance of reciprocating parts by contra-rotating masses 1895
Elimination of torque reaction by contra-rotating flywheels 1895
Torsionally stiff chassis frame 1895
Reversed-tiller steering control 1895
Worm-driven rear axle 1897
Compounding of simple epicyclic trains 1900
Splined shafts in place of keys 1900
Preselection of gears 1900
Cantilever springs with radius rods 1900
Forced, high-pressure engine lubrication 1905
Torsional vibration damper 1910
Harmonic balancer for 4-cylinder engines 1911

APPENDIX 4

LANCHESTER PATENTS AND PATENT APPLICATIONS 1888-1939

1888
16 432   Ruled parallel equidistant lines etc.

1889
19 868   Gas motor engines.
   650   Book marker, joint application with H. V. Lanchester.
   651   Book marker and leaf holder, with H. V.
  5840   Book markers, with H. V.
  7382   Advertising, with H. V.
 12 502   Governing gas oil engines

1890
  5479   Gas motor engines.
 14 381   Governing gas etc. engines.
 15 936   Gas engines.
 19 513   Gas and hydro-carbon engines.
 19 775   Starting gas motor engines.
 19 846   Igniting starting gear for gas engines.

1891
  1689   Igniters for starting gas engines.
  2504   Wheeled appliance for the feet.
  4222   Gas engines.
  4230   Gas engine starting arrangements.
  5072   Gas engines.
  5226   Valve-oiler arrangements of gas bags for gas engines.
  5956   Wheels of cycles.
  6094   Gas engines.
 11 861   Gas engine starting arrangements.

14 945	Engine governors.
16 147	Gas engines.
16 384	Bicycles etc.
18 711	Power hammers, stamps rock drills etc.
18 880	Holders for cutting tools.
21 406	Gas engines.
21 592	Changing word or figure apparatus.

1892

4210	Gas engines.
4314	Gas and petroleum engines.
5602	Starting gas engines.
8099	Gas engine starters.
9703	Velocipede pedals.
13 943	Starting gear for petroleum etc. engines.
14 153	Friction gearing and friction clutches.
18 691	Friction gear etc.
18 696	Velocipede pedals axle.
18 795	Gas etc. engines.
21 978	Driving gear and bearings for bicycles.
23 696	Gas and like engines.

1893

3538	Aerial machines.
11 407	Gas and oil engines.
14 175	Gas, petrol, etc. engines.
19 759	Dynamo machines.
20 152	Gas etc. engines.

1894

19 112	Gas and oil motor engines.
22 500	Gas engines.
22 946	Gas etc. engines.

1895

6849	Gas etc. engines.
15 045	Gas etc. engines.
16 548	Photography in colours.
18 908	Gas and oil motor engines.
21 954	Vehicle driving mechanism.
24 333	Brake mechanism.

1896

5748	Power propelled vehicles.
5814	Gas and oil motors.
7603	Gas and oil motors.
12 744	Aerial machines.
13 960	Fluid pressure engines.
14 917	Gear for transmitting power.
16 721	Gas etc. engines.
18 829	Gas and oil motor engines.
21 697	Power propelled vehicles.
21 772	Power propelled vehicles.
22 935	Gas and oil motor engines.
22 94I	Keys for shafting.
24 805	Gas and oil motor engines.
27 590	Clutch mechanism.
29 543	Gear for transmitting power.

1897

3608	Aerial machines.
10 043	Power propelled road vehicles.
10 044	Shaft couplings.
13 433	Gear cutting.
18 197	Gas and oil motor engines.
20 758	Transmitting power.
28 418	Blowing and exhausting apparatus.
30 592	Gas engine starting gear.

1898

| 5613 | Screw propellers. |
| 6272 | Gear for transmitting power. |

8076	Power propelled engines.
10 836	Fluid pressure engines.
11 738	Gas and oil motor engines.
13 915	Tyres.
18 959	Gas generators.
26 702	Screw propellers and shafts.

1899

281	Gas etc. engines.
12 243	Power propelled vehicles.
12 244	Engines.
12 245	Gas and oil motors.
13 467	Power propelled vehicles.
15 081	Governors.
15 082	Motors.
23 342	Packing piston rods etc.
24 395	Speed gearing.
20 570	Gas and oil engines.
23 341	Oil engines.

1900

4806	Transmitting power.
4951	Power propelled vehicles.
7909	Power propelled vehicles.
9983	Power propelled vehicles.
13 965	Oil motor engines.
15 037	Oil motor engines.
16 454	Change speed gearing.
17 001	Gear cutting.
17 503	Gas etc. engines.
18 060	Power transmission gear.

1901

1793	Self propelled vehicles.
2844	Oil motor engines.
5904	Tyres.
7739	Motor road vehicles.
10 500	Internal combustion engines.
13 491	Roller bearings.
17 032	Thrust bearings.
18 354	Internal combustion engines.
19 070	Motor vehicles.
19 159	Fluid pressure engines.
23 227	Roofing for marquees etc.
23 412	Lifting jacks.
23 500	Motor vehicles.
23 501	Self propelled vehicles.
23 617	Self propelled vehicles.
23 692	Shaft couplings.
23 698	Bearings.
25 121	Self propelled vehicles.

1902

10 375	Engine governors.
10 376	Gas etc. engines.
12 235	Level gauges for tanks.
12 715	Gas etc. engines.
12 847	Gas etc. engines.
12 848	Power propelled vehicles.
13 445	Screw propellers.
13 446	Internal combustion engines.
13 760	Gas·etc. engines.
14 792	Propelling boats.
22 768	Gas etc. engines.
23 774	Turbine motors.
26 407	Power propelled vehicles.
26 408	Turbine motors.
28 743	Road vehicles.

1903

| 477 | Oil engines. |
| 478 | Gas etc. engines. |

566	Gas etc. engines.
659	Spindle bearings.
1618	Gas etc. engines.
1619	Internal combustion engines.
1722	Road vehicles.
2422	Road vehicles.
2625	Gas etc. engines.
5105	Power propelled vehicles.
5106	Screw propellers.
7064	Electrical connections.
9850	Gas etc. engines.
9937	Internal combustion engines.
11 159	Electric generators.
12 599	Motor car fittings.
13 258	Pocket card filing device.
17 259	Road vehicles.
18 189	Internal combustion engines.
18 632	Road vehicles.
18 959	Vehicle wheels.
20 968	Gas etc. engines.
21 228	Internal combustion engines.
21 239	Gas etc. engines.
22 234	Gas etc. engines.
22 936	Power propelled vehicles.
26 514	Screw propellers.

1904

878	Motors driving gear.
879	Reciprocating engines.
1342	Internal combustion engine starters.
1343	Power propelled vehicles.
10 929	Gas etc. engines.
12 979	Road vehicles.
16 864	Road vehicles.
16 805	Motor vehicles.
16 959	Vehicle etc. clutch brake and change gear mechanism.
17 047	Internal combustion engines.
17 048	Oil valves.
17 049	Vehicle drive gear.
17 061	Engine ignition.
23 839	Transmission gear.
24 725	Driving gear.
24 726	Fluid pressure engines.

1905

186	Lubricating engines.
187	Brakes.
7949	Road vehicles.
7950	Motor cars.
17 935	Aerodromes.
20 149	Sound reproducing equipment.

1906

1340	Concrete building construction.
28 236	Vehicle speed mechanism.
27 136	Motorist etc. goggles.

1907

5835	Vehicle speed mechanism.
9413	Aerodromes.
9413	A Propeller driving mechanism.
9451	Internal combustion engines ignition.
9452	Internal combustion engines valve gear.
10 140	Clutch gear.
16 427	Grinding rollers and bushes.
22 431	Projectiles etc.

1908

3605	Sound-recording discs.
17 273	Motor vehicle steering mechanism.
18 065	Imparting stability to aerodrome in flight.

1909

2145	Internal combustion engine valve gear.
2428	Internal combustion engines.
2958	Piston packings.
8849	Steering flying machines etc.
9259	Motor vehicles.
10 421	Speed reduction gearing.
10 422	Flying machines.
18 303	Aeronautical machines .
18 384	Flying machines.
19 108	Internal combustion engines.
23 106	Internal combustion engines.
22 325	Integrating mechanism.
23 820	Internal combustion engine valves.
23 867	Propelling vehicles.
24 113	Lubrication of vehicles.

1910

5676	Aerial machines.
13 310	Resilient or spring arrangements.
14 700	Internal combustion engine valve gear.
15 851	Automobile brake.
18 630	Vehicle wheels.
18 631	Propelling vehicles.
19 452	Internal combustion engines.
21 139	Reciprocating engines.
26 123	Piano-players.
26 399	Electric lamps.

1911

3682	High speed engines.
8162	Power transmission change speed gear.
8745	Power transmission change speed gear.
9714	Screw propellers.
9873	Aeronautical machine engines.
15 810	Worm gearing.
15 811	Cutting worm gear.
16 815	Window cleaning apparatus.
21 322	Vehicle electrical installation.
21 360	Aeronautical machines.
21 361	Automobile vehicle bonnets.
22 502	Aeronautical machines.
22 545	Change speed gear box.
23 271	Flying machines.
26 038	Balancing reciprocating engines.
26 777	Balancing reciprocating engines.
28 538	Change speed gear.

1912

3604	Internal combustion engine reversing gear.
7041	Rectifying gear wheels.
9557	Piano players.
9610	Piano players.
11 016	Pianofortes.
12 418	Starting internal combustion engines.
12 522	Pianofortes.
13 284	Starting internal combustion engines.
21 993	Pianofortes.
25 074	Measuring efficiency of transmission.
27 375	Starting internal combustion engines.
28 817	Automobile wheels.

1913

179	Musical instruments.
346	Musical instruments pneumatic players.
7162	Projectiles.
9427	Change speed gear.
13 634	Internal combustion engines.
13 635	Piano players.
15 423	Lighting etc. vehicles.
15 424	Vehicle brake.
15 429	Vehicle windows.

15 430	Shaft-coupling joint.		133 156	Brakes of power propelled vehicles.
16 060	Engine starters.		135 582	Crankshafts and bearings therefor.
16 832	Engine starters.		135 756	Pneumatic tyres.
16 974	Wheels.			
17 026	Engine starters.		**1920**	
17 636	Vehicle windows.		137 125	Vehicle springs.

15 430   Shaft-coupling joint.
16 060   Engine starters.
16 832   Engine starters.
16 974   Wheels.
17 026   Engine starters.
17 636   Vehicle windows.
21 444   Projectiles.
22 508   Storing etc. liquid fuel.
23 349   Musical instruments.
24 210   Musical instruments.
25 275   Musical instruments.
29 407   Internal combustion engines.
29 461   Vessel propellers.

1914

 1563   Vehicle windows.
 2320   Pianofortes.
 3255   Spur gearing.
 5030   Ignition.
17 450   Signalling.
17 451   Bearings.
17 544   Rotating cylinder engines.
17 546   Radial engines.
17 775   Aeronautical engines.
18 064   Telephones.
18 146   Fuel supply.
20 638   Guns.
20 905   Projectiles.

1915

 441 1   Signalling.
 4412   Telephones.
 7366   Vehicle electric transmission.
 9376   Fuses.
10 517   Storing liquid fuel.
15 066   Water carriers.
17 367   Engine coolers.

1917

105 373   Valve-operating gear of petrol internal combustion engines.
108 970   Motor vehicles.
109 529   Motor vehicles.
110 182   Fuel feed valves and valve operating mechanism for internal combustion engines.
111 170   Railway coach propulsion.

1918

119 140   Clutch and change gear mechanism.
119 339   Tents.
121 243   Lubrication of high-speed reciprocating engines.

1919

131 618   Fire places.
121 765   Springing of vehicles.
121 767   Springing of vehicles.
127 620   Mechanism for receiving and launching aeroplanes at sea.
127 674   Internal combustion engines.
128 686   Internal combustion engines.
131 325   Internal combustion engines.
135 301   Internal combustion engines.
127 680   Floating mines and submarines.
127 859   Floating mines and submarines.
127 686   Hot air engines.
127 687   Hot air engines.
129 026   Projectile fuses.
129 374   Machine guns.
129 727   Lateral plumb indicator for aircraft.
130 025   Attachment of aeronautical propellers etc.
130 070   Aeroplanes.
132 363   Automobiles.

133 156   Brakes of power propelled vehicles.
135 582   Crankshafts and bearings therefor.
135 756   Pneumatic tyres.

1920

137 125   Vehicle springs.
141 096   Wheels and tyres.
145 193   Buildings for exhibitions etc.
150 009   Pianofortes.

1921

157 524   Vehicle wheels.
158 305   Apparatus for heating or cooling and ventilating buildings and ships.
166 017   Transmissions and brake mechanism of motor vehicles.
167 616   Motor vehicles.

1922

174 758   Magneto.
176 514   Motor vehicles.
180 383   Vehicle suspensions.
187 364   Propulsion of amphibious automobiles.
188 541   Steering wheels.

1923

195 684   Vehicle wheels.
198 527   Vehicle wheels.
196 643   Power propelled vehicles.
198 707   Vehicle brakes.

1924

209 837   Change-speed gear etc.
216 599   Internal combustion engines.
216 600   Pistons.
224 932   Vehicle brakes.

1925

229 722   Vehicle springing.
229 842   Reciprocating engines.
232 661   Liquid-level indicators.
232 772   Automobiles.
241 965   Automobiles.
238 921   Coating hollow articles with metal.
240 540   I.C. Engines.
243 304   Balancing reciprocating engines.
243 786   Vehicle steering mechanism.
244 007   Vehicle steering mechanism.

1926

253 173   Change speed gearing.
261 536   Vehicle pedal mechanism.
261 874   Steering-mechanism of vehicles.
262 174   Motive-power engines.
262 242   Automobiles.

1927

263 555   Vehicle steering-mechanism.
263 904   Vehicle brakes.
266 782   Electric motors.
268 859   Electric motors.
267 190   I.C. Engines.
271 133   Carburettors.
282 537   Vehicle windows.

1928

282 880   Dynamos.
293 148   Bonnets of automobile vehicles.
298 687   I.C. Engines.
299 552   Spindles for grinding wheels.
300 667   Change-gear mechanism.

1929

304 406	Vehicle steering-mechanism.
305 971	Mechanism for rectification of gear-wheels.
309 931	Vibration dampers for machinery.
312 103	I.C. engine ignition.
312 968	Buffers for locomotives.
317 169	Microphones etc.
318 279	Microphones etc.
317 339	Loudspeakers.
320 647	Loudspeakers.
321 328	Dynamometers.
321 967	Gramophones etc.

1930

325 784	Loudspeakers etc.
327 790	Loudspeakers etc.
327 145	Sound reproduction apparatus.
337 811	Sound reproduction apparatus.
338 656	Appliance for storage etc. of pins etc.
339 307	Warning-devices for motor vehicles.
339 949	Reproduction of music, speech etc.

Note: From April 1930 onwards the Patents Name Indexes ceased to be issued annually. Instead, they were issued as each 20 000 specifications were accepted. For each 20 000 series, the period covered was approximately one year.

340 001-360 000

341 574	Wireless reception apparatus.
356 246	Field magnets for loudspeakers.
356 367	Mechanism for reproduction of recorded music etc.

360 001-380 000

361 841	Reproduction of sound.
364 683	Diaphragm mountings for acoustical apparatus.
368 708	Loudspeakers.

380 001-400 000

382 952	Electric transformers.
383 376	Telephone receivers.
390 584	Telephone receivers.

400 001-420 000

409 821	Clutch etc. mechanism of motor vehicles.
410 589	Clutch etc. mechanism of motor vehicles.

500 001-520 000

509 786	Suspension of motor vehicles. Accepted July 21st, 1939.

THE YEAR OF THE SPRITE

By John Ridley

Not since going to collect my first car (a Lanchester Leda) had I been so apprehensive. Here I was investing all my savings in an everyday vehicle which not only had I never closely inspected but which also had a unique engine, unique body, unique upholstery and, worst of all, a gearbox which practically no one had heard of, let alone knew what to do if things went wrong. What's more it was April Fool's Day!

Post-War Lanchester output could hardly be described as exciting. The LD 10 got more expensive to the point of almost pricing itself out of its particular market and that market was dwindling. Some models, like the LD 10 Coupe and the LG 15, never went into production and, as far as I'm aware, only two chassis had the benefit of the special conversion to transform them from DE 27s to LE 27s. Great hopes were pinned on the two-litre Leda but the reaction from the public is best summed up by the nickname given to the car by the dealers which incorporated the model's name but began with a B!

The failing of the Leda was that it was somewhat underpowered. There were, of course, two ways to correct this mistake—either up the power or lessen the weight. We all know of the success of the former option. It took less than a year to change the LJ 200 (long stroke, four-cylinder, two-litre) to DJ 250 (short stroke, six-cylinder, $2^1/_2$ litre) and produce the best-selling Conquest. One might be tempted to think that the second alternative was just as straightforward but, fortunately for me, the story is much more interesting.

My saga does not really start with the Leda or, for that matter, with any other car of our marques. Indeed the story does not even begin in Coventry but in Paris at the Panhard & Levassor works. The BSA Group had in mind assembling the Dyna 850 in England. The Dyna was a most unusual, sleek, aluminium car powered by a flat-twin engine. It offered 75 mph and over 40 mpg but was by its very nature rather expensive to build. It would however have fallen nicely into the Lanchester image. Unfortunately, there was insufficient capacity within the BSA empire to make the aluminium bodies and the government of the day frustrated the import of ready made panels so the project was dropped but not the idea of producing a car along the same lines.

Thus a new Lanchester was conceived, code LM 150. For lightness the construction was integral, with the main floor forming a punt-like basis for the body from the rear seat pan to a massive bulkhead, from which triangulated box sections extended to take the engine and coil and wishbone i.f.s. Steering swivels were used but on ball joints rather than trunnions as had been the practice. Additional strength came from the transmission tunnel, front cross member, wheel arches and inner side panels. The whole bonnet and outer front wings could be swung upwards to give access to a brand new engine which, in reality, was a four-cylinder version of the Conquest

"worked over" by Westlake & Co., the combustion specialists. Very neat exit porting helped the power unit to the same 60 bhp as the Leda whilst giving away 346 cc and 1 cwt. Further weight savings were made by use of light alloy for doors, boot etc.

Although a fluid-flywheel (and, presumably, a preselector box) were originally envisaged, it was decided at an early stage to go one up on rival firms by claiming the world's first medium size car with automatic transmission. Daimler had toyed with various ideas since the war. Dr J N H Tait, the Experimental Engineer, had designed a semi-automatic version of the Wilson'box, probably for a DF 300, and both Freebourne and Sinclair units had been tried but it was to be the Hobbs system that became the first serious contender.

It must not be thought that the Hobbs 'box was just another bought-out component. To go into the full history of this unit would require an article in itself but briefly, the gearbox was originally designed by the Australian born inventor, Mr H F Hobbs, just after the war for a personnel carrier but the project was abandoned in a NATO amalgamation. With financial support from interested persons Mr Hobbs and his son John worked with a number of companies on the redevelopment of the "box" one of which was BSA. Dr Tait was detailed to assess the unit. He raised a number of criticisms but these were so speedily rectified that by 1955 a 51% share of Hobbs Transmissions Limited was taken with a view to marketing three versions, the $1^1/_2$ litre Sprite, $2^1/_2$ litre Conquest and the $3^1/_2$ litre Regency. Later a fourth, smaller, type was fitted experimentally to Austin A35s and the like. Much money was spent on buildings and plant and a sizeable contract to supply Borgward of Germany was landed but, unfortunately, this firm promptly ran into financial trouble and ceased production after some 500 Borgward cars had been fitted with Hobbs, in particular the "Big" Borgward. By this time BSA was in the midst of its apparent self-destruction and agreed to sell back to Hobbs Transmissions the 51% interest which was then sold to the Westinghouse Brake and Signal Co.

After further development, Fords were poised to use the Hobbs 'box for all its European light cars and about 250 Cortina and Classic cars were fitted with the Hobbs units on a dealer conversion basis, but a change of heart of a newly appointed American as technical director in England meant that hopes were finally dashed. The 'box deserved a better fate for it had proved itself in such wide ranging fields as door-to-door delivery vehicles, P.S.V.s and racing cars. With regard to the last use, Mr Hobbs' younger son David used to race a Lotus equipped with one of the 'boxes. His technique to beat the field off the starting grid was to wind the engine up to maximum revs. and slot the auto-box into lowest gear. Just try that with a pre-selector! Elite cars fitted with the transmission were used as personal transport by Stirling Moss and the late Jim Clark.

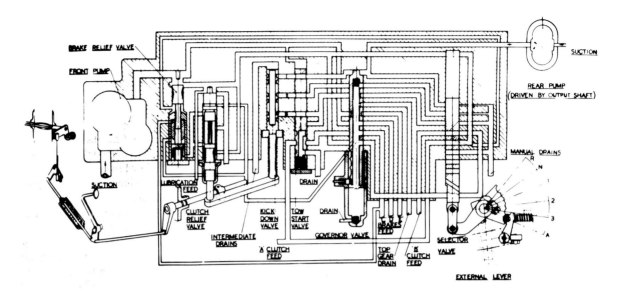

Power trains of the Hobbs gearbox.

Two philosophies make the design of the Hobbs 'box, both going contrary to the fluid-flywheel/Wilson combination we know so well. First, if the fluid coupling could be eliminated, so could its attendant power losses—an over riding consideration for smaller cars: second, if brake bands are to be used in selecting epicyclic gears, why not make them do the work of conventional clutches at the same time?

Notice that there are two clutches to take up the main starting loads and that the three (one doubled) geartrain or reaction brakes are similar to disc brakes—unlike bands as in the Wilson unit. However, there were no annulus or outer ring gears, eliminating them brought down the overall height of the box, and consequently the whole car, and required less critical gear cutting. (Mr Hobbs, by the way, had a very high opinion of the Daimler gear cutting shop). Oil pressure to operate the clutches and brakes was supplied by an engine driven pump, pressure and delivery being controlled by suitable valves in an hydraulic unit. A second pump was driven off the output shaft with the oil delivery being fed to the hydraulic unit, thus enabling gear changes to take place automatically as road speed varied. 1st, 2nd, or 3rd gears could be held to give semi-automatic operation and there was a kickdown facility. Other considerations, such as tow starting and prevention of inadvertant manual selection of too low a gear, were also taken care of.

It has been said that the 1954 car was merely a design exercise. I dispute this as no less than five chassis numbers (70010—70014) were allocated of which three were built. Furthermore, Mr Hobbs recalls that the main reason for not pursuing with the phase I type was the delay—not cost— involved in using new panels rather than adapting Conquest parts. Daimler's Chief Engineer, C M Simpson, believes that the Company wanted to make maximum use of the recently acquired Carbodies plant. Whatever the reasons, the result was, in my opinion, the prettiest post-war Lanchester although I admit the Dauphin has more style. Both the LD 10 variants seem to me like taxi cabs and the Leda suffered from rear-end lumpiness but with the Sprite the team got things right. I well remember my youthful doodlings on tracings of the Leda in attempts to improve its lines and

coming up with almost the same answer even though the Sprite was no more than a name to me then. Mark you, the improved back still required a midget to get under the open boot.

The phase two Sprite was more Conquest-like in other ways, too. Much of the i.f.s. was unchanged but the coil springs gave way to long torsion bars (rods, not leaves as in the DJ/LJ range, and adjustment was by simple screws) anchored to a tranverse I-beam half-way down the body. From the I-beam two legs of an embryonic chassis extended rearwards to take the back axle etc, an ingenious construction which gave rise to the apparent paradox that the weight of the car was carried on a "chassis" but the weight of a chassis was not carried by the car, (think about it). Running forward from the I-beam were two deep box sections. The bonnet was of the normal alligator type with the front valence and wings being structural. The earlier idea of a combined bonnet and wing structure opening forward had proved better in theory than in practice. The structure was too heavy and if the engine needed attention in the dark, the headlights pointed directly onto the ground thus giving the worms a bad night and making the vehicle dangerously inconspicuous. Rear wings, windscreen and rear window were all pure Conquest. Even more striking was the rear seat pan which still showed the indentation for the battery access even though the battery was housed, modern-style, in the engine compartment. Second series Sprites also had a tighter turning circle (33 feet) despite increases in wheelbase and front track to 8'4" and 4'4", better ground clearance (7 inches) and slightly larger tyres (5.90 x 15) of the new-fangled tubeless type. The A.C. instruments gave way to Smiths and there was a single bench front seat.

It is fascinating to see how the new model reflected current fashions, in particular the interior. In those innocent pre-seat-belt days, a family saloon was expected to carry at least six people, making a front bench seat and column gear change obligatory. What you sat on was no longer stuffy old leather but exciting new plastic. A T-spoked steering wheel helped the driver see better through the lowered windscreen but at least the Sprite did not have a wrap-around rear window. Also, in

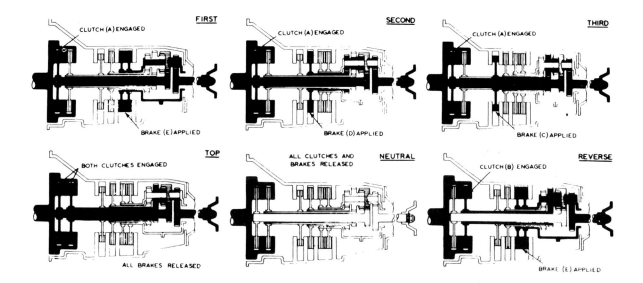

The hydraulic circuit.

response to another fashion, some adventurous colour schemes were proposed such as pastel blue/mid-blue with beige trim, and stone beige/scarlet, also with beige trim. "My" Sprite was supposed to have had a dark green exterior with green trim but, although no less than three different shades of green can be distinguished in the paint, the interior is entirely in beige.

There were relatively few problems in its development. Colin Bromfield was closely involved in the evaluation of the prototypes and he relates that the main fault was lack of torsional rigidity and a number of stiffeners were required. The other trouble spot was the gearbox, in particular the "A" clutch. After only a few thousand miles judder occured. This judder, which wasn't experienced with other installations, was probably the result of just the wrong combination of speed and engine torsional vibrations. Daimlers had used fluid-flywheels for many years and had not needed to take into account these vibrations. Various remedies were tried without success. The factory had little expertise in clutches and to complicate matters, this one ran in oil. The problem was only solved after ringing up the BSA motorcycle factory engineers (whose clutches usually ran in oil), and they advised changing the lining from the normal asbestos to a special neoprene/ cork material.

The 1955 Motor Show boasted two of the new Sprites, one in silver/maroon and the other in silver/black. Sales brochures and owners' handbooks were printed as deliveries were expected by mid-1956 at £1,230 (inc. tax). In all 13 of the later Sprites were built (chassis 70100—70112) of which the first three appear to have been out and out prototypes differing in many minor details. Comparing the promises of the sales bumph and the Show reports with the remaining example, it would seem that most of the differences involved bringing down the cost. Some sensible savings had already been made by cutting out unwanted chrome and the central chassis lubricator, (by some oversight the list of recommended lubricants in the handbook includes equivalents for the chassis lubrication but just where the punctilious owner would put his Girling-Bijur Chassis Oil or Shell Dentax 90 can only be a matter for interesting speculation). Aluminium panels for the doors gave way to steel and

the featured locker in the front arm-rest disappeared. But the biggest apparent cost cutting was in the upholstery. Now I don't mind plastic headlining, it's easier to keep clean, and I concede that leathercloth is a reasonable economy for door trimming but surely leather is the only material for seats? Just what the Sprite upholstery is I don't know, but it looks more like contemporary loudspeaker weave and is such an eyesore that it might have come straight out of a 1978 car. We all know that Lanchesters were advanced but it is a pity that this trend is backwards.

Production development continued. After the first 500 cars it was planned to replace the Zenith carburettor with an S.U., and from 1,000 on, minor modifications to the steering were scheduled. More exciting is that I have come across references to type LM 152/153. These refered to a twin-carburettor aluminium head which should have given a broadly similar performance to the Riley 4/72. The standard engine with its single carb. and 7.1 compression ratio was limited to 4,200 r.p.m. and so there was plenty of room for improvement.

Ironically Sir Bernard Docker (and with him the driving force behind the Conquest and Sprite), was ousted at almost the same time as potential customers had been promised the goods. It was said at the time that the £500,000 needed to put the car into production was too much but it smacks of a convenient excuse. More likely in my opinion was that the new managers, being of motorcycle backgrounds, backed away from committing themselves to any car with a question mark. The one unsolved but minor problem is alluded to in The Daimler Tradition, it concerned the behaviour of the gearbox on descending long, steep hills. The hydraulic pressure to operate the clutches tended to drop on the long overrun and so the linings could burn out with severe abuse. No one in the development team expected any problems in finding a solution.

Everyone that I have talked to and who was involved in the Sprite project thought it was a winner. After all, if you are producing your best selling model ever and you have a way of making practically the same thing only 20% cheaper, the market is yours. Instead - and against the strong advice of the dealers - the Conquest price was

The Lanchester Phase One Sprite. This early publicity photograph shows the resemblance between the Lanchester and the contemporary Hillman Minx.

dropped to just below that of the Sprite whose cost had risen to £1,300. It is difficult to see how the factory could have made a profit. For a week or so both cars were listed at virtually the same price but by the 1956 Motor Show, the Lanchester option had disappeared altogether.

By contrast to the Dockers, the Hobbs family parted from BSA on the best of terms and they were allowed to take with them most of the gearboxes along with, I fear, all the drawings. Many of the remaining Sprites were fitted with preselects, probably from LD10s as there would not have been room to fit larger units, and used as works hacks. Mr Simpson went touring in the Alps in one and experienced no trouble whatsoever. As far as I can trace from the registration numbers all the other Sprites have been broken up although the licencing history of one lasted until 1966. Sprite engines were to play a part in the development of the SP 250 as test beds to gain essential experience on clutches.

Just one Sprite, the very last Sprite, and hence the very last vehicle to carry the honoured Lanchester name, survived in its original form. It was first registered by the Lanchester Motor Co. Ltd. on 25th January 1957 but within a week was transferred to the Triumph's Meriden Works. In late 1957 it was purchased by Mixintransit Ltd. of Manchester for use by a Mr. Thompson on business purposes and came into the possession of Lime-Sand Mortar Ltd. (part of Thomas Tilling Group) when L.S.M. acquired the assets of Mixintransit Ltd. and the car was eventually transferred to Conyngham Hall, Knaresborough until its eventual sale via, it is thought, Leeds Motor Auctions for approximately £300. As far as can be recalled the Sprite gave excellent performance whilst in L.S.M.'s possession.

It was pure chance that this historic Lanchester came into the hands of the Lanchester Historian. Mr Hutton-Stott has friends in Cornwall and one of them just happened to be passing a showroom in Truro when he saw a "Leda" which didn't look quite right. A telephone call to Newbury sent him west and he bought the Sprite

on the spot. Five years of enjoyable motoring followed, with overheating and back axle the only trouble areas, but by the end of the period, the car was showing the usual Conquest body problems. Alec Norman purchased it and his works did a very creditable job of restoration although I have personal reservations on changing the colour from Conquest green to Ford velvet blue as Daimler never used dark blue with beige interior. Interestingly the "chassis" needed very little attention .

With retirement ahead, Alec Norman decided to reduce his collection and I was able to convince him that it was in the car's best interest that he sell it to me at a price I could afford. And that is why John Whitney was persuaded to divert many miles to give me a lift from Reading to Gamlingay so that I could start my first "Year of the Sprite".

Getting into the driver's seat I was immediately struck by the family resemblance. Set in the dash. of the usual walnut, (I believe the first three Phase two prototypes to have used a metal dash., like the Leda,) were a clock, speedometer and combined petrol gauge/ammeter/water temperature indicator. True to form there was no oil pressure gauge. The instruments were grey faced Smiths with the two largest having crystal centres like the black type used on the Daimler Ladies Model. The feminine trend continued with control knobs of the satin chrome variety (late Conquest) designed, according to Mr Hobbs, by Lady Docker herself for easy use by women with long finger nails. There was no petrol reserve. The quadrant gear lever had A for automatic instead of the pre-select T for top and was lit at night (why on earth was that not done before, I wonder?). On the floor were only two pedals, arranged so that both were operated by the right foot. The rationale against using the left foot for braking was that in emergencies unaware drivers might revert to slamming the right pedal with disastrous consequences. Looking through the windscreen I might just as well have been in a Leda until I put my foot on the throttle. The difference between the

Above: David Hobbs seated in the Sprite.

Below: John Hobbs, Mr Hobbs Snr., David Hobbs, and John Ridley (seated in car).

Sprite and the earlier car was really quite striking and could have landed me in trouble had I not been aware of it. A second habit to unlearn was that of putting the gear lever down to position 3 once in top. I always do this with the Wilson 'box but the Hobbs immediately changes down. It is difficult to be subjective but the visibility to the sides and rear seemed better than with a Conquest.

Ahead of me lay 90 difficult miles home. In my previous car, a Daimler Special Sports, they had been pretty grim. How, I wondered would this Sprite fair? Would it follow the dictionary definition of a disembodied spirit (not a bad description of some cars) or realise the fantasies of the sales blurb? I am happy to report that the latter was not too far from the mark. True, the gearbox seemed to be determined to change up at far too low speeds making manual selection advisable but the car was very lively to about 40mph and cruised happily at around 55 with top coinciding with the legal maximum. The kick-down worked perfectly and was a blessing on the Berkshire Downs. The steering was very light and the body was amazingly free from rattles, which shows that in this respect integral construction could be superior to the traditional chassis plus body. Wind noise was above average, so too was the exhaust note with only a single silencer about the same size as one of the LD10s. The all-hydraulic brakes inspired confidence and at last a handbrake alongside the seat - much safer than the grope and hope type underneath the dash. The heater was first class, helped by the engine appearing to run hot. There was just a hint of pink on two star. In fact, by the end of my very first drive, I realised that I'd made an outstanding buy and had acquired a very delightful car with a character entirely different to that of any other Daimler/Lanchester/BSA experienced.

During the next twelve months I had a continuous stream of good luck in overcoming the potential problems thrown up by the Sprite's unique features. To be truthful, my good fortune had started before collecting the car as I had persuaded Harry Aldridge to do the servicing, a great help when one considers that the omission of the central chassis lubricator meant a service interval of only 500 miles, or ten round trips to work.

The apparent one-off engine problem was solved by Alec Norman who had an almost complete spare with a packet full of head gaskets. The unique body shares many panels with the Conquest range although it is a pity that the front wings are welded and so I cannot make use of the glass fibre alternatives.

As for the unfamiliar steering linkages, one track rod end looked suspiciously more worn than the rest and a search for another model in common began. It wasn't Conquest and it wasn't LD10 and it wasn't substantial enough for the larger cars. Heavy expenditure on a special machining job loomed large until I showed the doubtful part to George Bennett at the Gamlingay Stores. A look came over George akin to Archimedes at bathtime. I do not claim that he actually raced naked down the main street chanting "Eureka" but he did lead me to four bins of parts which had been rescued from the Daimler cellars and did not seem to fit any known model. I now have enough track rod ends to last well into the next century.

Common spares for other items were found: the back axle is similar to a Morgan 4/4; the brakes are largely Austin A60; the door handles were used on many Triumph models and some industrial 'fridges; the boot handles could have fallen off the side of a Foden lorry, the radiator grill is the same as the Leda and many interior fitments are shared with other Daimler models, particularly the Majestic. But the biggest success was a meeting with the Hobbs family at Browns Lane, organised by the ever helpful Andrew Whyte on the grounds that as David Hobbs had been a Jaguar racing driver, the publicity would be of benefit to all. Father and sons could not have been more interested. The Sprite was taken for a test run and the gears pronounced to be in fine shape but that there was indeed a fault in the control unit - a blocked jet perhaps - and the "A" clutch needed attention. This was the clutch mentioned earlier which gave trouble in development until the asbestos lining was changed to a neoprene cork but, after about 100,000 miles, a replacement was not unreasonable.

After a three day search the Coventry Museum's document room revealed that the composite used to be called Neolangite 55. A Buyers' Guide of the '60s listed this as a trademark of the Cork Manufacturing Co. who were most helpful. Neolangite 55 was some 15 years out of date, the modern equivalent being SP 220. What a pity the firm's code had not been advanced by thirty so that I could have claimed to have at last found a proper use for bits of Daimler SP 250.

In the twelve months, the Sprite took me to many meetings and innumerable local gatherings. In addition I got engaged and married in it. The car never failed to start first or second try and it only came to an involuntary stop once, in a cloud of smoke outside Chipping Norton, when the carburettor insisted on spraying petrol over the exit manifold. There have naturally been a number of minor incidents, like the time a plug lead disappeared (just like that), but nothing one would not expect of a vehicle a tenth of its age. As for the overheating, only a thorough clean out of the water system plus a new radiator block had the slightest effect on the temperature reading. Perhaps a design problem. The original two-bladed fan has been uprated to four while the capacity of the cooling system is less than the Lanchester LD10s.

On the return from the MOT (it passed first time, naturally), the first annual mileage was noted as 6,570 at a consumption rate of 31.2 mpg - pretty good by any standards. Current usage is around 1,000 miles a month.

The future? The Conquest type panels need continuous watching and a respray every few years seems inevitable. Choice of colour poses a problem. I rather fancy the stone beige and scarlet proposed by Lanchesters, it should liven up any rally line, but I suspect a return to green is more likely. Something will have to be done about the seats and, as the upholstery material appears to be unobtainable, it would seem logical to remove the originals and store them and replace with contemporary leather items. Century rear seats fit but the side handbrake means that DJ fronts would have to be modified. Split fronts would not be as unoriginal as they sound because Lanchesters were about to abandon the bench seat. The one other factory proposed modification I would agree with is to change the Zenith carb. to S.U., but this would mean casting a new inlet manifold and I have yet to find the appropriate Daimler drawing. These diversions aside, I see no reason why my Lanchester should not continue to give me unique, enjoyable and economical motoring for many more years to come...

XXIIIme RALLYE AUTOMOBILE
MONTE-CARLO
JANVIER 1953

One of the last Lanchester appearances in a competition event, this Lanchester Fourteen featured in the 1953 Monte Carlo Rally.

THE 20 H.P. FOUR-CYLINDER LANCHESTER.

ANY PRODUCTION EMANATING FROM THE LANCHESTER MOTOR WORKS IS PRODUCTIVE
OF GREAT INTEREST IN THE MOTORING WORLD ON ACCOUNT OF THE ORIGINALITY SHOWN
IN DESIGN AND THE EXCELLENCE OF THE WORK PUT INTO THE VEHICLES.

As will be seen from the illustration, the engine is a four-cylinder vertical type, now more or less regarded as standard.

The valves are arranged horizontally, and are mechanically operated by means of side levers arranged vertically, and enclosed in cam boxes, which form oil reservoirs, so that the cams and the portion of the levers on which they operate are always immersed in oil. Flat springs are used in place of the usual coil springs to return the valves to their seats, thus effecting a considerable saving in the weight of the moving parts, and obtaining in consequence a

There is a separate throttle to each inlet valve, these being of the ordinary butterfly valve type. They are linked together, and opened or closed simultaneously by the centrifugal governor, or by means of a foot accelerator attached to the footboard.

The system of pressure lubrication is as follows: The oil pump is driven off the crankshaft, and is at the left-hand end of the engine, within the crank case. This oil pump delivers into a tube running longitudinally, and having branches leading to each main bearing. The oil then flows to the connecting rod heads through diagonal holes in the crankshaft, and

Fig. 1.—Side view of the Lanchester 20 h.p. four-cylinder engine and change-speed gear.

A top of crank case	G, magneto armature
A1, crank pit	H, ignition shafts and tweakers
A2, motor support brackets	J, ignition shaft skew gears
A3, cylinders	K, camshaft
B, change speed gear box	K1, cam box
C, clutch case	K2, valve springs
C1, clutch oil pipe	K3, camshaft motion lever for advancing or retarding the ignition
D, brake box	K4, camshaft gear box
E, driving pot or universal coupling	
F, flywheel	

L, feed valves	R, change speed hand lever
M, throttle valves	R1, change speed handle
M1, throttle coupling link	R2, change speed bell crank lever
M2, throttle lever	R3, reversing link
M3, centrifugal governor	R4, clutch and brake link
N, vapour inlet pipe	R5, reverse lever
O, exhaust pipe	R6, low speed lever
P, water outlet pipe	R7, compound or second speed gear lever
Q, water inlet	

valve motion that is very silent, even at high speeds.

The inlet, exhaust, and water pipes are disposed practically parallel to one another along the top of the engine.

The flywheel containing the magneto electric generator is at the front end of the engine, and attached to the crank case at the rear end is the countershaft containing the three change-speed gears, the clutch, and the main brake. This arrangement of the countershaft ensures perfect alignment, and avoids the necessity of a universally-jointed shaft, such as is often necessary between the engine and the gear box on the more common design of cars.

thence up the centre of the connecting rods to the small ends and cylinders. Small holes through the cylinder walls near the lower extremity convey oil to the cams and camshaft bearings. There are also small tubes running from the cylinders to the vertical ignition shafts. The lowest piston ring when overrunning this hole causes oil to be blown up the tube, and supplies ample lubrication for these vertical shafts.

The ignition plugs are identical in design with those fitted to Lanchester engines for the past five years, and have proved themselves extremely reliable, get-at-able, and free from trouble.

Reference to the index and fig. 1 will enable the

reader to trace the various parts of this ingenious engine and the fittings thereto.

The Countershaft.

The countershaft box consists of three portions—the change-speed gear box B, the clutch case C, and the brake box D (fig. 1).

The change-speed gear box B is attached direct to

The brake box D (fig. 1) contains rings similar to those used in the clutch, the difference being that the inner or internal rings are carried by the arborshaft, and the external rings are mounted in grooves in the brake box casting, and therefore cannot revolve.

The clutch and brake (fig. 2) are actuated by means of one lever, operated on the outside by a link connected to the hand lever, and operating within the clutch case on the clutch in the forward direction, or on the brake in the backward direction.

It will be seen from fig. 2 that the clutch-actuating lever carries on trunnions a thrust sector, which through a ball bearing acts on a thrust ring and the clutch pins. A forward movement of this sector will

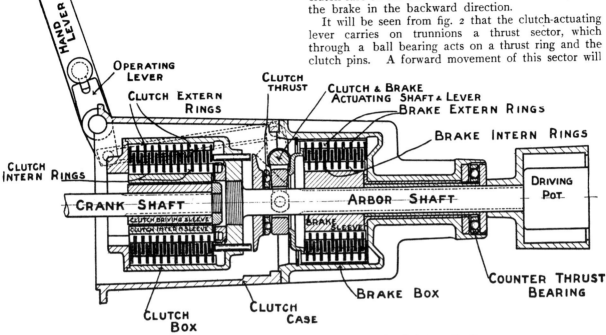

Fig. 2.—Showing the direct drive plate clutch and brake plates and method of operation.

the rear end of the crank case, as previously described. This box contains two forward speeds and one reverse on the epicyclic principle, and similar to that used on the 10 h.p. and 12 h.p. twin-cylinder cars, over three hundred of which are now in use on the road. The forward speeds are the low and compound, or second, speed, and each gear is brought into action by applying a brake to a drum carrying one of the elements of the epicyclic train.

The clutch case C contains the high speed gear, which gives a direct drive through a Weston type of clutch (fig. 2), composed of several steel discs, these discs being mounted alternately on a sleeve carried on the motor crankshaft, and in a box attached to the arborshaft.

depress the clutch pins and clamp the clutch discs together. In a similar way, the sector, if moved backward, acts on the brake discs, but in this case there is no necessity for a ball thrust, as the parts operated on do not revolve.

At the rearmost end of the brake box is arranged a counter thrust for the main clutch, and the arborshaft also carries the universal coupling for the propeller shaft. This coupling the makers prefer to term the "driving pot." The coupling is similar to the one used on the 10 h.p., 12 h.p., and 16 h.p. cars to connect the propeller shaft to the wormshaft, and is capable of sliding telescopically. as well as having universal radial movement.

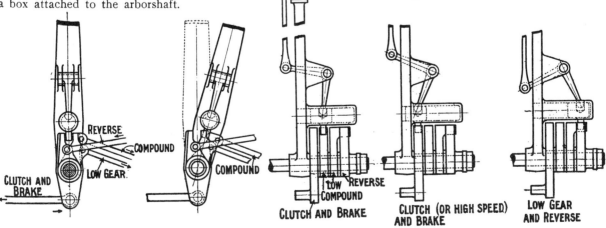

Fig. 3.—Showing the change-speed lever in various positions to operate the gear mechanism, clutch and brake.

The 40 h.p. Lanchester Sporting Model.

A New Supplementary Model with a Six-cylinder Engine arranged in Front under a Bonnet.

SINCE long ago in the early history of the motor car—one might almost call it the tube ignition age—the Lanchester car has been a law unto itself in the matter of its design both outwardly and inwardly, and yet, although almost all the original features as time went on were absorbed into the appearance is of the utmost simplicity, and its balance seems to have been obtained by careful attention to the needs and proportions of the two units, *i.e.*, the chassis and the body, which merge indissolubly into each other. It may be noticed from the drawing of the new car that the radiator is not vertical, but

A sketch of the new 40 h.p. sporting model Lanchester car, showing its exceptionally graceful lines. The engine has six cylinders, 102 × 114 mm., and embodies several departures from previous Lanchester practice.

standard practice of other manufacturers, its appearance has remained unique. For this reason the announcement that the Lanchester Co. are now putting on the market a new car in which the engine is placed under a bonnet in front—and a long and most comely bonnet at that—will come in the nature of a surprise to motorists in general.

It must be understood that this new car does not take the place of the standard 38 h.p. six-cylinder model—which has no bonnet in the ordinary sense of the word—but has been produced simply as an additional, open touring car type to meet the demands of those who prefer the conventional outline and arrangement.

The Lanchester Co., having decided to make a car with a bonnet, have set about it in a characteristically thorough fashion, and, in the opinion of the writer at any rate, have achieved lines more graceful than those of any five-seater touring car yet on the road. Of course, one man's ideas of automobile beauty generally do not agree with those of all others, but it would indeed be a captious critic who could find fault in this case. The car recalls the lines of a war vessel or some great express engine, in that it has the same indescribable harmony of outline. The

Front view of the new 40 h.p. Lanchester car.

lies slightly back at the top. The swell of the body as it continues vertically downwards and inwards towards the frame is followed up horizontally also, right through to the end of the bonnet and the radiator, and the complete absence of unnecessary beadings and so forth is noticeable.

Although of a novel appearance for a Lanchester car, the mechanical details of the car, with the exception of the engine, follow closely the recognised Lanchester practice, inasmuch as a three-speed epicyclic gear box bolted to the engine, and a worm-driven rear axle slung on cantilever springs, are employed. The six-cylinder engine, however, is of a new design. It has a bore of 4in. and a stroke of 4½in.; approximately 102 × 114, equal to 5,588 cubic capacity. It is rated at 40 h.p. and can develop 75 b.h.p. at 1,800 r.p.m., whilst the power curve does not commence to drop until 2,200 revolutions are exceeded. The car complete weighs 33 cwt., and on top gear has a speed of 30 m.p.h., with the engine running at 1,000 r.p.m. The ratios are: top speed direct drive 3.3 to 1, second speed 5.5 to 1, and first speed 11.5 to 1.

The cylinders are cast in pairs, and the valves are on the near side. The valves being arranged vertically

B19

The 40 h.p. Lanchester Sporting Model.

form a distinct departure from Lanchester practice, *i.e.*, horizontal valves, one on each side of the cylinder head. They are operated from a single chain-driven camshaft by rockers and adjustable tappets. These rockers are in pairs, the fulcrum pin of each pair being carried in a small detachable plate held up to the side of the crank case by a dog.

An interesting point is to be found in the valve tappet guides. These are arranged in pairs, and the base flange of each pair is provided with a raised lip or tray around the edge in such a way that any oil issuing from the top of the guide drips down into the tray, and is able to return to the crank case by a tortuous passage. There are detachable cover plates around the valves, and, owing to the device mentioned, there is no likelihood of oil oozing from these cover plates and giving the engine a dirty exterior. Both the inlet and exhaust manifolds are separate castings held up to the cylinder facings by dogs. The carburetter is a special Smith four-jet.

The cams are separate on their shaft, which is carried in four phosphor bronze bearings. The six-throw crankshaft has seven white metal-lined bearings. The crankshaft is of large diameter and stiff, the shaft and pins being hollow.

The piston has four compression rings, and one scraper ring at the bottom of the skirt. Some special

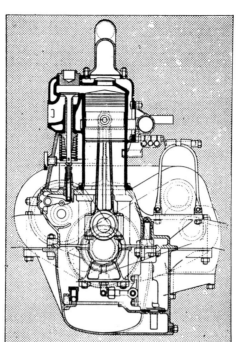

End elevation of the new Lanchester engine.

interest attaches to the use of this scraper ring, inasmuch as it has been the standard Lanchester practice since 1904. This ring is fitted to the very edge of the skirt of the piston, and the lower flange which holds it in position is reduced in diameter and the top edge of the ring is slightly bevelled. At the bottom of the ring groove are small holes communicating with the interior of the piston.

Generally speaking, the Lanchester engines do not suffer from "pinking" caused by excessive carbonisation, and it is owing to the arrangement of this scraper ring. Supposing the walls of the cylinders to be covered with a film of oil, the piston on the down stroke presents to the oil the sharp cutting edge of this lower scraper ring, and, as it were, planes the oil cleanly away, there being plenty of room for the film to curl over against the cutting edge and peel away. On the up stroke, such oil as remains on the cylinder walls is not removed by the scraper ring, owing to the upper bevelled edge sliding over the oil rather than cutting through it. Any surplus oil which may collect in the bottom of the ring groove is able to find its way out into the interior of the piston through the small holes already referred to.

The Lanchester Co. have always been in favour of pressure lubrication, and a fairly high oil pressure at that. An oil pump of the gear variety is used,

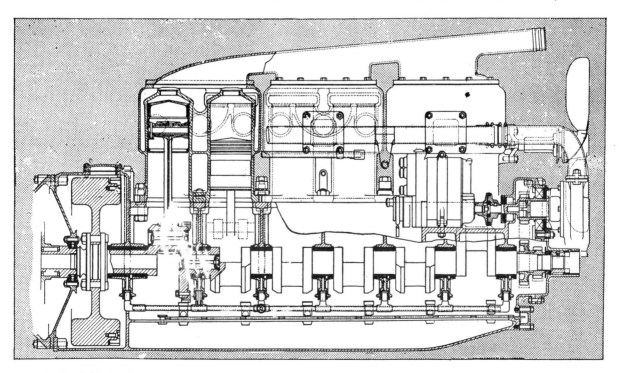

Sectional side elevation of the new 40 h.p. six-cylinder Lanchester engine. The bore and stroke are 4 × 4½in. (102 × 114 mm.)

The 40 h.p. Lanchester Sporting Model.

and the gear wheels in this are of small diameter and great width of tooth, after the fashion of a Roots blower, the object being to reduce the peripheral speed of the wheels to the smallest extent, and thereby to avoid frictional loss. The oil pump picks up its oil from a large sump at the bottom of the crank

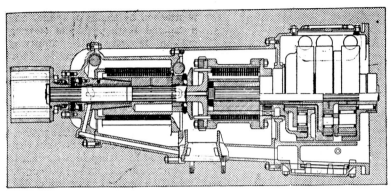

Sectional side elevation of the three-speed epicyclic gear box of the new 40 h.p. Lanchester car. The casing of this gear box forms an extension of the casing of the engine, the two being bolted up together to form a single unit. The multi-plate foot brake is contained in the rear of this casing.

case, and delivers it to the main bearings, whence it finds its way into the hollow crankshaft to the big ends, and up pipes on the connecting rods to the gudgeon pins. The surplus oil drops back into the crank case and finds its way into the sump by percolating through a gauze filter plate of large size, which can be removed from the engine without any dismantling being necessary.

An oil gauge of an interesting pattern is fitted on the dashboard. It consists of a needle registering on the left side zero and on the right a short black scale. If the needle be at zero no oil is circulating. So long, however, as the pointer is touching the black scale all is well. This gauge has been designed to show when the pressure is good and sufficient for all purposes. What the pressure may be above the low limit mark is held to be of no particular moment to the user, within certain limits, and in any case a release valve for the pressure is provided which short-circuits excess oil back to the sump.

On the off side of the crank case towards the rear is a large oil-filling funnel, which is really conveniently placed for filling, and slightly to the rear of this funnel is a lever which opens, through the agency of a rod, a tap on the side of the crank case giving the oil level; that is to say, if the tap be opened and no oil issues, replenishment is necessary. If too much oil be there the surplus can be run off through the tap.

A dual ignition, consisting of a Lodge battery system and a Simms magneto, is employed. The magneto is carried on the off side of the engine close up to the front. On the near side at the rear of the engine is placed a Lucas free-wheel electric engine starting motor.

On the front of the engine is mounted a water pump of considerable size, and also a fan for assisting the cooling of the radiator. The top water lead to the radiator is cast in one piece for the three sets of two

cylinders, and the same applies to the bottom water lead. On the top lead, however, a lug is arranged through which a bolt passes to the top of the radiator and thereby braces the latter to the engine. The radiator itself is carried on trunnions provided with rubber buffer bushes.

The chassis frame is rather remarkable; the inside edges of the frame members lie parallel, but from the front dumb iron the side member swells in section, both vertically and horizontally, to a maximum at the position of the second main tubular cross member; the frame remains parallel to the rearmost tubular cross member, and then, at the point where the upward sweep to clear the back axle commences, again narrows down to a fine section.

The tubular cross members are of large size, and from the point where the front pair of arms of the engine are attached, back to the second tubular cross member, a channel section liner is inserted as an extra interior stiffening piece, this liner being largely cut out along its neutral axis. The front springs of the new car are of the semi-elliptic pattern, whilst the back are of the well-known and well-copied Lanchester cantilever type.

The rear ends of the frame members provide attachment for a neat pressure-feed petrol tank remarkable for its bevelled edges and its strength. It might be mentioned in passing that pressure for the petrol tank is obtained from a suitable pump driven by the engine, and not from the exhaust gases.

The engine and the three-speed epicyclic gear are bolted together in one unit, and the unit is bolted rigidly to the frame at four points on four bearer arms. There are several points of interest about the Lanchester gear. The shafts are on plain bearings, but only oil is used in the box, and this oil is fed round to the various bearings by means of a high pressure pump of the same pattern as that used in the engine, and provided like the engine with a dashboard indicator. This has been a feature of Lanchester practice for many years past.

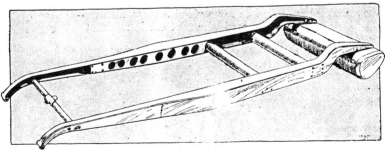

The frame of the Lanchester sporting model car. The considerable cross-section of the frame in the middle portion and the large size of the two main tubular cross members are noticeable.

The direct drive of the Lanchester gear is obtained through the agency of a multi-plate clutch running in oil, and to the rear of this clutch is situated on the driven shaft a multi-plate foot brake on the same principle. These clutches are also lubricated by the pump, and provision is made that the box may not be

B21

The 40 h.p. Lanchester Sporting Model.

filled beyond a certain height, so that no trouble can occur through over-lubrication. The brakes of the epicyclic gearing are adjustable from outside the box, and an arrangement is made so that they cannot by inadvertence be adjusted too tightly.

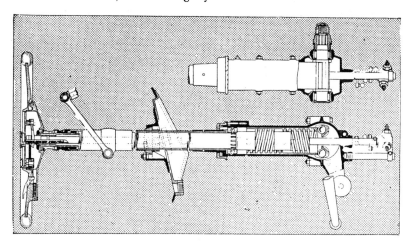

The steering gear of the Lanchester car. Right and left-hand threads engage right and left-hand half sleeves respectively, one half sleeve rising and the other falling as the steering wheel is rotated. This movement oscillates the cross shaft through the agency of a rocking arm, the shaft itself being mounted on rollers.

Although the Lanchester car is equipped with an epicyclic gear, the operation of this is exactly the same for the driver as the ordinary sliding gear; that is to say, one has a change speed lever and a clutch pedal, the change-speed lever actuating a very ingenious form of selector. Of course, it is practically impossible to damage the gear through bad changing. The only thing one can do is to estimate the relative speeds of the engine and car so badly that one causes the engine to drive the car with a bad jerk, or the car to drive the engine with a similar jerk at the time that the change is made.

The drive from the gear box to the back axle is by means of an unenclosed universally-jointed propeller-shaft, the joint at the front end being of the sliding square block type, whilst at the back a star joint is utilised. The final drive is the well-known Lanchester worm.

In the rear axle the wheel hubs take their bearings upon the inside of the casing, and again close up to the worm wheel, thus obtaining a wide supporting base and making it possible to provide adequate thrust ball bearings to take the load when the car is rounding a bend.

The internal expanding shoes for the hub brakes are actuated by the side lever, the latter by the way, being of the type which has no trigger, but which is moved sideways in order to engage or disengage it from the rack. The brake cross-shaft and its compensating gear are carried on the axle casing, a tie rod being used to connect the compensator to the brake lever. The rocker of the compensator is ball-ended, and these joints are protected from grit by rubber rings held over conical seatings by small cover plates.

Accompanying this description will be found a section of the Lanchester steering gear. The column has right and left-handed worms cut on the same shaft, and each of these worms engage with half a sleeve. Thus the right-hand worm engages half a sleeve with the right-hand thread, and the left-hand worm the half sleeve with the left-hand thread in it. Rotating the steering wheel in one direction will, therefore, cause

the right-hand worm to move its sleeve upwards or downwards as the case may be, whilst the left-hand worm causes its sleeve to move in the opposite direction. The ends of these two half sleeves bear against rollers carried on a rocking arm. The rocking arm in turn is borne by a cross-shaft, to the end of which the steering lever is attached by means of splines and a tapered seating. The steering column is very well supported additionally on the scuttle dashboard and the ramp. Down the centre of the wheel main tube pass smaller tubes for the switch, ignition, and the throttle controls respectively.

The boss of the steering wheel is of very much larger size than usual, and in reality forms a box in which the throttle and spark control levers are housed, with only their button ends visible. The rim of the wheel has spokes leading inwards to a ring which embraces the control lever box, and is attached thereto by means of a hinge and locking device, so that the wheel can be tilted up in line with the column to allow easy access to the driver's seat. The front axle is of an easy curved H section, and when in position on the spring pads the top of it is canted slightly backwards so as to give the front wheels a slight caster action in steering similar to that of a bicycle steering head.

A neat device is attached to the front tubular cross member, intended to retain the starting handle in a

The steering wheel of the Lanchester car, showing how the spark and throttle levers and the switch are concealed in the central boss of the wheel. The gate gear change and side brake lever can be seen also.

convenient out-of-use position. It consists of the provision on the cross member of an arm free to swing, at the end of the arm being a piece of tube open along the lower side. This tube is of sufficient size to embrace the starting handle, and the spring in the arm of the handle itself is sufficient to cause the latter to lock itself against the bottom of the tube when the device is forced over into use. To operate the starting handle it is only necessary to lift up the swinging tube.

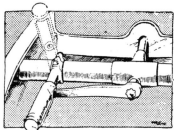

The device to keep the starting handle clean and hold it out of use.

The construction of the body is interesting, inasmuch as it is built on to a subsidiary frame of its own which fits over the main frame when the body is in position. The verticals of the body are attached to the horizontals by means of massive aluminium brackets, with the result that rack in the body is reduced to the smallest possible extent, and undesirables in the form of rattling or jamming doors in after life are not encouraged.

It may be of interest at this point to give the dates when various features which have been adopted by many other makers were originally introduced into the Lanchester car, so we give the short table below:

1906.—Oil in the gear box pressure fed to important bearings.
1904.—Scraper piston rings to prevent carbonisation.
1899.—Magneto ignition.
1899.—Cantilever suspension.
1897.—Wire wheels.
1896.—Live axle.
1896.—Mechanical feed lubrication, the forerunner of modern pressure feed, and the first substitute for the drip feed.
1895.—Raked steering.
1895.—Mechanical inlet valves.

With regard to the performance of the car on the road we have had the opportunity of driving it and being driven in it over some very varied roads, from the big open straight to the tortuous and remote bylanes in the Cotswolds, where gradients are very severe and surfaces in many cases abominable; in fact, the car was used to explore one or two places we did not care about exploring on our own car. It is only fair to say that it was with the full consent and approval of Mr. George Lanchester, who would have driven the machine up the roof of a house had we provided any sort of ramp by which he could attack the roof. However, nothing so heroic as that was in our minds. All we wanted to do was to satisfy ourselves that the car had that all-round adaptability which is essential in a vehicle which may be used one day for a twelve or thirteen hours straightaway run over big main roads, and the next for work in steep and twisty lanes.

To take the open road first. The turn of speed which the car showed was, to say the least of it, fully up to our expectations; there is no need to specify the precise maximum attained, and we concern ourselves rather in saying how it was done. At all speeds from a crawl up to a strenuous maximum the engine running was delightful, no suggestion of a period and no irritating noises. One felt there was a big insistent " something " which induced an exhilarating pressure in the small of one's back and necessitated the closing of the throttle long before the summit of a slope was breasted.

The hold on the road was excellent, and we mention this because many maintain that cantilever springs will not give a good road hold, though their comfort is not disputed. The new Lanchester combined both road hold with great comfort and dropped into potholes without any nasty jar, while side roll was conspicuous by its absence. The steering is very easy and light without showing any nasty tendencies at any speeds.

Perhaps the most noticeable advantage of the control is that which is common to all Lanchester cars—gearchanging is a matter of the utmost ease. All one has to do is to depress the clutch pedal fully, move the gear lever, and then release the pedal. What is more, it is precisely the same operation whether changing up or down. After all, what baffles the ordinary driver more than anything else is the fact that if he perfects his method of changing down, he has trained himself to do automatically the reverse of what he should do if he were changing up. Now with the Lanchester, the operations are the same each way, and, provided one does not change without intelligence, one cannot go wrong. For instance, if one changed down at thirty miles an hour, and then let the clutch in without accelerating the engine to approximately the speed it should be revolving at when doing thirty miles an hour on the second, there would be a shock, depending as to its magnitude upon the difference between the engine speed and the gearshaft speed; but so long as the engine be quickened up to meet the change of gear nothing could be easier. At any rate, as every Lanchester driver knows, the gear-changing is ease itself, and, as we have said, we believe it is mainly due to the fact that the procedure is uniform.

The brakes are very powerful and smooth in action, and, although the car has a long wheelbase and a

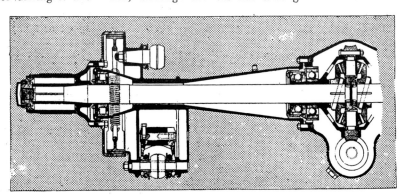

Part sectional view of the Lanchester back axle.

wheel track in proportion, it can be driven in narrow lanes with every security, ease, and comfort, despite the fact that it is such a fine open road vehicle. Probably few new models have been tested as thoroughly as this. It is over a year ago since we tried the first car in its finished form, and from that time to this the car has been in constant hard service, and the strength and suitability of every new part for its work have been very thoroughly proved.

B23

Reprinted from " THE AUTOCAR."

IN SURREY ON A 23 H.P. LANCHESTER.

Comfort, Speed, and Flexibility. Outstanding Features of the Latest Model of a High-grade British Production.

DATA FOR THE DRIVER.
23 h.p., six cylinders, 78'7 x 114 m.m. (3,327 c.c.) Tax £23.
Weight of complete car, less passengers, 38 cwt.
Weight per c.c., 1 2 lb.
Gear Ratios : 19'2, 11'5, 7'7 and 4'8 to 1.
Worm final drive.
Semi-elliptic front and cantilever rear springs.
31 x 5¼ in. tyres. on detachable disc wheels.
Brakes on four wheels.
Wheelbase, 11 ft. 1 in,
Track. 4 ft. 8 ins.
Fuel Consumption, 18 m p.g
Tank Capacitp, 16 gallons.
Price : Chassis, £1,050.

Of handsome and dignified appearance the 23 h.p. Lanchester enclosed-drive limousine can be taken along narrow country lanes with confidence.

NO longer are cars of the highest grade spoken of in the same manner as vintage wines. New models are not now produced with unfailing regularity once a year, but modifications dictated by experience on the road are adopted as and when they are perfected.

Accordingly the 21 h.p. Lanchester now has a bore of 78.7 mm. for its six cylinders, instead of 74.5 mm., giving it an actual rated horse-power of 23. This change has been made because the chassis was originally designed to accommodate four-seater bodies, whereas the general demand is found to be for six-seaters, and in consequence the slight increase in bore gives a greater reserve of power and renders the car more suitable for the larger and heavier coachwork. Another engine modification concerns the ignition, for, in addition to the magneto, a coil system may now also be fitted, the distributor being located

midway along the near side of the overhead valve gear cover and driven from the overhead camshaft. The magneto and coil systems are carefully synchronised, and both are very accessible for inspection and adjustment.

One of the latest type chassis, fitted with a roomy and comfortable enclosed-drive limousine body, we recently tested in the Surrey hills, and, despite its size and weight, it proved as tractable on rough and narrow lanes as some small sports car of half its rating, while in traffic the smoothness of the clutch and flexibility of the engine leave little for the driver to do. Normally, one starts from rest on the level in third gear, letting the clutch in without speeding up the engine, and changing into top just as soon as one feels inclined. Thereafter top gear suffices, however slowly the traffic stream may flow, and only if forward motion actually ceases is it necessary to change down again to third.

With the ignition retarded and the air control lever set slightly towards " rich " on its quadrant, the car runs smoothly on top gear at about 2 m.p.h. without any sign of unevenness of firing or snatch in the transmission. This it will do either on the coil or magneto ignition. It will, moreover, accelerate at once without labouring in response to a greater throttle opening. The top gear acceleration is, in fact, decidedly good, for from a steady 10

respectively, while on top gear 66 m.p.h. was comfortably reached, and in more favourable circumstances could have been bettered.

SILENCE AND POWER COMBINED.

Throughout its range of speed the engine retains its smoothness in a remarkable degree, and only when fully extended on the lower gears does it exhibit a tendency to become less silent. At a comfortable cruising gait of 45-50 m.p.h. the hiss of the wind round the joints of the wind-

Owing to the rigid construction of the frame, and the use of a cast aluminium foundation for the body, no distortion is apparent when rough ground is encountered, and the doors showed no signs of binding when the above photograph was taken.

m.p.h. a speed of 30 m.p.h. can be attained in the brief space of 12 seconds.

On the indirect gears the Lanchester exhibited a liveliness which one does not, as a rule, associate with an all-enclosed six-seater, for the 10-30 m.p.h. acceleration was accomplished in 7 one-fifth s. on third, and in 6 two-fifths s. on second—no mean performance in view of the weight. The maximum speeds attained on third and second were 46 m.p.h. and 33 m.p.h.

screen, and the purr of the tyre treads on the road, are the most prominent noises, while the reserve of power is sufficient for the car to spurn ordinary main road gradients without the speedometer needle varying its reading.

With four up, the hill to Newlands Corner was taken on top, the speed on the steepest part falling to about 8 m.p.h., but the engine pulling evenly and sustainedly none the less. At the foot of the succeeding hill, just before reaching Shere, a sharp left turn was made up a narrow and rough lane, which has before now figured in trials. As the gradient steepened, third was engaged, and the hill climbed as fast as the deep ruts would allow, until the worst portion, reputed to be 1 in 5 or less, was reached. Here the car was turned and reversed up the hill, then turned again and, with first engaged, allowed to run back, being brought to rest and driven forward by the somewhat brutal method of letting in the clutch. Despite this treatment, no transmission harshness or judder could be detected, while it was, incidentally, proof positive that the clutch was more than up to its work.

Not many motorists attempt the direct road up Box Hill from the first left-hand bend to the second right-hand bend, especially with a heavy enclosed car. The Lanchester made light work of the climb, despite the surface, on second gear. This is a tribute to the excellence of the suspension system, and no other comment is necessary, for the name Lanchester has always been synonymous with springing more than ordinarily good. On descending the hill the steering lock allowed the hairpin corner to be taken with feet to spare— a performance not often achieved with a car of fairly large dimensions, for the corner in question is really acute.

As regards the four wheel brakes, which are direct operated by the pedal, an improvement has been effected in the method of adjustment. The shoes are pivoted at their upper ends, and a vernier adjustment is provided at this point, so that lost motion may be taken up and the maximum braking efficiency always retained. From a speed of 40 m.p.h. the car was brought to rest smoothly and without deviation from the straight in a distance of 100ft. A fair, but not exceptional, pressure on the pedal is necessary.

REMARKABLE COACHWORK SUSPENSION.

Of the steering and controls generally it is sufficient to say that they are in keeping with the high character of the chassis. The coachwork, also, is worthy of the chassis bearing it, and is remarkable for the cast aluminium body frame, which is mounted on rubber buffers, so that road shocks and mechanical vibration are intercepted. The result of this method of body construction is great rigidity, which, combined with the very stiff frame construction, gives entire freedom from body noises and from such troubles as warping doors. Even on the most uneven surfaces the four doors showed no signs of binding, or, if opened, of fouling the door frames when being closed.

Some idea of what can be done with the Lanchester in this respect is shown by one of the photographs on the previous page.

In brief, the present 23 h.p. Lanchester may be summed up as a medium-powered high-grade car eminently suitable for the needs of the owner-driver, whether he requires an open tourer or a luxurious all-enclosed six-seater. The increase of cylinder bore has given the car a snappiness of performance which formerly it lacked, although the smooth, silent, and effortless running of its predecessors has not been impaired.

A modification has been effected in the front wheel brakes by means of a vernier adjustment of the pivots of the shoes, situated over the top of the steering head. Lost motion can be easily taken up at this point.

Reprinted from " THE AUTO MOTOR JOURNAL,"

The 21 h.p. Six-Cylinder Lanchester.

A Car of Fine Repute—The Result of over Twenty-Five Years' Experience—Splendid Engineering Design.

THE name Lanchester has always been associated with the soundest practice in automobile construction, and the eminent engineers who have produced the wonderful succession of Lanchester designs have been responsible for many details of design which have been largely adopted as current practice by automobile builders of both hemispheres.

For a number of years the Lanchester Motor Co., Ltd., followed a one-model policy. They concentrated on the production of the high-class, high-power car, a policy culminating in the production of the renowned "Lanchester Forty," which to-day stands as a pre-eminent example of the highest class automotive design and engineering.

But, in order to meet the ever-increasing demand for a high-grade, medium-powered

This view of the near side of the 21 h.p. Lanchester shows the overhead rocker-operated valve gear, the double exhaust manifold, the thermostat, etc.

car making a special appeal to the owner-driver, they have now produced a second model—the six-cylinder car of 21 h.p.

This new car upholds the traditions of its predecessors in rigorously maintaining the high standard of design, workmanship, and quality of material which has made the name of Lanchester famous amongst automobile engineers.

And, while the new smaller powered model maintains the qualities essentially Lanchestrian, it also represents a distinct advance in design and is, at the same time, a car of moderate price—when price is considered in relation to mechanical efficiency and super-comfort, refinement, and luxury.

The 21-h.p. Lanchester, while resembling the "forty" in appearance, neither supersedes the latter nor competes with it.

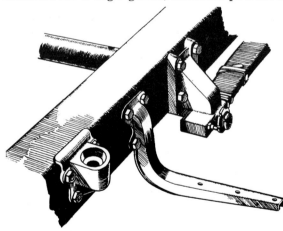

This view of the chassis side of the 21 h.p. Lanchester shows the cup which locates the rubber buffers, a set of which isolate the body from the frame. The sliding forward anchorage of the spring is also shown.

It is a junior member of the same family and possesses, in common with its big brother, the following features :—It has a six-cylinder engine, unit construction of engine, clutch and gear, forced high-pressure lubrication, overhead valves and camshaft, thermostat water-temperature regulator, silent worm drive, flexible cantilever rear suspension and exceptionally long torque tube, an underslung front suspension, a very stiff chassis frame, a mounting of the body on rubber buffers, and Lanchester patent four-wheel brakes of special design.

The engine of 21 h.p. has a Treasury rating of 23 h.p. The six cylinders are 78.7 mm. bore, and the piston travel is 114 mm. The engine, clutch, and gear form a single unit. The valves are enclosed overhead and operated by a worm-driven, overhead camshaft. The engine is supported in the deep steel chassis frame by bearer brackets cast integral with the crankcase and gear-box.

The crankshaft is of nickel-chrome steel machined from a solid forging and is hollow. There is a bearing of large area between each of the six throws and two end bearings—seven in all; and the big bearing next the flywheel is divided to admit the worm wheel driving the vertical shaft which drives the overhead camshaft.

All the main bearings and connecting rod big ends are lubricated under pressure by a positively driven gear pump. The connecting rods are stampings in high tensile steel and completely machined to matched balanced weights. The big end has a white metal bearing cast under pressure which gives great density of bearing metal and long life. Oil is forced from the crank-pin bearing to the little end of the rod by a steel tube.

The pistons are of die cast aluminium with four rings—one a scraper ring at the bottom of the skirt. The gudgeon pin floats and is tubular and ground after hardening.

The overhead valves are slightly inclined

and are operated from the centrally placed camshaft by rocker arms with adjustment by eccentric fulcrum pins with a screw adjustment which allows of the greatest nicety in adjusting the clearances and ensuring accurate timing. The valve gear is entirely enclosed in a detachable cover.

An automatic specially designed carburettor is fitted to an induction manifold which is the result of long experience gained by extensive trials and research. The carburettor is fed from a special vacuum tank mounted in front of the dash. The main supply being from a tank at the rear of the chassis frame.

Cooling is by a honeycomb radiator of distinctive design, and a centrifugal pump located at the end of a transverse shaft gearing with the vertical camshaft driving shaft ensures a complete and efficient circulation of water around the cylinders and the detachable cylinder head. A thermostatic temperature regulator is embodied in the water circulation system. There is a four-bladed, V-belt driven fan behind the radiator. Thermostat and fan are shown in one of our illustrations.

The transverse shaft, which drives the pump situated on the off side of the engine, drives at its other end the high-tension magneto. Delco ignition with coil and contact breaker worm driven from the camshaft at the side of the engine can be fitted as an extra to give dual ignition at £21. The electric starting and lighting equipment is by the Lucas Electrical Co. The generator has an output of 9 amps. at 12 volts' pressure and is of 56 ampere hours' capacity, ample to meet all reasonable demands for charging batteries, lighting, starting, and accessory equipment.

The starting motor will turn the engine when cold, at 120 r.p.m. The clutch is of large diameter and is a steel plate gripped between two Ferodo-faced discs mounted in the engine flywheel.

The clutch and speed gear are mounted

On the off side of the 21 h.p. Lanchester engine is seen the automatic carburettor, the transverse-driven centrifugal water pump and the Autovac tank on the dash.

in unit with the engine with wide bearer arms at the end of the gear-box as seen in our photograph. The gear shift lever is at the right-hand side, the box gate being rigidly connected with the gear-box. Four forward speeds are arranged for and the reverse gears remain motionless when not in use.

Power is taken from the gear by way of a metal lubricated universal joint inside the spherical mounting of the forward end of the torque tube through which the propeller shaft runs to the under geared Lanchester worm gear of the back axle bevel differential. The rear axle is practically a replica of the axle of the 40 h.p. model on a reduced scale. The central portion is divided horizontally so that the upper portion may be removed for inspection without interfering with any of the adjustments.

The axle casings are steel "draw through" pressings of taper formation, and exceedingly strong yet of light weight. The axle shafts are semi-floating, having one big ball bearing mounted on the axle casing approximately in the plane of the wheel track—the central plane of the wheel. The axle shafts are connected with the wheel hubs by combined splines and cone in the same manner as is adopted in the case of the 40 h.p. model.

The suspension is by the well-known Lanchester flexible cantilever springs at the rear. This method of springing may be said to have been originated by Lanchester, and has been a feature of Lanchester construction since the inception of the Lanchester car. The springs are of the firm's own manufacture, an entirely new and original method being employed in their manufacture. They are encased in leather gaiters. No shackles are used, the spring ends sliding in trunnions which are housed in oil-retaining boxes. The front springs are long semi-elliptic, the springs being underslung and encased in gaiters. The front axle is of tubular construction—another feature which has been always included in the mechanical design of Lanchester cars. The new axle is specially designed to resist the torsional loads imposed by the action of front-wheel brakes.

The braking system is another exclusive Lanchester feature. Brakes are, of course, on all four wheels. The drums are of large diameter, and the shoes possess a correspondingly large area of frictional surface, thus making for exceptional durability.

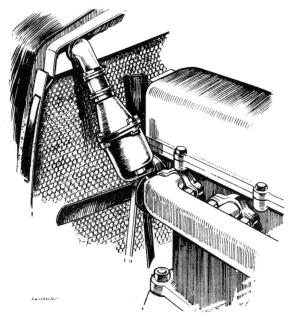

The forward end of the cylinder block of the 21 h.p. Lanchester, showing the detachable cover of the overhead valve gear, the belt-driven fan, the front section of the exhaust manifold, and the thermostat.

This view of the 21 h.p. Lanchester chassis shows the substantial mounting of the rear of the power and transmission unit, also the accessible position of the starter motor, the big diameter tubular cross-members and the spherical housing of the forward end of the torque-tube.

The front-wheel brakes are actuated by universal cams beneath, and in alignment with, the steering head pivots. Both front and rear brakes are operated simultaneously by the pedal and a very neat and simple compensating device is provided to ensure that each pair of brakes takes an equal share of the retardation. The hand-brake lever applies brakes in the drums of the rear wheels only, and by independent link work. A great feature of the brake work is that all adjustments are readily made by hand, and are comfortably accessible.

The steering is in principle identical with that on the 40 h.p. Lanchester. In the steering box, which is oil retaining, a right

and left-hand square thread actuates two plungers which bear on rollers equi-distant from the axis of the rocking trunnion, and all the joints of the steering gear are of the self-aligning ball type.

The wheelbase is 11ft. 1in. and the track is 4ft. 8in. A short chassis with a wheel base of 10ft. 9in. is made to order. The overall length of the chassis respectively are 15ft. and 15ft. 4ins., and the overall width 5ft. 6ins. The width of the chassis frame is 2ft. 10ins., and the length available for bodywork from the dash is 8ft. 5ins. on the short model and 8ft. 9ins. on the long. The wheels are detachable disc or wire as desired and carry 31ins. by 5¼in. tyres. A 16-gallon petrol tank with a special gauge shown in our sketch is carried at the rear of the chassis frame.

The equipment of the chassis includes the electric generator and starter, head lamp pillars with a pair of Lucas head lamps, a Lucas tail lamp, switchboard with distributor box and fuses, accumulator, tray and brackets, and an electric horn. The instrument board is mounted with speedometer, clock, oil gauge, switchbox, ignition and starter switches, etc. Four Dunlop cord tyres 31 ins. by 5¼ ins. are supplied, and a spare wheel and wheel carrier. A full tool kit and a comprehensive assortment of spare parts are included in the full chassis equipment.

The aluminium and duralumin body frame construction of the 21 h.p. Lanchester It makes for strength with rigidity and lightness.

65

The chassis price is £1,050. The prices of complete cars depend on the coachwork selected. Lanchester bodies are designed and built in the Lanchester works. The bodies are mounted on the chassis on indiarubber buffers positioned in metal cups attached to the chassis frame, and illustrated in one of our drawings. These effectually intercept the road shocks. The body framing is of special design in which aluminium and duralumin play a prominent part in ensuring strength and rigidity with wonderful lightness.

Lanchester cars are made throughout by the Lanchester Motor Co., Ltd., of Montgomery Street, Birmingham. Their London showrooms, where Lanchester cars can be examined and tried, are at 95, New Bond Street, and they have a northern depot at 88, Deansgate, Manchester. They have a very well-equipped repair and overhaul works at Star Road, West Kensington, W.14. The telephonic address of the Bond Street showrooms is Mayfair 6138.

Reprinted from " THE BYSTANDER,"

A SHORT time ago I had an unexpected opportunity of trying a 21 h.p. Lanchester. I was suddenly called upon to transport a relative at a moment's notice to catch the Channel boat at Newhaven. My own car was temporarily out of commission, so I tore round to all my friends, and was finally successful in borrowing the Lanchester, all complete with one of those three-seater boat-shaped bodies, finished in brown and white, of which too few are about at the moment. I started my Lanchester motoring after dark, and, apart from certain trouble with the petrol feed, which was in no way the fault of the Lan-

chester, but rather the result of neglect, I had a perfectly wonderful journey. Perhaps it was as well that the dash-lamp had ceased to function, and I had therefore no opportunity of seeing the speedometer readings until the next day, but, judging from the apparent acuteness of the corners on a road which I knew well, the Lanchester must have been extraordinarily fast. Confirmation of this is afforded by the fact that our speed, according to distance and time, was remarkably high. In any case, we caught the boat by four minutes, an achievement which I should have made on few other cars.

Road Tests Showing Principal Characteristics

THE STRAIGHT-EIGHT LANCHESTER

The Latest Product of One of the Oldest of British Car Manufacturers

The car tested, which was fitted with a five-seater saloon body of handsome appearance.

THE Lanchester has always been a high-grade car. It ranks among the best-made and most highly priced automobiles in the world. It combines a good performance with the greatest comfort and luxury which modern motor engineers can provide.

The 30 h.p. straight-eight Lanchester was first introduced about two years ago. Since then it has been systematically improved in detail, and the model which we recently tested was a fine example of British automobile engineering at its best.

Although fitted with a four-speed gearbox, the Lanchester "eight" is for all practical purposes a two-speed car. On all ordinary occasions one starts on the fairly high third gear of 6.75 to 1. The clutch is so smooth that the drive is taken up almost unobserved by the passengers, and at walking pace one can engage top gear and stay in it.

No Driving Fatigue.

The steering is so light, the suspension so cushioned, yet firm, and the operation of the brakes so easy that long distances can be covered without a vestige of fatigue being felt by the driver. Very often driving a really large saloon car through dense traffic is something of an ordeal to those not accustomed to cars of this type. The driver of the smallest "baby" car could, however, step into the Lanchester and

drive it in busy streets without finding it in the slightest degree clumsy or awkward to handle.

We took over the car in the heart of the City and drove out of town as if we had been used to handling the car for years. On reaching one of the new arterial roads we only realized that we were travelling at 50 m.p.h. when this was pointed out by one of the passengers. From the silence of the engine and the smooth

---

CAR TESTED: Lanchester straight-eight ; chassis price £1,325.
ENGINE: Eight cylinders ; overhead valves and camshaft ; magneto and coil (dual) ignition ; bore 78.7 mm. ; stroke, 114 mm. ; capacity, 4,440 c.c. ; R.A.C. rating, 30.8 h.p.
TRANSMISSION: Single-plate clutch, four-forward-speed gearbox, enclosed propeller shaft, worm-and-wheel final drive.
SPEED ON GEARS: Top (4.375 to 1), 72 m.p.h. ; 3rd (6.75 to 1), 55 m.p.h. ; 2nd and 1st speed ratios are 11.5 to 1 and 17.5 to 1 respectively.
SUSPENSION: Semi-elliptic front springs, cantilever rear springs, Luvax shock absorbers, Dunlop 32-in. by 6-in. tyres.
BRAKES: Pedal-operated four-wheel brakes with Dewandre servo motor ; hand lever controls rear brakes by independent linkage.
PETROL SYSTEM: 16-gallon rear tank and vacuum feed ; consumption, 14 m.p.g. approx.
TURNING CIRCLES: Right, 55 ft. ; left, 48 ft.
DIMENSIONS: Wheelbase, 11 ft. 10 ins. ; track, 4 ft. 8 ins. ; overall length, 16 ft. 4½ ins. ; width, 5 ft. 7 ins.
WEIGHT (as tested, unladen): 42 cwt.

LANCHESTER MOTOR CO., LTD.,
Montgomery St., Birmingham, and 95, New Bond St., London, W.1.

---

running of the car we would scarcely have imagined that we were doing more than half that speed. Indeed, the speed is so deceptive and effortless that it was necessary to slow down sooner for cross-roads and bends than one would otherwise have thought of doing, although, as there is no sign of rolling on corners and riding is steady even on bad surfaces, ordinary curves in the road can be taken without appreciably slackening speed.

Brooklands was our objective, but the conditions, unfortunately, were as bad as they could possibly be. Rain fell in torrents and was swept along by a strong wind. Water lay in sheets on the concrete. What with the low barometric pressure it was not to be expected that the engine would give of its best, while tyres with a tread designed in the first instance for silent running could not be expected to grip well on wet and sometimes slippery concrete when the brakes were fully applied. Under these conditions the results obtained may be regarded as most satisfactory.

Acceleration Tests.

The acceleration on top gear proved all that the average driver of a large car could desire, while a drop to the relatively low third gear gave acceleration figures which would satisfy the most critical.

As the gear change is singularly easy and rapid a driver anxious to

B7

67

THE STRAIGHT-EIGHT LANCHESTER—Contd.

make the most of his acceleration could therefore use third gear when required up to speeds of about a genuine 55 m.p.h., but, as a matter of fact, so smooth and easy is the acceleration on top gear that there is really no temptation to improve the get-away by changing down.

Thanks to the fitting of an efficient thermostat, which commences to open at between 160-165 degrees Fahrenheit, the engine rapidly attains its most efficient running temperature, and only a lap or so of Brooklands track was necessary to work the car up to its maximum speed. This was found to be in the region of 72 m.p.h., which, considering the weight of the car (42 cwt.) and the wind resistance of the large saloon body, may be regarded as very creditable.

When we came to try the brakes, however, we were handicapped by two factors; one was the rain-drenched condition of the track, so that a certain amount of water was inevitably splashed into the brake drums, thus reducing the effective friction of the linings, while the specially made tyres, to give silent running, had circumferential ribs, which offered no resistance to sliding in a forward direction. We have no doubt at all that had the track been dry and tyres with transverse grooves in the tread been fitted, very much better results would have been obtained.

The layout of the brake gear provides for a comparatively easy application of the brakes, apart from the additional force applied by the Dewandre vacuum servo.

We subsequently essayed the climb of the Brooklands test hill, which has an ultimate slope of 1 in 4 for a distance of over 154 ft., the

average gradient of the entire hill being 1 in 5. From a standing start at the foot of the 1-in-8 section the test hill was climbed very easily on the second-speed ratio of 11.5 to 1 in 17.4 secs., which is equivalent to 13.8 m.p.h. The top of the hill was crested at 20 m.p.h. by speedo-

The impressive overhead-camshaft engine ; note the two ignition units.

meter. A second attempt on first speed reduced the time to 15 secs.

For such a large car—the wheelbase is 11 ft. 10½ ins.—the turning circles were most satisfactory.

The general design of the straight-eight 30 h.p. Lanchester, as can be seen from the condensed specification which we publish, has remained

unaltered, for the policy of the Lanchester Motor Co., Ltd., is to incorporate improvements from time to time instead of definitely dating their models as leaving the works, for example, in 1928 and 1929 or 1930.

Changes which have been made since we last tested this model include new spring mountings, the adoption of Luvax shock absorbers and a Dewandre servo-motor, the use of Elektron light alloys in place of aluminium for many parts, a redesigned exhaust manifold, and the standardizing of Lucas P.100 D.B. headlamps.

Summing up our impressions of the car, therefore, we may say that the Lanchester 30 h.p. straight-eight is a really well-designed automobile of the highest grade, in which quite obviously no expense has been spared in striving for what the designers believe to be the ideal.

Our only regret was that the exigencies of time did not permit us making our test so long as we should have preferred, for the charm of driving the car is such that we should have thoroughly enjoyed a journey to Scotland and back.

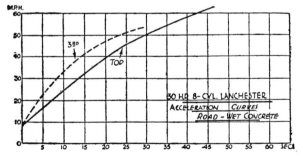

(Left) Acceleration figures on top and third gears.
(Below, left) Proportions of the saloon body.
(Below) Braking figures obtained under bad weather conditions.

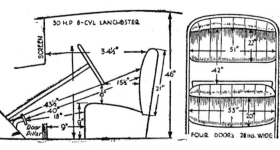

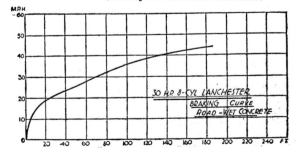

"THE AUTOCAR" ROAD TESTS—*(continued)*

No. 711 (*Post-War Series*).—15-18 h.p. LANCHESTER SALOON

WHEN the 15-18 h.p. Lanchester was introduced last autumn its design occasioned a great deal of interest. Much was expected of the car, and now expectations are being realised, for its running on the road is exceptionally good and exceptionally pleasant. A speed range on top gear from half a mile an hour up to 71½ miles an hour, controls that a child could handle, a capacity to make high average speeds from place to place without apparent effort, and quietness at all times, these features present an unusual combination, especially when found in a car costing less than £600.

Possibly the outstanding feature of the car is, paradoxically, that it has no single outstanding feature, since the design is so well balanced as to make it universally good throughout. As a commencement the six-cylinder overhead-valve engine, although of a modest two and a half litres capacity, pulls with "Pomeric" energy, if the coining of a word may be permitted. The top gear ratio is not particularly low, as the maximum speed figure shows, yet the engine will pull the car up hills on top gear in virile fashion, to the point of accelerating up gradients of 1 in 10 instead of slowing down.

This engine is delightfully smooth, is dead quiet at slow speeds, so that the noise of the tyres on the road is the only sound to obtrude on the consciousness, whilst the rise of the speedometer needle to 40, 50, 60, or more miles an hour produces very little change in the "engine-room" quietness. Thus the prescience of the designer in using a special cam contour which allows a 50-thousandth inch valve clearance is fully justified in practice.

To the driver the Lanchester presents many attractions. In the first place the driving position is comfortable, the seat cushions are unusually deep from back to front, and the steering column is sufficiently long to give tall people leg room without a cramped posture. The steering is light, and has just the right degree of caster action to give an automatic return to the straight and yet be free of undue heaviness on a steeply cambered surface. As to the suspension, it is sufficiently flexible to give great riding comfort in the rear as well as the front seats, and this point is backed up by the fact that the occupants sit well down in the car, and thus experience a feeling of safety. The car can be driven fast over bad surfaces and keeps its course exactly because it holds the road well.

In the brakes there is a unique combination of the Lockheed hydraulic and compensating operating mechanism, assisted by a Dewandre vacuum servo, so that only light pressure on the pedal is necessary. The brakes are smooth and very comfortable in general use. When applied hard for emergency stopping purposes they lock the rear wheels first. Brake adjustments are made on the master rod, and also individually on the fulcrums of the shoes of each drum. There is an en-

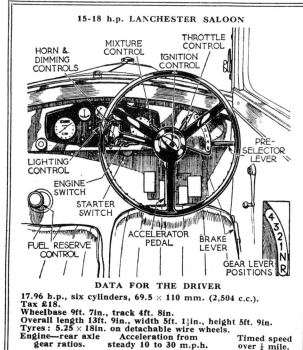

15-18 h.p. LANCHESTER SALOON

HORN & DIMMING CONTROLS · MIXTURE CONTROL · THROTTLE CONTROL · IGNITION CONTROL · PRE-SELECTOR LEVER · LIGHTING CONTROL · ENGINE SWITCH · STARTER SWITCH · FUEL RESERVE CONTROL · ACCELERATOR PEDAL · BRAKE LEVER · GEAR LEVER POSITIONS

DATA FOR THE DRIVER

17.96 h.p., six cylinders, 69.5 × 110 mm. (2,504 c.c.).
Tax £18.
Wheelbase 9ft. 7in., track 4ft. 8in.
Overall length 13ft. 9in., width 5ft. 1½in., height 5ft. 9in.
Tyres: 5.25 × 18in. on detachable wire wheels.

Engine—rear axle gear ratios.	Acceleration from steady 10 to 30 m.p.h.	Timed speed over ¼ mile.
19.44 to 1		
11.15 to 1	6¼ sec.	
7.16 to 1	7½ sec.	
4.86 to 1	10⅜ sec.	71.43 m.p.h.

Turning circle: 40ft.
Tank capacity 16 gallons, fuel consumption 20 m.p.g.
12-volt lighting set cuts in at 8 m.p.h., 11 amps. at 30 m.p.h.
Weight: 31 cwt. 14 lb.
Price, with saloon body, £565.

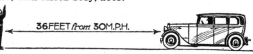

36 FEET *from* 30 M.P.H.

Chassis described in "The Autocar" of October 2nd, 1931.

"THE AUTOCAR" ROAD TESTS—(continued)

15-18 h.p. LANCHESTER SALOON

tirely separate brake at the rear of the gear box, operated by a right-hand lever, and this brake will hold the car on the 1 in 4 gradient of the Brooklands test hill. Incidentally, the Lanchester will climb this hill from a standing start, the driver changing up into second gear, in 15½ seconds.

Momentary stopping and starting on an ultra-steep hill is the easiest thing in the world because of the marvellous fluid flywheel and self-changing gear box. On a low gear the car is allowed to slow and come to rest merely by permitting the accelerator to rise a little, and then the running engine will hold the car in place. To restart, the accelerator is pressed down again; the brakes need not be used. By the same means, driving in traffic is simplicity itself, and the need for gear changing is at an absolute minimum.

So much has been written at various times about the fluid flywheel and transmission that there is no need to refer to it in detail, but merely to remark that it is all that is claimed for it, and a very great advance in automobile design at that. During this test a girl of nineteen, who had never seen the Lanchester before, was given merely a few verbal instructions and sent to fetch the cold car from an awkward private garage, where reversing several times is necessary to make an exit. She arrived at the front door of the house with the car intact in less than five minutes. Yet an old hand at driving can make perfect racing changes without a mistake or having to learn new tricks.

As regards the general controls, the hand brake lever is well out of the way for getting in or out, and there is plenty of room between the pedals.

Basically, the whole car has been designed to permit a large body to be mounted on a compact chassis, the engine being farther forward in the frame than usual to make this possible. The resulting weight distribution gives good riding, and secures plenty of body space in a car of economical size. The saloon body is very well finished inside and out, and has a fine appearance.

There is a folding centre armrest for the rear seat, and side rests as well. The body has six lights and four wide doors with drop windows, three having winding handles, whilst the driver's window has a quick-lift lever for easy signalling. Triplex glass is used.

Ventilation is good, and no draughts, exhaust smells, rattles, or squeaks were noticeable in the car tested. Pleated hide upholstery is used, and the interior woodwork is dark well-polished walnut.

The wings are particularly shapely, besides being efficient. Bumpers are fitted fore and aft, and are of a special design to harmonise with the general scheme of the contours.

There are so many special points as to preclude mention of them all. However, general accessibility for maintenance is very good, excepting only the position of the starting motor, which is not too easy to get at.

NEW LANCHESTER
LIGHT SIX

Six-cylinder engine 57 mm. × 90 mm. bore and stroke. 1378 c.c. capacity. Tax 1934 £12, 1935 £9. Wheelbase 8ft. 5½in. Track 4ft. 0½in. Overall length 13ft. 2in. Overall width 4ft. 9in. Daimler Fluid Flywheel Transmission and self-changing four-speed gear box.

The Autocar

September 21, 1934.

THREE SPECIAL NEW CARS

An Entirely New 18 h.p. Lanchester, a Light Six Lanchester and a Light Six B.S.A., All With Daimler Fluid Flywheel Transmission

WHEN an entirely new car bearing the classic Daimler-Lanchester-B.S.A. hall mark is announced the motorist who is also a good judge of car vintage may be certain of immediate interest. In particular, the largest of the three new cars about to be described exhibits fresh combinations of design, whilst all three possess similar cardinal points in engine construction and have the unique Daimler fluid flywheel transmission.

These three cars are a new 18 h.p. Lanchester, which takes the place of the model first introduced in 1931; a light six-cylinder Lanchester, which carries similar coachwork to the latest type of the well-known Lanchester Ten; and a light six-cylinder B.S.A., with coachwork similar to that of the longer wheelbase model of the B.S.A. Ten.

Certain very definite ideals are the basis of the new 18 h.p. Lanchester, which is intended, above all things, to be an ultra-refined car—one with a really capacious five-seater body, yet compact in overall size; one in which fine road performance is almost concealed by silence of running and by a system of spring suspension aimed to eliminate pitching, so that the vehicle, at all speeds, rides smoothly on an even keel, and the occupants of the rear seats are as comfortable and serene as those in front. Finally, extreme ease of handling is given by the fluid flywheel transmission, whilst the addition of light controls and excellent brakes relieves the driver of nervous strain and so makes for safety.

These points are more than mere words, for any driver of long road experience comes to realise in the end that quietness and light controllability have a great influence upon the degree of his ultimate fatigue. Taking first of all the suspension of the new car, a careful study of the problem of weight distribution has resulted in the mounting of the engine fairly far forward in the frame, which allows the body to be brought well within the wheelbase, so that the loading is more uniform. Pitching in the fore-and-aft sense is largely governed by the relationship between the periodicity of the front and rear springs. As a rule, front springs have a faster period than the rear ones. By altering the weight distribution, the periodicity of the front springs can be brought more closely into step with the rear.

Next, on the Lanchester, the amplitude of front spring movement can be made greater than normal because axle movement is controlled by radius rods. These are spring steel links mounted above

each half-elliptic spring, one end being attached at a point fairly high above the front axle bed and the other attached to the frame side-member. These radius rods also have a torsional steadying effect upon the relative move-

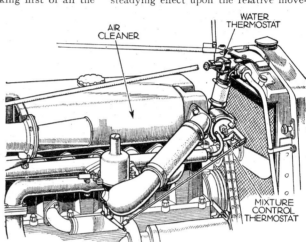

AIR CLEANER

WATER THERMOSTAT

MIXTURE CONTROL THERMOSTAT

Showing the two thermostats and air-cleaner on the 18 h.p. model.

ment of axle and frame. Incidentally, the axle beam is shaped in an even curve from end to end, without a sudden rise from the spring pad to the swivel head. Luvax shock absorbers are anchored to the centre of each front spring at a point coincidental with the radius rod.

Now comes another particularly interesting item—the frame. This has been designed to give regular rigidity throughout its length, and to avoid localised whip. As in the frame of the "40" Lanchester of a few years ago, the new design utilises the box section principle.

The side-members are of channel steel, joined by a large cruciform member in the middle portion, whilst from this point the extremities both front and rear have steel lattices welded on and thus closing the channel section into a box form. This section possesses much greater torsional stiffness than an open channel. The lattice blades have stiffening ribs pressed into them.

This latter construction is applied not only to the frame sides but also to the extremities of the cruciform and to an exceedingly stout compound front

The 18 h.p. car has lattice-work box frame construction at front and rear.

SIDE MOUNTINGS GIVING RESTRICTED MOVEMENT

FRONT & REAR MOUNTINGS

Engine mounting of the 18 h.p. power unit.

Lanchester "18" six-light saloon with folding baggage grid, Model 316.

the case, for it is definitely stated that the official servicing charge of the company for these operations will be no greater than for the same operations on such of their engines as have detachable heads.

The reasons are that the cylinder block by itself is not heavy, when clear of the car one man can lift it and carry it without difficulty; after the valve cover has been removed and the side plate taken off it is not very bulky; and, lastly, a simple form of jig can be used to enter the six pistons back into the cylinder bores without difficulty or fear of breakage of rings. One simple pulley block in the roof of the garage is all that is

cross-member, upon which the front rubber mountings of the engine rest.

Conservation of weight has been carried right through the whole design, including the engine, which is particularly interesting. Its dimensions are: six cylinders, 69.5 by 105 mm. (2,390 c.c.), rating 17.97 h.p.; tax now £18, in 1935 £13 10s.

In common with all the engines of the Lanchester range the new design has overhead valves operated by push rods and rockers from a side camshaft, which has special wide-clearance cams giving exceptionally quiet running.

But there is a fresh and remarkable feature: the detachable type of cylinder head has been abolished. The cylinder block and head are one piece; this is mounted on a two-piece aluminium crank case and sump, the crank case being stiffly designed and arranged to support the balanced web type of crankshaft in four main bearings.

There are many excellent reasons for this adoption of the integral cylinder head. First, it avoids complicated castings on which a considerable series of lugs for holding down bolts adds masses of metal at awkward places. It avoids distortion in the upper end of the cylinder barrels due to unequal thickness of metal and unequal water spacing. This is a most important point, because lack of absolute roundness in the cylinder bores at the top is one of the chief causes of cylinder wear and of erratic oil consumption. Then the integral head abolishes the troublesome gasket; there is no possibility of water leakage; the valves can be of adequate size without

Locker containing the spare wheel on the 18 h.p. Lanchester, Model 316.

"masking"; the valve seats may be evenly water cooled, and the necessity for valve tappet adjustment is reduced to a bare minimum.

It might be supposed that the integral head would make decarbonising the cylinder heads and regrinding the valves a difficult process. This apparently is not

The Lanchester Light Six streamline saloon, Model 321.

needed to enable any mechanic, professional or amateur, to tackle the job.

To deal with the problem of avoiding piston and cylinder wear the cooling system is controlled by means of a thermostat, so as to attain a high temperature as quickly as possible after starting from cold. A second thermostat is coupled to the mixture regulator of the S.U. carburetter, so that richness is reduced automatically as the engine warms up. The air intake to the carburetter is both silenced and warmed.

Then the bi-axial engine mounting is another special point. It is a rubber-cushioned mounting at five points, disposed at different levels, two in front of the engine, two more adjustable points higher up and adjacent to the centre of the unit, and one below the rear end of the gear box. This mounting gives a restricted freedom, sufficient to permit the unit to absorb, as it were, its own vibrations, but not so free as to allow it an excessive movement likely to cause vibration in controls and so forth.

It is hardly necessary to deal at length with the fluid flywheel transmission and

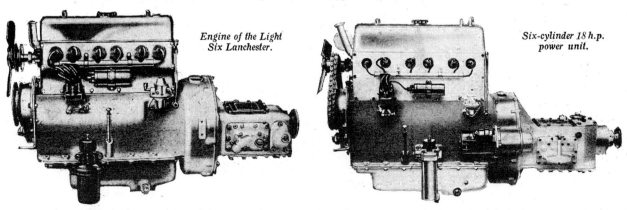

Engine of the Light Six Lanchester.

Six-cylinder 18 h.p. power unit.

Lanchester Light Six, Model 313, priced at £365.

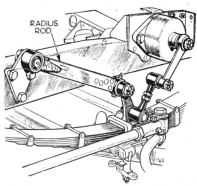

Radius rod for front axle on the " 18."

self-changing preselective gear box, because it is well known, well proved, and tremendously appreciated by skilled and unskilled drivers alike. The transmission has recently been improved by a new multi-disc top gear mechanism, which ensures positive engagement and disengagement at all times, reduces pedal pressure, and eliminates hum in the neutral position.

The principal dimensions of the new 18 h.p. Lanchester are: wheelbase 9ft. 3in., track 4ft. 8in., overall length 14ft. 11½in., body space from front of toe board to centre line of rear axle 7ft. 1½in. The tyres are of 5.50 × 18in., on wire wheels.

Forward View For Driver

There is a wide range of coachwork for the new car, in which special care has been taken about one important point apart from the dictates of comfort, luxury and room: the forward view is particularly good. The scuttle and bonnet are not too high, and consequently a driver of short stature is able to see the tips of the front wings on both sides.

The six-light saloon Model 316 has a capacious body with most comfortable seating and plenty of head and leg room. The interior trimming is very attractive, control of ventilation is secured by hinged flaps on the front and rear quarter lights, the wings are ample, and at the rear of the body is a locker containing the spare wheel. Concealed in this locker is a stout steel luggage grid which can be brought into position

Ample room is available in the rear seats of the B.S.A.; foot wells are not used.

and the lid of the locker closed again, leaving a tidy appearance.

Coachwork models and prices are: six-light saloon, Model 316, £580; six-light saloon de luxe, Model 318, £710; four-light saloon, Model 317, £595; four-light saloon de luxe, Model 319, £710; Wingham cabriolet, Model 322, £695.

Next comes the Lanchester Light Six, which has been produced to meet an evident demand for a car of similar coachwork size to that of the successful Lanchester Ten, with the added refinement of a six-cylinder engine. The engine size is six cylinders, 57 by 90 mm. (1,378 c.c.), rating 12.09 h.p., tax now £12, next year £9. The capacity of the Ten engine, by the way, is 1,203 c.c., so that the new six-cylinder engine is slightly larger.

Most of the foregoing description of the new 18 h.p. engine applies to the new 12 h.p., the differences being merely of detail. The chassis is identical with that of the latest Lanchester Ten, the special features of which, in addition to the fluid flywheel transmission, include a low-built underslung cruciform type frame, which in conjunction with the

The Lanchester Light Six drop-head coupé, Model 314.

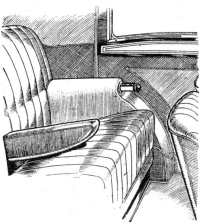

On the Lanchester Light Six the floor is flat at the rear, and telescopic ashtrays are provided.

Streamline saloon on the B.S.A. Light Six chassis.

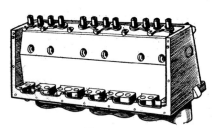

Cylinder block with non-detachable head on the Lanchester "18."

The B.S.A. Light Six fixed-head coupé, priced at £315.

worm final drive gives a flat floor level and easy access to the body, besides a great deal of room in a compact design of saloon, mechanically operated four wheel brakes that are powerful and particularly progressive in action, and a suspension system which is notably easy riding.

The wheelbase is 8ft. 6⅝in., track 4ft. 0⅞in., and the tyre size 5.0 by 18in. The prices are: six-light saloon, Model 311, £365; streamline saloon, Model 321, £375; fixed-head coupé, Model 313, £365; Romney coupé, Model 324, £430; drop-head coupé, Model 314, £390.

Last, but by no means least, is the new B.S.A. Light Six. Here again a demand has been felt for a similar type of car to the sturdy and reliable B.S.A. Ten, but fitted with a slightly larger six-cylinder engine. The B.S.A. Ten has been the lowest-priced car obtainable with the Daimler fluid flywheel transmission. The new Light Six has a chassis similar to that of the latest longer wheelbase Ten, a car notable for its steadiness, and dependability,

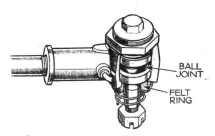

12 h.p. Lanchester adjustable steering joint.

and its responsive lightness of handling.

The Ten has a four-cylinder side-valve engine, the capacity being 1,185 c.c., but the Light Six engine is larger, 57 by 90 mm. (1,378 c.c.). It is an overhead valve design with integral cylinder and head arrangement, four-bearing balanced crankshaft, and possesses the chief features of the latest Lanchester engines as already outlined.

Three styles of coachwork are available for the B.S.A. Light Six: six-light saloon, Model 107, £315; streamline saloon, Model 108, £325; fixed-head coupé, Model 109, £315; and four-light sports saloon, Model 111, £325.

The B.S.A. Light Six engine, with overhead valves and silent cams, has a four-bearing crankshaft.

10,000 PEDESTRIAN CROSSING PLACES FOR LONDON

LAST week the Minister of Transport informed London local authorities of proposals to increase pedestrian crossing places in the Metropolis from the existing 2,000 to the number of 10,000 before the end of next month. The Road Fund will provide 60 per cent. towards the cost of these crossings provided the work is finished by October 27th. The representatives of local authorities approved the scheme.

Steel studs 4in. in diameter are to be adopted to mark the crossings. These will be placed 18in. apart and can be laid down at a cost of £20 per crossing. No charge for maintenance is involved. White painted lines, on the other hand, cost about £30 a year to maintain.

When the complete system of crossings is installed the Minister will issue regulations which will safeguard pedestrians at uncontrolled points, where they

will have complete priority. Before the regulations come into force there will be sufficient crossings to make it unnecessary for pedestrians to cross at other points, and they will be warned that if they do so it is at their own peril. Pedestrians will be able to signal that they are about to make use of the crossings; motorists, on the other hand, will have to slow down and exercise every care at all crossings.

EUROPE'S FINEST GARAGE IN CARLESS CITY

ONE of the finest garages in Europe is situated in Venice, just about the only city in the world where you cannot drive a car! However, you can drive almost into Venice by crossing the splendid mile-long bridge, at the end of which stands this enormous garage. From a distance it looks like some modern factory.

It has at either end a circular ramp, up one of which cars can be driven to

any of its six floors; the other is for descending. On the ground floor there runs the whole length of the building what amounts to a complete street. Here is an information bureau with at least three assistants who are expert linguists. Next to the bureau are hairdressing saloons, for men and women, and several car showrooms where the latest Italian models are on view. On the other side are more offices, a com-

plete post office and some telephone booths.

There are a restaurant, a snack bar, a tobacconist's shop, and many other features which make this garage as complete as any luxury hotel. From the garage, luggage is carried by porters to the canal side where further progress has to be made by water, either in the slow, swaying gondolas, or by the modern motor boats.

D 8

The Autocar Road Tests

No. 926 (*Post-War Series*)

12 h.p. LANCHESTER LIGHT SIX SALOON

Extreme Ease of Control in a Smooth Running Car Which Has a Good All-round Performance

IN the Lanchester Light Six, which was introduced at the beginning of the 1935 season, is found a car of remarkably good balance. Each one of its features as a roadworthy vehicle reaches a decidedly high standard of refinement. Although it has no pretensions towards being a large and fast car, it can nevertheless offer much the same ease of quite fast travel when required, as well as a capacity to tour along in exceptional comfort and quietness when lane exploration happens to be the order of the day.

To be able to make a good average speed over a twisting and not smooth road—most drivers know the conditions implied—is one of the hall-marks of a good car, for such work entails that many points must be just right, steering, suspension steadiness, certainty of acceleration, ease of gear change, and smooth regularity of braking. All these features the Lanchester definitely does possess, and that is what is implied by describing it as having a good balance.

In the first place, the spring suspension is not only very comfortable over all kinds of road surfaces, but there is a minimum of the fore-and-aft pitching which used to be associated with cars of relatively short wheelbase. Again, the car is unusually steady on curves and corners, and displays no tendency toward side sway or slow roll. Then the steering, too, is very good, light to handle even at the very low speeds of turning in confined spaces, yet not too low-geared, and able to give a pre-

cise sense of direction without sponginess. The caster action is sufficient to give quick return of the wheels after cornering.

Added to these points is the excellence of the brakes, for their action is definitely progressive, meaning that a light pressure on the pedal produces light braking, and an increase in the pressure increases the braking power in direct relationship. This gives an excellent sense of control. The brakes are extremely powerful if applied really hard, but are not at all inclined to cause swerving in such circumstances, and that is a valuable attribute for brakes to possess.

It may perhaps seem to be curious to deal with these facets of the car's character before making reference to the power unit, but in point of fact it is the soundness of these points which makes it possible to utilise and enjoy to the full the refinement of the motive mechanism.

The six-cylinder engine is admirable. It runs with smoothness throughout its speed range, and is never harsh or noisy. When idling it is difficult to tell that the engine itself is actually running.

This car has, of course, an infinite range of flexibility on top gear, within the limits of literal loitering up to a maximum of well over a mile a minute. The fluid flywheel transmission allows such exceedingly slow speeds on top gear, and also makes it possible to stop and restart on the level with any gear in engagement, or on a gradient with a lower gear en-

DATA FOR THE DRIVER

12 H.P. LANCHESTER LIGHT SIX SALOON.

PRICE, with four-seater saloon body, £365. Tax, £9.
RATING : 12.09 h.p., six cylinders, o.h.v., 57 × 90 mm., 1,378 c.c.
WEIGHT, without passengers, 22 cwt. 3 qr.
TYRE SIZE : 5 × 18 in. on bolt-on wire wheels.
LIGHTING SET : 12-volt ; automatic voltage control.
TANK CAPACITY : 10 gallons with 2 in reserve ; fuel consumption 28 m.p.g.
TURNING CIRCLE : 39ft.   **GROUND CLEARANCE** : 5⅜in.

ACCELERATION From steady m.p.h. of				SPEED		
Overall gear ratios	10 to 30	20 to 40	30 to 50			m.p.h.
				Mean maximum timed speed over ¼ mile		62.07
5.38 to 1	14¼ sec.	16⅗ sec.	21¼ sec.			
7.776 to 1	10 sec.	12 sec.	19⅗ sec.	Best timed speed over ¼ mile...		64.29
11.983 to 1	9¼ sec.	—	—			
22.012 to 1	—	—	—	Speeds attainable on indirect gears—		
From rest to 50 m.p.h. through gears, 27⅘ sec.				1st		21
				2nd		40
From rest to 60 m.p.h. through gears, 45 sec.				3rd		52
				Speed from rest up 1 in 5		
25 yards of 1 in 5 gradient from rest, 7 sec.				Test Hill		12.64

Performance figures of acceleration and maximum speed are the means of several runs in opposite directions.

(Described in " The Autocar" of September 21st, 1934.)

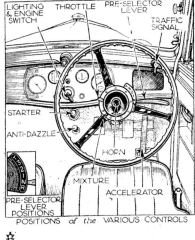

POSITIONS *of the* VARIOUS CONTROLS

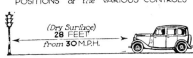

(Dry Surface) 28 FEET *from* 30 M.P.H.

"The Autocar" Road Tests

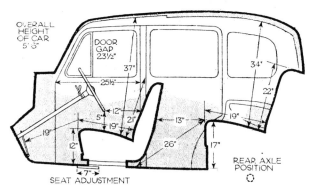

OVERALL HEIGHT OF CAR 5' 3"
DOOR GAP 23½"
SEAT ADJUSTMENT
REAR AXLE POSITION

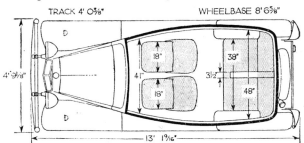

TRACK 4' 0⅝" WHEELBASE 8' 6⅝"

gaged, by use of the throttle pedal alone, that control of the car is appreciably simplified.

The engine pulls well and has plenty of reserve for acceleration, nor does it die away quickly when climbing gradients. A long slope of 1 in 10 can easily be surmounted on top gear. The car has no best cruising speed; it remains pleasant, quiet, and easy to handle right up to its maximum, and as a result rather tempts the driver to go quickly because the going is so easy.

Incidentally, the car tested proved to have a speedometer accurate within approximately 1 m.p.h. The car was able to finish a climb of the Brooklands Test Hill on second gear, but proved slightly faster when making a plain ascent on first. The hand brake would pull the car to a standstill and hold it down a gradient as severe as a genuine 1 in 4.

Of the attractions of the fluid flywheel transmission generally there is scarcely need to write in detail, because the features of this combination are by now very well known. The fluid flywheel is an automatic hydraulic device which gradually and softly takes up the drive as the engine is accelerated, until at a certain engine speed the drive is practically solid. It is a form of clutch which asks the driver to exhibit no skill or care at all. It also relieves the transmission of much shock.

Combined with it is a four-speed preselective self-changing gear, and this is operated from a fingertip lever below the right-hand side of the steering wheel. When changing gear all that is necessary is to move the lever to the desired notch, depress a pedal to its full extent, and then release it. That is really all, except that for changing up the piano-type accelerator pedal is released, whilst when changing down the pedal is slightly depressed. This trans-

mission is most attractive to handle and gives an unskilled driver a quick and complete mastery over gear use.

The arrangement of the controls affords an additional boon besides ease of handling, for the driver can enter or leave the car as easily by the left door as by the right, the gear lever is out of the way, and the hand-brake lever lies beside the right of the seat cushion.

Within the four-door six-light saloon body the seating positions are arranged very comfortably as regards width and depth of cushions and angles of back support; the seats are on the generous side. The body has wide doors and a low floor level but not an ultra-low roof, so that there is plenty of head space. The low floor makes entry to the rear seats easy. The rear seat has a folding centre arm-rest besides elbow-rests.

Above each of the drop windows is a glass draught-preventing louvre, the front windows also have a triangular ventilator flap, and the main glass is of the self-balancing type for raising and lowering. The front door handles are countersunk below the level of the trimming so as to avoid unnecessary projections. The interior door handles lock the doors when turned in the direction reverse to that for opening.

In the centre of the spring-spoked steering wheel are controls for the slow running and mixture setting; the latter automatically returns from the rich to the normal position after use. The switch of the hand-cancelling traffic indicators is on the right-hand side of the instrument board, and the control for the dip-switch of the head lamps takes the form of a plunger on the floor within reach of the driver's left foot. Above the sloping windscreen are twin electric wipers, and there is a sliding roof with centre-locking control.

The Lanchester Light Six is a car of very real attraction, it is easy and pleasant to drive, able to get over the ground fast if required, and possessed of genuine refinement.

ARW 177

B 4

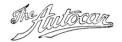

"THE AUTOCAR" ROAD TESTS—*(continued)*

No. 937 (Post-War Series) 18 h.p. LANCHESTER SALOON

An Exceptionally Well-balanced and Pleasant Car Which, Among Many Virtues, Has Exceedingly Comfortable Suspension

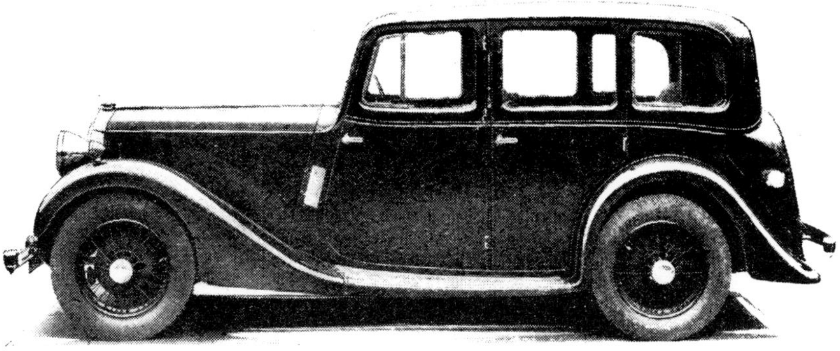

RIGHT from the start the Lanchester Eighteen, the 1935 type, exerts an immediate fascination. It has that indefinable quality which rouses an instinctive appreciation. Like charm in human beings, this quality is not a single virtue, but a compound of many.

Thus it is not easy to say what is the chief point of attractiveness about the way in which the Lanchester handles and runs. Amongst many good features there is one which perhaps stands out most, because it is a point wherein cars, even good cars, frequently leave something to be desired.

This is the suspension—it is quite outstanding in its comfort. The car swims along smoothly on a perfectly level keel. Pitching, which gives that sharp little jerk to the head familiar to motorists, is reduced to such a negligible quantity that its absence is for some time remarked. It seems odd to traverse a familiar bump and not to receive the usual pitch.

A special part of the design is the positioning of the engine mass well forward, and the use of rather flexible springs of about equal periodicity at back and front, so that both ends of the car rise and fall in harmony. Radius rods to the front axle prevent this suspension from interfering with steering stability. Be the design as it may, however, there is no doubt about the results. In back and front seats the riding is much above the average and exceptionally comfortable. It was found possible to write legibly whilst sitting in the rear seats and travelling at 70 m.p.h. on Brooklands track, which is no billiards table.

Despite this smooth flexibility of the suspension, the Lanchester does not give that feeling of "riding in a balloon" which is often experienced on flexibly sprung cars; it rides with certainty and follows its light steering with precision. To drive the car fairly fast over a road section chosen for multitudinous curves and many sharp corners is to appreciate its many good points—the stability, the ease of the steering, its freedom from road shock and its automatic return to the straight, the progressive way in which the brakes operate (the car slows in direct ratio to the pressure applied to the pedal), the beauties of fluid flywheel transmission, and the smooth willingness of the six-cylinder engine over a wide variety of speeds.

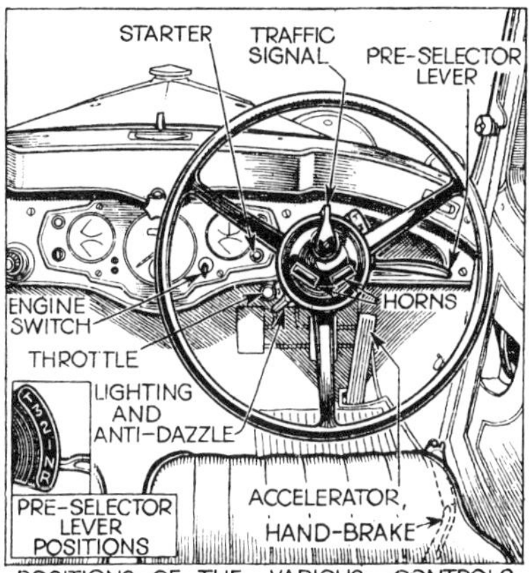
STARTER
TRAFFIC SIGNAL
PRE-SELECTOR LEVER
ENGINE SWITCH
HORNS
THROTTLE
LIGHTING AND ANTI-DAZZLE
ACCELERATOR, HAND-BRAKE
PRE-SELECTOR LEVER POSITIONS
POSITIONS OF THE VARIOUS CONTROLS

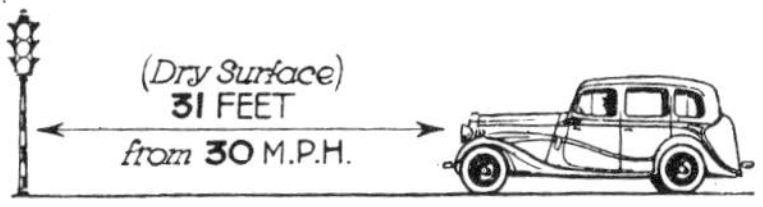
(Dry Surface)
31 FEET
from 30 M.P.H.

This engine is very sweet running indeed, right from a snail's pace on top gear up to the 70 m.p.h. or so of which the car is easily capable. It is also exceptionally quiet; indeed, such sound as there is in the car is confined almost entirely to the rushing of wind. The Lanchester is a car which can be driven comfortably and easily at any average the driver chooses, and it can make decidedly fast times from place to place.

There is no sign of exhaust or body boom, no trace of fumes or heat in the body, and a good control of ventilation is afforded by hinged half-window flaps in front and rear quarters. The driving position is very comfortable, and the view outwards and forwards particularly clear even close up to the car, because the bonnet and scuttle are not too high. This is a commendable point. The side view is slightly less unobstructed, because the screen pillars are rather wide and the front-window ventilator flaps tend to introduce a minor obstruction in the field of view. These flaps are controlled by winding knobs, by the way.

The sliding roof has a centre lock, and in front of the driver is a neat little self-locking blind for use as an anti-sun-glare shield. The instruments are neatly grouped in the centre of the board, and the large-dial speedometer, as fitted on the car tested registered 74 when the car was timed to be

DATA FOR THE DRIVER

18 h.p. LANCHESTER SALOON.

PRICE, with five-seater saloon body, £580. Tax, £13 10s.
RATING : 17.97 h.p., six cylinders, o.h.v., 69.5 × 105 mm., 2,390 c.c.
WEIGHT, without passengers, 31 cwt. 3 qr.
TYRE SIZE : 5.5 × 18in. on centre-lock knock-off wire wheels.
LIGHTING SET : 12-volt ; automatic voltage control.
TANK CAPACITY : 18 gallons with 2 in reserve ; fuel consumption, 20 m.p.g.
TURNING CIRCLE : (L.) 38ft. ; (R.) 38 ft. GROUND CLEARANCE : 6in.

ACCELERATION.

Overall gear ratios	From steady m.p.h. of 10 to 30	20 to 40	30 to 50
4.86 to 1	12 4/5 sec.	14 sec.	15 1/5 sec.
7.58 to 1	9 4/5 sec.	9 1/5 sec.	13 1/5 sec.
11.27 to 1	8 1/5 sec.	—	—
19.82 to 1	—	—	—

From rest to 50 m.p.h. through gears, 19 sec.
From rest to 60 m.p.h. through gears, 36 4/5 sec.
25 yards of 1 in 5 gradient from rest, 5 sec.

SPEED.

	m.p.h.
Mean maximum timed speed over ¼ mile	70.31
Best timed speed over ¼ mile...	71.43
Speeds attainable on indirect gears—	
1st	22
2nd	39
3rd	55
Speed from rest up 1 in 5 Test Hill	15.60

Performance figures of acceleration and maximum speed are the means of several runs in opposite directions.

(Latest car described in "The Autocar" of September 21st, 1934.)

The Lanchester Eighteen saloon exhibits a well-balanced appearance ; it is seen on the road in its native county.

travelling at 71.43 m.p.h. As Brooklands track was still under repair at the time of the test, the maximum speed obtained may be regarded as conservative.

So much has been written in the past about the fascination of the fluid flywheel transmission and the pre-selective self-changing gear that the temptation arises to put forward one aspect of it that is important, if not superlative, namely, that a gear control consisting of a finger-tip lever below the steering wheel, when combined with a pull-up brake lever tucked down at the right-hand side of the driving seat, does secure absolute ease of entry or exit by the left-hand as well as by the right-hand door. So often is this a boon when using a car for shopping.

The gear lever is a new roller-cum-quadrant device that ensures the lever going right home into any notch however carelessly used, so that there is no chance of accidentally missing a selection.

To recapitulate some of the major points of this trans-

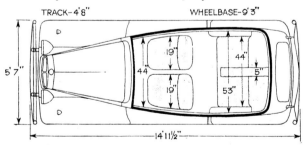

mission, with the engine running at idling speed and the car stationary any gear can be selected, and the pedal released. Because of the fluid flywheel the car does not move forward unless the accelerator pedal is depressed.

A start can be made on any gear. The car can be driven in traffic merely by using the accelerator to go forward and the brake to stop—the "clutch" pedal need not be touched. The car can be driven up a hill, allowed to come to rest, and then be started again with the accelerator, provided, of course, that the gradient is not too severe for the gear ratio in use. On first gear this can be accomplished on a 1 in 4 section.

Gear changing requires no skill, only the common-sense method of releasing pressure on the accelerator pedal when changing up and depressing the pedal when changing down.

This gear change not only presents no difficulty to the unskilled, but the skilled driver can play any of his pet fancy "tunes" on it without making a mistake.

As regards the rest of the performance, the figures speak for themselves, particularly the acceleration from a standing start to 50 m.p.h., which is always a measure of the gear change as well as of the heartiness of the engine and the power-to-weight ratio. What the figures do not tell, however, is that the performance is particularly easy and regular and that the car is in all ways especially pleasant to handle.

The coachwork offers a great deal of room ; the seats are generous, particularly the front seats, there is leg-room to spare in the rear compartment, and no fear of heads bumping the roof with this specially good springing. The usual fittings include such items as a rear blind controlled by the driver, twin roof lights with a switch on the centre pillar, pockets in the doors, elbow-rests, a folding centre arm-rest, a roof net, balanced drop windows in the forward doors, and, of course, separate adjustable front seats.

In the tail is a compartment to house the spare wheel and wheel tools, and also a folding luggage platform which does not necessitate the lid of the compartment being left open. Besides a Daimler-built body the car has the special Daimler type of bonnet, the top of which lifts up on rear hinges and is held by struts, while the sides may easily be removed altogether if required. The tool-kit proper is in a locker under the bonnet. Accessibility of the mechanism for ordinary maintenance has been carefully studied.

Altogether, the Lanchester Eighteen is one of the most pleasantly running cars that has yet emanated from this famous stable of high ideals.

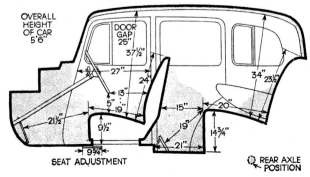

SEAT ADJUSTMENT   REAR AXLE POSITION

A 36

The Autocar Road Tests

The Lanchester near Iping, close to the borders of Sussex and Hampshire.

No. 1,007 (*Post-War Series*) LANCHESTER TEN SALOON

Benefits of the Fluid Flywheel Transmission on a Comparatively Small Car : A Roomy and Well-equipped Body

AMONG the smaller cars on the market the Lanchester Ten has a rather special position. It is only to be expected that, produced as it is by the oldest firm in the British motor industry, with a fine reputation for building cars of quality, this, their smallest model, should be on a distinctly different plane from that occupied by the average small car.

This year the engine size of the Ten has been increased, so that the rating is now actually 10.8 h.p., and this has had a material effect in improving the performance from the ordinary driver's point of view. It is a car to which people turn who want the economy, ease of handling, and other advantages of a comparatively small car, yet definitely desire a measure of comfort and refinement that is not to be found at the lowest prices of all.

Wishes such as these are met extremely well by the Lanchester Ten. It travels with a very satisfactory smoothness and quietness at the sort of speeds the majority of people employ—that is, round about 40 m.p.h. ; it gives good comfort as regards both the suspension and the seating, and it is a handy size of car on crowded roads. By no means least, it is exceptionally simple to control by virtue of the fluid flywheel transmission, which includes the Wilson type of self-changing preselective gear box.

No chassis space is wasted by overhang or a sweeping tail to the body, and, as a result, this four-door six-light saloon is remarkably roomy for a car with an engine of 11 h.p. rating. It is a car that suits admirably those who value quiet and peaceful motoring. At higher speeds the engine loses some of the quite unusual refinement apparent over the normal range, and is not silent above 50 m.p.h. and towards the limit, but it is still able to make a driver who wishes to travel fast feel that it is working well within its capabilities.

In point of fact, this car is faster in sheer maximum speed than might be expected, or needed, by the majority of owners. It was tested at Brooklands on a day when a strong wind was favourable in one direction, and achieved in that direction a timed speed which can be regarded as

The engine is particularly neat with the main auxiliaries accessible.

equivalent to definitely helpful conditions on the road. The speedometer then showed a highest reading of 73 ; at 30 the instrument read a little more than 3 m.p.h. fast, and at 50 was 4.3 m.p.h. fast.

The ordinary kind of main road slope is taken without appreciable lessening of speed and without any necessity to rush the gradient ; but gear changes are so easily made, and third gear in particular is so quiet—as to be almost indistinguishable from top—that it is intriguing to employ the gears sometimes by way of improving the performance. There are good pulling powers on third, which will cope with a gradient of 1 in 8, whilst a steeper hill of 1 in 6½ maximum gradient can be climbed about half-way on third and finished on second, with a reserve in hand, including the rounding of an acute left-hand corner at the summit.

Gear changing on this car is indeed child's play. The finger-tip control lever is moved to the position on the quadrant for the required lower or higher ratio, the left-hand, or transmission, pedal is depressed, and the gear at once obtained without possibility of making a noise or missing the gear.

One advantage of the fluid flywheel is that the take-up of the drive is smoothed out after gear changes have been made, but another and more important feature of it is that the car can be controlled largely by the throttle pedal and brakes alone. When waiting in traffic it is not necessary to go into neutral ; the car will rest stationary with the engine ticking over, and first or second gear engaged—second gear starting is recommended by the makers. As soon as the throttle is opened and the engine accelerated sufficiently, the fluid flywheel takes up the drive and the car moves away, when the gear changes in succession through to top can be made in the usual manner.

Also, the car can be held on a gradient by the engine without use of the brakes. According to the severity of the hill, second or first gear may be engaged, and the engine accelerated sufficiently, when the car will "hang" on the hill, moving forward as soon as the throttle is opened enough to produce the necessary

" The Autocar " Road Tests

power. That this can be done on a hill as steep as 1 in 4, which is seldom paralleled in main road motoring, is distinctly a point of interest. The engine is always available as a brake when descending hills with a gear engaged—the fluid flywheel is in no sense a free wheel.

Certainly more can be done with the car on top gear, at low speeds in traffic and on gradients as well, because of the presence of the fluid fly-wheel, than would generally apply to a four-cylinder car of this size carrying a quite big saloon body. When accelerating from the crawling speeds thus permitted there is a trace of fine pinking from the engine, which passes off almost at once ; a fairly high compression ratio is employed in the interests of efficiency.

The entire control is light. The steering turns easily, and does not become heavy when the car is being manœuvred in a confined space. It has perceptible caster action to return the front wheels after a corner, though not very much automatic sense of direction. Slight movement is sometimes transmitted back, according to the surface which is being traversed. It is fairly high-geared steering, two turns of the wheel giving full lock from right to left, and rather less from left to right.

The gear changing pedal action is particularly light on third and top, a little heavier where first and second gears are concerned, but it is not intended that the pedal shall be used as a clutch. With the fluid flywheel the proper method is to depress it fully for engagement of a gear and then leave the pedal alone, whether going forward in the ordinary way or reversing.

Brakes of the rod-operated Girling pattern are fitted. These are notable for lightness of operation and for the

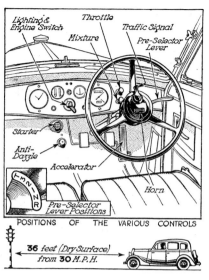

POSITIONS OF THE VARIOUS CONTROLS

36 feet (Dry Surface) from **30** M.P.H.

DATA FOR THE DRIVER

LANCHESTER TEN SALOON.

PRICE, with four-door six-light saloon body, £298. Tax, £8 5s.
RATING : 10.82 h.p., four cylinders, o.h.v., 66 × 105 mm., 1,444 c.c.
WEIGHT, without passengers, 23 cwt. 1 qr. 23 lb.
TYRE SIZE : 5.00 × 18in. on bolt-on wire wheels.
LIGHTING SET : 12-volt ; three-rate charging ; 6-7 amps. at 30 m.p.h.
TANK CAPACITY : 10 gallons ; fuel consumption, 26-30 m.p.g.
TURNING CIRCLE (L. and R.) : 37ft. **GROUND CLEARANCE** : 5½in.

ACCELERATION				SPEED	
Overall gear ratios.	From steady m.p.h. of				m.p.h.
	10 to 30	20 to 40	30 to 50	Mean maximum timed speed over ¼ mile	62.07
5.43 to 1	14⅘ sec.	17⅘ sec.	22 sec.	Best timed speed over ¼ mile...	66.18
8.20 to 1	10 sec.	13¼ sec.	—	Speeds attainable on indirect	
12.65 to 1	8⅘ sec.	—	—	gears :—	
23.33 to 1	—	—	—	1st	12–17
From rest to 50 m.p.h. through gears,				2nd	23–31
28⅘ sec.				3rd	38–45
25 yards of 1 in 5 gradient from rest,				Speed from rest up 1 in 5 Test	
6⅘ sec.				Hill (on 1st gear) ...	13.20

Performance figures of acceleration and maximum speed are the means of several runs in opposite directions.

(Latest model described in " The Autocar " of August 16th, 1935.)

---

door yet instantly to hand, with a pull-up action to apply it. It holds the car securely on 1 in 4.

The springing has a fairly soft action for comfortable riding under almost all normal conditions, but permits neither an undue amount of fore-and-aft motion nor noticeable side sway unless appreciable corners are taken faster than is general practice. It is a suspension which has a good capacity for smoothing out poor surfaces, without being actually outstanding where a really bad, almost freakish, surface is concerned.

The spaciousness of the body has already been mentioned. This is a particularly noticeable point of the Lanchester Ten. In front there is ample elbow room as well as leg room, the driving position is comfortable, and the thin-rimmed steering wheel is not set so high as to interfere with the vision of a short driver. The off-side wing is visible to anyone of average height sitting up normally. The windscreen, too, is of good depth, and the bonnet and radiator are not specially high. The front seats have rather sharply inclined back rests, which is not everyone's taste, but the cushioning effect is very good.

In the back compartment there is full leg room for two tall passengers. At the centre of the seat is a folding armrest, and there are softly padded armrests at the sides. A centre-locked sliding roof is fitted, also a twin-blade electric screenwiper, and special provision for ventilation is made, the forward door windows being divided, with a hinged section. The interior generally is very nicely finished. The instruments are neatly panelled, and well illuminated at night ; they include an engine thermometer. The view in the driving mirror is very good, just falling short of all-embracing.

Starting is ready on a cold morning, and the engine gains temperature quite quickly, having a thermostat in the water circulation system. The retention of an external radiator filler cap is a pleasing, not to say practical, point, and the reserve petrol tap fitted is an excellent feature. Luggage is accommodated on a tubular grid at the rear.

This car is capable of pleasing many people of a critical frame of mind, who appreciate quality.

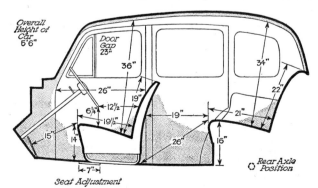

Seat Adjustment

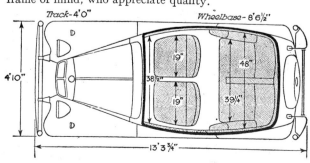

high proportion of braking effort obtained for a given pressure on the pedal. On this Lanchester they reduce speed smoothly and inspire confidence. The hand-brake lever is of a special type, placed at the right of the driving seat, where it is entirely out of the way of the driver's

C 10

Lanchester Fourteen Roadrider coupé, a smart body with luggage boot and external covered spare wheel.

New Lanchester Fourteen

Four Styles of Coachwork Available on a Carefully Designed Six-cylinder Chassis

INSPIRING the design of the latest Lanchester, the six-cylinder Fourteen Roadrider, is the desire to produce a car of comfortable size, smooth road performance, extreme ease of driving, and complete dependability, so that the owner will find a very sound all-round balance of the features which are of essentially practical value to himself.

This car is in no sense a flamboyant one, but is a modern version of quiet taste, and has been developed from the de luxe series of the Lanchester Twelve Light Six. Therefore, it presents no untried features; on the contrary, every feature of the Twelve has been carefully studied in the light of experience gained from "service," and improvements have been incorporated wherever desirable, so that the new model starts off with every prospect of showing particular reliability.

It has, of course, all the regulation Lanchester special features of construction, including the fluid flywheel transmission, but it is nevertheless the lowest-priced six-cylinder Lanchester so far placed on the market.

The prices, in fact, are as follows: Chassis £250, saloon (fabric top) £325, saloon (panelled top) £330, sports saloon £340, and coupé £330. These cars are already in regular production, and a number are in the hands of agents around the country.

In appearance the various styles are distinctly attractive, although they might not be recognised immediately as Lanchesters, because the radiator has been redesigned and modernised; moreover, it is mounted farther forward, and the three-piece bonnet is considerably longer and more imposing than on pre-

D 7

vious types. The radiator and front wings are carried on a cross beam, centre-point-mounted on rubber to the front cross-member of the chassis, whereby any weaving of the frame is prevented from affecting the front end of the bonnet and body. Short brackets issue from each side of the radiator, and carry the head lamps, whereby the directional adjustment of the beams is kept accessible.

Of the various styles of coachwork, the saloon is a coachbuilt body of conventional shape, with a flowing back panel in which the spare wheel is concealed under a circular cover, the luggage problem being met by a large and substantial folding grid. This body is a four-door six-light design with ample head room, and a perfectly flat floor in the rear compartment, a point

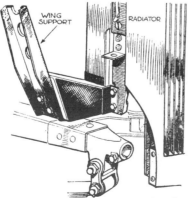

Wing supports and radiator are slung in one piece on a central rubber mounting.

which is secured by the low level of the underslung worm-driven rear axle.

One of the features of the design is that the scuttle is particularly wide; hence the windscreen—centre-controlled by a winding handle and fitted with independent twin concealed wipers—is extra wide, so that visibility is good, especially as the scuttle is not too high. A short driver can see both wings easily. Again, the rear window is large and the backward view clear. Separate seats of very comfortable shape are provided, with easy adjustments for reach, and the base of each front seat is recessed to give extra toe room to the rear seats. Large rolled elbow rests and a folding centre arm-rest add to the comfort of a rear compartment which has a recessed roof to add to the already generous head room.

A sliding roof, draught-preventing louvres to the four drop windows, and scuttle ventilators take care of ventilation. The instruments are neatly grouped on the right-hand side in front of the driver, leaving the left side free to provide a cubby hole of large size.

To those owners who prefer coachwork of a more sporting type, the new sports saloon should prove attractive. It is a four-seater four-door four-light body with a large boot built into the back to contain the spare wheel and to offer plenty of room for luggage under cover. There is about this body something different from the appearance of the average modern car, for flowing curves and bulbous lines have deliberately been eschewed, and fine curves with sharp corners and level lines have been adopted instead. This scheme is both

New Lanchester Fourteen

refreshing and attractive to the eye.

The coupé is more orthodox in style, and is a smart four-light two-door body with a luggage boot and external covered spare wheel. With both these models there is a choice of two styles of upholstery—either leather, or a combination of leather and cloth. This latter is a new scheme likely to set a fashion, for the roll at the front of each seat cushion and the edging of the squabs are of leather, whilst the rest is of cloth to match the leather in colour. Thereby, not only is a distinctly smart appearance obtained, but also leather is found at the points of wear and cloth in the places where cloth is most comfortable. On all models there is a wide range of exterior colour schemes.

The chassis has a wheelbase of 8ft. 7in., track of 4ft., and overall length of 13ft. 10in., the width being 5ft. Wire wheels of the Magna type are shod with 5.00 by 18in. tyres. Rated at 14 h.p., and taxed at £10 10s., the 1½-litre engine has six cylinders of 60 by 90 mm. (1,527 c.c.) and develops over 40 b.h.p. As compared with earlier designs, the new engine has an extra stiff crankshaft with webs of increased size, and considerably longer pistons are fitted.

The construction embraces the use of an integral cylinder head, with push-rod-operated overhead valves, and large-clearance silent cams. The carburetter draws its air through a silencer and fume pipe and feeds the inlet valves through a straight type of hot-spot manifold; the carburetter receives its fuel from a mechanical pump. The coil ignition is neatly arranged, with the distributor and coil as close as possible to the sparking plugs, which enter the cylinder heads at a convenient angle, and are partly concealed in pockets. On the same, or left, side of the engine are the oil cleaner and the dipstick, whilst the oil filler is on top of the valve cover. The dynamo, with a tandem water pump, is driven by a triangular belt in conjunction with the fan. The aluminium crank case of the engine is continued to form the housing of the fluid flywheel, and to this housing the four-speed preselective self-changing gear box is attached to form a complete unit mounted in the frame on rubber pads at five points. Final drive is by

Entirely changed—the latest Lanchester radiator design.

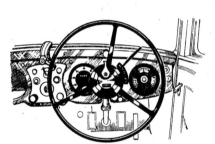

Grouped controls: finger-operated gear lever and two large dials containing all the instruments.

Strengthened and redesigned chassis cross-bracing.

means of an open propeller-shaft passing through the centre of the cruciform of the frame to the worm-drive rear axle.

This car's frame is an interesting piece of work, the side-members being reinforced with a prolonged cruciform, and box section, or lattice box section, is used wherever desirable to give the utmost rigidity. The centre of the cruciform has been greatly strengthened. At the rear of the frame is a 10-gallon fuel tank, 1½ gallons being held in reserve, and brought into use when a plunger on the dash is pulled out. This plunger makes a visible reminder of the need for replenishment. Long and flexible half-elliptic springs are employed, and form a part of a suspension scheme whereby careful weight distribution secures comfortable riding on an even keel. To add to the comfort and maintain the efficiency, Luvax shock absorbers of a greatly increased size are now used, and are carried on extra stiff brackets. The front ones are mounted laterally, and their arms are linked to the axle ends close to the steering swivels, so as to obtain a wide base to control roll. Girling four wheel brakes are used, and the hand-brake lever is of the pull-up type, out of the way of easy entry to the front seats. Easy entry is, in fact, one of the features of the car, as there are no control levers whatever in the way.

These, then, are the major points of the new Lanchester Fourteen, which is pre-eminently a type of quiet, comfortable car to suit the needs of a discerning owner. It has a good road performance, and is particularly easy to handle.

As regards the remainder of the Lanchester programme, the 11 h.p. four-cylinder car is to be continued, and particulars will be issued towards the end of September, whilst complete car prices will range from £298. The Lanchester Eighteen is also to be continued in an improved form, but details will not be available until the Olympia Show in October.

(Left) The Fourteen coupé showing the Magna wheels now used.

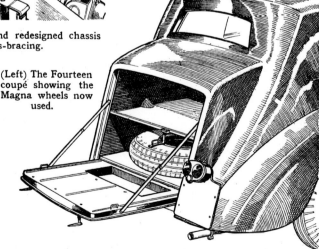

"Well-cut" lines and useful rear compartment of the new sports saloon body.

D 8

The AUTOCAR ROAD TESTS

No. 1,107.—LANCHESTER EIGHTEEN SALOON

A Worthy Example of One of the Oldest of British Makes

THERE must be many people who appreciate the kind of motoring the Lanchester Eighteen provides. It is a car of quality which exhibits a definite character in its road behaviour, and which is not expensively priced for what it is and gives. At this moment it is specially appropriate to deal with a car from one of the oldest firms in the British industry, and a make that is in Royal service.

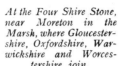

At the Four Shire Stone, near Moreton in the Marsh, where Gloucestershire, Oxfordshire, Warwickshire and Worcestershire join.

This car is thoroughly comfortable, has a smooth and quiet 20 h.p.-rated six-cylinder engine, and handles well. It travels in a more than usually pleasing way, the engine never obtruding itself upon the driver's or passengers' consciousness, and the car as a whole riding evenly. Given a chance to get moving, it runs with train-like regularity and steadiness at speeds between 50 and 60 m.p.h. on open main roads. Forty miles or thereabouts can be put into an hour, in the dark, for instance, the car's running in the process being so easy that passengers are found to be dozing.

That is characteristic of this Lanchester. Both to ride in and to drive it is a soothing car. It calls for no showy handling to make a really good day's mileage. It may be mentioned that this car was tested during the first 1,100 miles of its life, over a distance exceeding 500 miles.

Equal in importance to the effortless manner of the car's progress is the sense of control that a driver strange to it at once experiences. He has mastery over the car; it does not seem big or unwieldy. A merging of good qualities in it gives a balance on the road that is unusually satisfactory. That one thinks so well of this Lanchester goes to show how many things count besides sheer performance.

This can be very much of a top gear car. The Daimler fluid flywheel transmission is fitted, of course, in conjunc-

tion with a four-speed preselective gear box. Unless the driver chooses to the contrary, for the sake of extra performance, he need seldom use a lower gear. Particularly pleasing is the manner in which this car will glide through town streets. It is possible, indeed, to handle it entirely on top gear in dense traffic, taking right-angle turns and using top even for getting away from a standstill. This may hardly be good regular practice, but it can be done easily, and is a rather remarkable feature. The now not uncommon modern engine

"flutter" is absent when accelerating from the lowest speeds on top gear. This extreme flexibility makes town driving as nearly a pleasure as it can ever be, and the driver is left free to concentrate upon the traffic.

As to hill-climbing, about 1 in 12 can be managed on top gear, though actually there is an advantage in dropping down to third. The usual 1 in 6½ hill required second, and the climb was completed at about 16 m.p.h.

Gear changing is the easiest possible matter. All that the driver has to do is to select the gear he wants and depress the transmission pedal, preferably adjusting the engine speed accordingly. Pedal pressure for engaging forward gears is moderate, but there is a considerably stronger action on reverse, and, from cold, there is apt to be a jerkiness when coming backwards out of a garage first thing in the morning. The preselector lever is well placed, and moves nicely. The Wilson-type gears are very reasonably quiet. First is purely an emergency ratio, and the car is normally started from rest on second gear.

It is an interesting variation in traffic allowed by the special transmission to move away on the hand throttle, for that lever is conveniently situated on the steering wheel. When waiting in traffic, second gear can be left engaged, and, with the engine tick-

---

DATA FOR THE DRIVER

LANCHESTER EIGHTEEN SIX-LIGHT SALOON.

PRICE, with Daimler-built six-light saloon body, £595. Tax, £15.
RATING : 19.3 h.p., six cylinders, o.h.v., 72 × 105 mm., 2,565 c.c.
WEIGHT, without passengers, 31 cwt. 3qr. 24lb.
LB. (WEIGHT) PER C.C. : 1.40.
TYRE SIZE : 5.50 × 18in. on centre-lock wire wheels.
LIGHTING SET : 12-volt. Automatic voltage control.
TANK CAPACITY : 20 gallons ; approx. normal fuel consumption, 17-20 m.p.g.
TURNING CIRCLE : (L. and R.) 38ft. **GROUND CLEARANCE :** 7in.

Overall gear ratios.	ACCELERATION From steady m.p.h. of			SPEED	m.p.h.
	10 to 30	20 to 40	30 to 50	Mean maximum timed speed over ¼ mile	68.57
4.86 to 1	12.6 sec.	15.0 sec.	18.3 sec.		
7.58 to 1	8.7 sec.	11.1 sec.	15.8 sec.	Best timed speed over ¼ mile...	70.87
11.27 to 1	7.5 sec.	—	—		
19.82 to 1	—	—	—	Speeds attainable on indirect gears (normal and maximum.) :—	
From rest to 30 m.p.h. through gears, 9.4 sec.				1st	10-19
From rest to 50 m.p.h. through gears, 24.4 sec.				2nd	25-35
From rest to 60 m.p.h. through gears, 36.8 sec.				3rd	48-53
25 yards of 1 in 5 gradient from rest, 6.3 sec.				Speed from rest up 1 in 5 Test Hill (on 1st gear)	14.39

BRAKE TEST : Mean stopping figure from 30 m.p.h., 34.5ft. (dry concrete).
Performance figures for acceleration and maximum speed are the means of several runs in opposite directions.
(Latest model described in "The Autocar" of September 25th, 1936.)

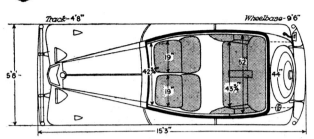

ing over, the fluid flywheel temporarily isolates the engine from the transmission. At this point the engine can be felt to some slight extent. Then, as the engine is accelerated suitably, the drive takes up and the car moves off.

Although this car possesses good stability, the suspension shows up to excellent advantage from the comfort point of view. The springing is soft, but not too soft. Slight deflection of the wheels may be apparent over minor inequalities in the road surface, but they do not affect the occupants. The most considerable movement in ordinary conditions is a series of mild tremors. Yet this car can be taken accurately round an appreciable corner at between 40 and 50 m.p.h. and the steering achieves a good degree of positiveness. In the right sense the front wheels can be felt, and occasionally a very slight "shiver" is noticeable, but this never becomes considerable. It is not "dead" steering, and, indeed, is moderately geared, requiring about 3½ turns from lock to lock. There is sufficient caster action. It is light steering for general control, requiring more effort for a sharp turn or manoeuvring. The lock, or turning circle, is distinctly satisfactory.

Smooth, Progressive Brakes

Also helping materially in the impression the driver has of full control, the Girling brakes are light to apply but not undesirably so. A gentle, progressive pressure upon the pedal draws the speed down smoothly, exactly as required, and there is braking power in reserve for an excellent emergency pull-up or sudden slowing down. The hand-brake lever calls for praise, too. It is of pull-up type, placed to the right of the driving seat, well out of the way but within instant reach, and it is powerful for holding the car. The small incidental controls are also particularly well within reach.

All in all, this is a car to appeal to those who set store by some of the finer points and who place the greatest value upon quiet and comfortable progression in a manner that does not imply dullness. Estimation of the Lanchester is increased also by the fact that the speedometer is unusually conservative; when it shows 30 the car is actually doing 31 m.p.h., and, at 50, 49.6 m.p.h. The highest reading when the car was being timed for maximum speed was 70-71.

Again of considerable importance is the position of the

steering wheel, which is thoroughly well raked, the top of the rim coming sensibly below eye level. There is a broad, deep windscreen, for which reason the windscreen pillars do not obtrude, even though they are not thin. Again, the bonnet level is kept at a satisfactory level. Actually, the driver could not set himself sufficiently close to the wheel by means of the adjustment provided, and used a supplementary cushion, but the whole range of the adjustment could easily be altered to give a similar result. The seats afford excellent support, and are really comfortable.

Finished quietly and well equipped in detail, the Daimler-built four-door saloon body is of restrained external appearance. Everything about it is of good quality. A centre-locked, easily operated sliding roof gives a really practical size of opening. A specially appreciated item is

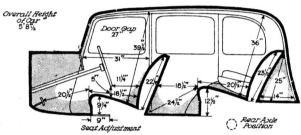

Seating dimensions are measured with cushions and squabs uncompressed.

the high mounting of the instruments. To read them calls for minimum deflection of vision.

A tell-tale warning lamp replaces the oil pressure gauge, and there is the interesting and practical fitment of an engine sump oil thermometer, in addition to a water thermometer. A reserve petrol tap is fitted within reach of the driver, and a 20-gallon tank gives a wide range without replenishing. Twin horns are controlled by separate switches. Door and window handles are well placed, and the doors shut solidly in the way that betokens a soundly built body. For the rear seat there is a central folding armrest, and the floor is free from any tunnel owing to the underslung worm final drive, whilst it is equally easy for the driver to get in or out by either door. Luggage is provided for only by an external folding grid.

Neat and accessible in the main items, the overhead-valve six-cylinder engine carries a good finish. It starts readily, and, from cold, automatic regulation of the S.U. carburettor mixture takes effect, there being no hand strangler control. Temperature is soon gained, but the engine is inclined to be a little uneven at first when stone cold, it being best, apparently, to drive straight off. Almost the only additional items of equipment that might be thought of is automatic chassis lubrication. A neat external radiator filler cap is appreciated. Also, the engine oil filler and dipstick are particularly convenient.

Showing the driver's view through the windscreen of the Lanchester as revealed by the new visibility test.

N I*

1938 Cars : New Lanchester Fourteen

Independent Front Suspension a Feature of an Entirely New Design Which is Offered with Fluid Flywheel Transmission or a Synchromesh Gear Box : Final Drive Now by Spiral Bevel Instead of Worm Gear Formerly Used

A neat appearance is shown to the front. Plain bumpers are used fore and aft.

ONE of the most successful models of the Lanchester range during the last season has been the Fourteen Roadrider, which is a car of considerable refinement, and of a type particularly to appeal for family use, partly because it is roomy and quiet and partly because the fluid flywheel transmission renders it so extremely easy to handle. This car is to be continued at a price of £330 for the saloon.

At the same time, however, an entirely new edition of it has been put into production, with many innovations and improvements which necessitate a slightly higher price range, as follows: Lanchester Fourteen Roadrider de luxe saloon £365 ; sports saloon £375 ; or with a synchromesh gear box instead of fluid flywheel transmission, £25 less in each case.

Rated at 14.06 h.p., tax £10 10s., the new engine has six cylinders of 61.47 by 101.6 mm. (1,809 c.c.), and the overhead valves, which are operated by rockers and push rods, are carried in a detachable cylinder head.

The valve rockers are carried on unusually rigid supports, whereby noise is avoided. Incidentally, cams of a new form have been developed, and these secure a high standard of silence in operation.

Cylinder Block

Many points are to be found in the cylinder block construction. The cylinder barrels are completely separated, with water space between so as to avoid distortion, and the water jacket is carried right down to the foot of each cylinder. Furthermore, the T-slotted aluminium alloy pistons, which have four rings, one a scraper, are designed with extra long skirts and a low position for the gudgeon pin. These features should combine to reduce cylinder wear to a minimum.

The crankshaft is counterweighted and carried in four bearings. In general layout the engine follows usual Lanchester practice, a refinement being that the distributor head and coil are close together, and close to the long-reach sparking plugs, the plug wires being very neatly concealed in a bakelite cover. A

mechanical fuel pump draws petrol from the twelve-gallon rear tank, which has a reserve control, and feeds it to an S.U. carburettor fitted with an air silencer.

As already indicated, this new car is

A synchromesh gear box is an alternative to this fluid flywheel.

obtainable with the fluid flywheel and pre-selective self-changing four-speed gear, or with a four-speed central change gear box with synchromesh on second, third and top, in con-

junction with a Borg and Beck single dry-plate clutch. In each case the gear box is in unit with the engine, and the unit is flexibly mounted in the frame on a three-point rubber suspension with an additional damper arm.

Particularly deep in section, the new frame has side members underslung at the rear to provide a low centre of gravity and a low floor to the body, and is formed into box section at the extremities by extensions of the limbs of a cruciform bracing. The centre point of the cruciform is of a particularly rigid type.

At the front of this frame is the independent suspension for the front wheels. The system employed is a development of the Andre-Girling, and is similar to that used on the latest Daimler 2-litre car. On the Fourteen Lanchester the new suspension is equally effective and gives the car, besides a comfortable, smooth "ride," noticeably good stability on corners. Also the steering is light, direct and very easy to handle even at the lowest speeds, whilst it is unaffected by bad road surfaces.

In the new car there is another departure from previous Lanchester practice, inasmuch as the final drive is by spiral bevel instead of worm gear. The rear axle casing also is of the steel banjo type. A point about the half-elliptic rear springs is that a special form of rubber pad is interposed between the spring and the axle pad to damp out the transmission of sound. Front and rear, the springs are checked by hydraulic shock absorbers, and each pair is cross-coupled by a torsion bar which improves lateral stability. It may be noted that the chief components are situated in the frame in such a way as to equalise weight distribution and to permit all the seats to be brought within the wheelbase, whereby comfortable riding is assured.

The six-light four-door saloon has plenty of window space. Window louvres are fitted.

C 10

Bendix mechanical four-wheel brakes are standardised on this car, and the hand brake is operated by a pistol-grip pull-out handle placed just beneath the instrument board on the right-hand side. The steering gear is a Marles, and the wheel has telescopic adjustment. Whilst on the subject of the steering, it may be remarked that the wheel is well placed and the forward visibility from the driving seat noticeably good.

Spoked disc easy-clean wheels are fitted, and are shod with Dunlop E.L.P. tyres, 5.75 by 16in. A portable D.W.S. hydraulic jack is part of the equipment. The wheelbase of the new car is 9ft. 2in., and the track 4ft. 4in., overall length 14ft. 8in., and width 5ft. 4½in.

Seating accommodation within the saloon body of the new model is ample in capacity, and the seats themselves are notable for the generous height of the back squabs, besides a well-chosen arrangement of angles which affords excellent support and comfort. The body itself is a four-door six-window design of smooth outline, and within the sloping back panel there is a large compartment for luggage under cover. The petrol filler cap is in the near-side rear wing, and the pipe does not obstruct the luggage container. The lid of the latter can be swung down into an horizontal position to act as an extra luggage platform. The spare wheel is carried horizontally in a separate compartment beneath the tail.

For the rear seats there is a folding centre arm rest besides elbow rests, and folding foot ramps are in the base of the separate adjustable front seats. A recessed roof gives extra rear headroom. The body has a sliding roof. The windscreen is operated by a central winding

1938 Cars : New Lanchester Fourteen

handle and is equipped with separately controlled wiper blades driven from a remote electric motor. There are pockets in all the doors, and the roof light is conveniently controlled from switches carried on the door pillars.

Across the scuttle is a facia board with large-dial instruments grouped in front of the driver, the minor controls and switches in a panel in the centre, and a large shelf on the left side.

Externally, this interesting new model has several points to note. The wings are large in size and deeply valanced, with concealed gutters to ensure their efficiency. The head lamps are carried by the structure of the radiator shell. The bonnet is particularly easy to open, for there is a single handle, like a door handle, on each side for locking purposes. Plain bumpers are fitted fore and aft.

NEW LANCHESTER FOURTEEN FOR 1938

Choice of Fluid Flywheel Transmission or Synchromesh Gear Box Offered : Independent Front Suspension

FULL DESCRIPTION OF THIS NEW
MODEL APPEARS IN THIS ISSUE

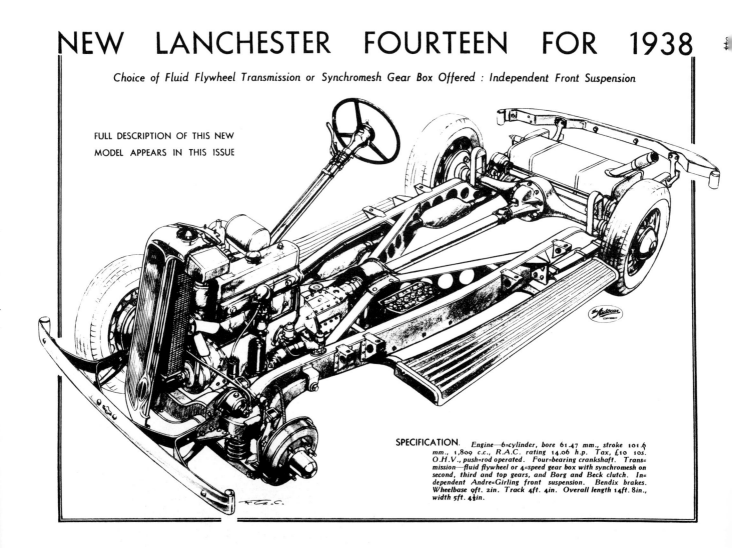

SPECIFICATION. *Engine—6=cylinder, bore 61.47 mm., stroke 101.6 mm., 1,809 c.c., R.A.C. rating 14.06 h.p. Tax, £10 10s. O.H.V., push=rod operated. Four=bearing crankshaft. Trans= mission—fluid flywheel or 4=speed gear box with synchromesh on second, third and top gears, and Borg and Beck clutch. In= dependent Andre=Girling front suspension. Bendix brakes. Wheelbase 9ft. 2in. Track 4ft. 4in. Overall length 14ft. 8in., width 5ft. 4½in.*

The AUTOCAR ROAD TESTS

No. 1,234
LANCHESTER ELEVEN SALOON

A SURPRISING feature, in fact an outstanding impression of the latest Lanchester Eleven, is the size of the body. There is the suggestion of being in a car of 14 or even 16 h.p. as regards roominess, and this illusion is helped by a bonnet of considerable length and width.

Always this model has been of de luxe character among the smaller sizes of car, and especially in its present form it gives rise to some rather unusual reflections as it comes to be judged. Not only is it exceptional in the seating accommodation provided in conjunction with an 11 h.p. engine, but also in the quality nature of the whole car, its finish and its equipment. The quietly furnished interior is that of an expensive style of vehicle.

Thus this model has a specialised appeal to those who appreciate a good type of car, but want economical running and set more store by comfort and general motoring convenience than they do by sheer performance.

It is not to be expected in the circumstances that this Eleven will give brilliant acceleration, for it is fairly heavy, but it does prove well capable of holding its own on the road, and, what is more important to most people, of offering a quiet and restful form of travel. The four-cylin-

der overhead-valve engine is smooth and self-effacing practically throughout its range, from the low speeds to the high, and when required is able to take the car along at 50 m.p.h. or so in an untroubled and effortless fashion, with something in reserve.

The Daimler fluid flywheel transmission that is fitted is of considerable advantage in giving added flexibility to the engine at traffic speeds and during leisurely driving, though with the preselector self-changing gear box gear changing is as simple as it can be. As is well known, with this system a lever mounted on the steering column is moved to the required position, and the next gear is obtained by nothing more than depression of the gear-changing pedal, no possibility existing of making a noise.

Since gear changes can be quick as well as certain, a good deal can be done by use of the indirects to assist acceleration at times or to keep up speed on a gradient where otherwise it would fall away. The car's low-speed acceleration on top gear is, however, satisfactory by normal standards, and certainly smooth and progressive.

Fluid Flywheel Benefits in Traffic

During town driving the fluid flywheel allows the car to remain stationary with a gear engaged ready to move off, the restart calling for no more effort on the driver's part than depressing the throttle pedal. The gear pedal should not be used as a clutch when starting from rest and manœuvring, for a jerky result is then likely to be obtained. First gear is a low emergency ratio, and allows restarting on a gradient as steep as 1 in 4.

There is a good feeling of firmness on the road and of

DATA FOR THE DRIVER

11-11-38

LANCHESTER ELEVEN SALOON.

PRICE, with four-door six-light saloon body, £295. Tax, £8 5s.
RATING : 10.82 h.p., four cylinders, o.h.v., 66 × 105.4 mm., 1,444 c.c.
WEIGHT, without passengers, 25 cwt. 0 qr. 2 lb. LB. PER C.C. : 1.94.
TYRE SIZE : 5.00 × 18in. on bolt-on wire wheels.
LIGHTING SET : 12-volt. Automatic voltage control.
TANK CAPACITY : 10 gallons ; approx. normal fuel consumption, 26–28 m.p.g.
TURNING CIRCLE : (L. and R.) : 42ft. 6in.   **GROUND CLEARANCE :** 6in.

ACCELERATION				SPEED.	
Overall gear ratios.	From steady m.p.h. of				m.p.h.
	10 to 30	20 to 40	30 to 50	Mean maximum timed speed over ¼ mile	60.81
5.43 to 1	15.9 sec.	17.9 sec.	25.4 sec.		
8.20 to 1	11.3 sec.	14.3 sec.	—	Best timed speed over ¼ mile ...	63.38
12.65 to 1	10.1 sec.	—	—	Speeds attainable on indirect gears (normal and maximum) :—	
23.23 to 1	—	—	—	1st	12—17
From rest to 30 m.p.h. through gears ... ... 11.7 sec.				2nd	26—33
To 50 m.p.h. through gears 35.8 sec.				3rd	42—49
25 yards of 1 in 5 gradient from rest ... ... 6.8 sec.				'Speed from rest up 1 in 5 Test Hill (on 1st gear)	12.84

BRAKE TEST : Mean stopping distance from 30 m.p.h. (dry concrete), 32.5ft.

WEATHER : Warm, dry ; wind light, S.E. Barometer : 29.80in.

Performance figures for acceleration and maximum speed are the means of several runs in opposite directions, with two up.

(Latest model described in " The Autocar " of September 23rd, 1938.)

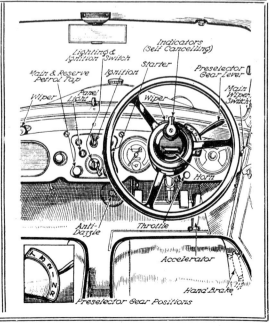

"The Autocar" Road Tests

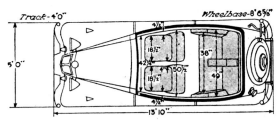

the car being solidly built, whilst the stability is sound for fast driving and cornering. The suspension of this smallest Lanchester is by half-elliptic springs all round. A praise-worthy level of riding comfort is attained, and back-seat passengers speak favourably of the springing. Very little tendency to pitching is noticeable, and also it is not a harsh suspension over distinctly bad surfaces.

A high-geared and fairly "quick" steering is employed, only two turns of the wheel giving the full lock-to-lock movement. It has useful caster action, is light during ordinary driving, and not heavy at low speed or when manœuvring. It is sufficiently accurate at medium and fast speeds.

Braking Points

The brake system is Girling, and light pedal pressure slows the car surely or stops it rapidly, as the case may be. Good reserve braking power is possessed for an emergency. The hand-brake lever is in an exceptionally convenient position, rising from the floor to the right of the driving-seat cushion, where it is out of the way of the door. The separate front seats place the occupants rather low, but the steering wheel mounting is such as to give a comfortable driving position. With the seat set well forward there is a tendency for the knees to be raised more than some drivers like.

Due to the placing of the gear and hand-brake levers the front compartment is clear of controls, which is a big advantage, and both doors become equally usable. Also, the floor is flat, as it is in the back compartment, too. This is decidedly unusual in the smaller cars, and an outcome of the Daimler-Lanchester underslung worm transmission employed, allowing a low-mounted propeller-shaft.

Generous Leg-room and Width

In the back seats as well as the front the upholstery affords plenty of support, leg-room is generous, and there is outstanding interior width for a car of this horse-power. Three reasonably sized people could be carried on occasion

at the rear. There is a comfortable folding arm-rest at the centre of the seat, in addition to elbow-rests.

No special method is provided of controlling ventilation in bad weather, nor are sun-glare visors fitted. The rear-quarter windows do not open. The centre-locked sliding roof forms a big opening. Quality is shown not only in the kind of leather upholstery employed and in the use of polished wood fillets and so forth, but also in the way in which the doors open and close.

The instruments are grouped in clear view of the driver, and include an engine thermometer. In the Daimler-Lanchester manner there is not an ordinary oil-pressure gauge, its place being taken by a warning lamp similar to the ignition tell-tale. The instruments are well lit at night, but not too brightly. The speedometer proved to be nearly 1 m.p.h. slow at 30 and slightly less than 1 m.p.h. fast at 40, becoming 2.4 m.p.h. fast at 50, and showed a highest reading of 67-68.

Within reach of the driver is that most valuable fitting, a reserve petrol control, and one of a type which is not

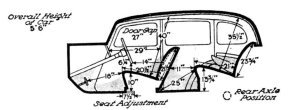

Seating dimensions are measured with cushions and squabs uncompressed.

liable to be overlooked after use. The driving mirror shows a sufficiently good view behind, if not a comprehensive one. The horn note is dignified as well as effective, and the head lamp beam good.

Exceptional body space is secured by making full use of the wheelbase, and there is no built-in luggage compartment, an external folding grid being fitted. The spare wheel is recessed into the rear panel of the body and neatly covered.

It is pleasing to see a tidy and well-finished engine; it has an accessible oil filler and dipstick, and the sparking plugs and carburettor are conveniently placed. There is no hand strangler control, enriching of the mixture for starting from cold being automatic, but a hand throttle is provided. The engine starts at once and pulls well from cold. The bonnet is of one-piece type, without a central hinge, opening up from the front and being then held securely by a strut. The side panels are easily removable if necessary, without need for using a spanner. Jacking is carried out from the sides.

Deep side windows and a deep, reasonably wide windscreen are features, but the screen pillars are fairly thick. The off-side wing is visible from the driving seat, though not the near-side one. The steering wheel comes a trifle high. Vision over the bonnet to the left is satisfactory.

The AUTOCAR ROAD TESTS

No. 1,279.—14 h.p. LANCHESTER ROADRIDER DE LUXE SPORTS SALOON

A RESTFUL atmosphere is induced by the 14 h.p. Lanchester Roadrider De Luxe, and is a singularly appealing quality. It is not accompanied by dullness—far from it—but the combination of a quiet and particularly smooth-running six-cylinder overhead valve engine, and a chassis and car as a whole which are unusually free from disturbing small noises, gives a machine of exceptional refinement.

Also it is very light to handle, and ease of control is materially contributed to by the preselective self-changing gear box and fluid flywheel transmission. It is of interest, however, that, if desired, a normal four-speed synchromesh gear box can be provided on this model.

Sufficient evidence of performance capabilities is afforded by the possession of a maximum speed in the neighbourhood of 70 m.p.h., but whilst it is a car that shows itself able to cover the ground very satisfactorily, one is apt, somehow, to consider it less in terms of performance figures than is often the case. Probably this is due to the engine remaining unobtrusive, yet getting on efficiently with its work.

Soothing Style of Travel

To an exceptional extent journeys are made in this Lanchester without becoming irksome to either driver or passenger. The engine is happy at maintained speeds between 50 and 60 m.p.h., likewise, with the assistance of the fluid flywheel, pulling the car away from low speeds on top gear without any form of vibration or mechanical effort. It is quiet, though at some speeds a subdued under-current of drone is detectable. This is not unpleasing and would pass unnoticed if it were not a particularly quiet engine in the general sense.

Complete top gear flexibility is the outcome of the fluid flywheel, it being even possible to make a start from rest on top. With so easy a form of gear change as is provided, however, it is not necessary to leave the engine to work at the very lowest speeds on top.

Gear changing is a matter of nothing more than moving the preselector lever, mounted conveniently on the steering column, to the required position and depressing the transmission pedal. For the smoothest take-up on the next gear it is desirable to level up engine speed, as with any form of gear change, but a noise cannot be made. Lightness of control extends to the gear-changing pedal.

In traffic the car can be kept in gear with the left foot off the transmission pedal and the brakes lightly applied to check any creeping-forward tendency, and then a move is made simply by depressing the throttle pedal. On an up gradient it can be held "on the engine," without using the brakes. It is a satisfactory method to start on second gear on the level.

On the usual 1 in 6½ gradient, which is of sufficient severity to pull down appreciably the rate of the smaller cars, second gear was only just required by the Lanchester, and there was power in hand for rounding the acute corner at the top.

The way in which this car makes journeys pleasantly is linked up as much with the character of the riding as with the performance provided by the engine. The Roadrider De Luxe has independent front wheel suspension by means of a big-diameter coil spring at each side, and a notably good result is obtained. The car is strikingly free from pitching tendency, and even minor disturbances due to surface defects, so that an untiring course is pursued.

At times the springs may be heard to be taking up a considerable reaction, but shock is not felt. Also it is a

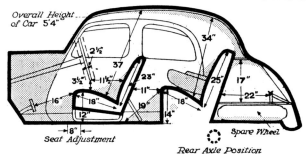

Seating dimensions are measured with cushions and squabs uncompressed.

good suspension as regards lateral stability. The Lanchester can safely be cornered a good deal faster than is usually required of this kind of car.

Although the steering is exceptionally light, being on the low-geared side, since it needs 3⅜ turns of the wheel from lock to lock, it is accurate and gives a definite sense of control over position on the road or when passing through a comparatively narrow space, and again during cornering. It has very satisfactory caster action and is not subject to road wheel tremors. This car is particularly easy to manœuvre.

The Bendix cable-operated servo-shoe brakes are smooth and progressive in their action, meaning that as pedal pressure is increased the retarding effect is increased proportionately. They are not over-sudden brakes, but can be used confidently from the higher speeds.

This is one of those cars that, dissected point by point, show up favourably because each component does its work

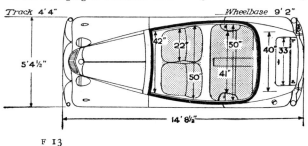

" The Autocar " Road Tests

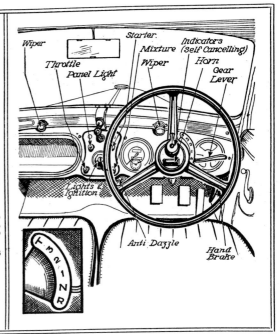

DATA FOR THE DRIVER   12-5-39

14 H.P. LANCHESTER ROADRIDER DE LUXE SPORTS SALOON.

PRICE, with four-door four-light sports saloon body, £375. Tax, £10 10s.
RATING : 14.06 h.p., six cylinders, o.h.v., 61.47 × 101.6 mm., 1,809 c.c.
WEIGHT, without passengers, 28 cwt. 0 qr. 0 lb. LB. PER C.C. : 1.73.
TYRE SIZE : 5.75 × 16in. on bolt-on perforated pressed-steel wheels.
LIGHTING SET : 12-volt. Automatic voltage control.
TANK CAPACITY : 12 gallons ; approx. normal fuel consumption, 22–24 m.p.g.
TURNING CIRCLE : (L. and R.): 40ft.   **GROUND CLEARANCE :** 5½in.

ACCELERATION				SPEED.	
Overall gear ratios.	From steady m.p.h. of				m.p.h.
	10 to 30	20 to 40	30 to 50	Mean maximum timed speed over ¼ mile	66.55
5.25 to 1	12.4 sec.	14.0 sec.	18.6 sec.	Best timed speed over ¼ mile ...	68.18
7.74 to 1	9.1 sec.	10.6 sec.	—	Speeds attainable on indirect	
11.55 to 1	7.7 sec.	—	—	gears (normal and maximum) :—	
20.16 to 1	—	—	—	1st	15—19
From rest to 30 m.p.h. through				2nd	29—34
gears			10.4 sec.	3rd	45—49
To 50 m.p.h. through gears			25.8 sec.		
25 yards of 1 in 5 gradient				Speed from rest up 1 in 5 Test	
from rest			8.1 sec.	Hill (on 1st gear)	13.96

BRAKE TEST : Mean stopping distance from 30 m.p.h. (dry concrete), 33.5ft.

WEATHER : Dry, warm, bright ; wind fresh, N.W. Barometer : 29.55in.

Performance figures for acceleration and maximum speed are the means of several runs in opposite directions, with two up.

(Latest model described in " The Autocar " of September 23rd, 1938.)

---

efficiently, but one that also is essentially to be judged as a whole for its mechanical excellence and practical arrangement of coachwork, controls, and detail fittings, making up a machine that is a pleasure to own and drive and have about one. In appearance it is distinctive, but the opposite of ornate, and the seating is most comfortable, the driving position also being thoroughly good.

The separate front seats have upholstery which not only avoids becoming noticeable on a long journey, but also affords excellent support to the back. A thin-rimmed steering wheel is placed at a natural angle, and is telescopically adjustable. The hand-brake lever moves horizontally and is in a convenient position under the scuttle, on the right. The absence of controls to get in the way allows the driver to use either door with equal convenience, always a material point. There is quality in the whole arrangement of the interior, as in other respects. This four-light sports saloon is offered at the same price as a six-light saloon.

Ample room is provided in all measurements, and at the rear a central folding arm-rest is provided. For ventilation purposes in bad weather useful louvres are fitted over the door windows. They are efficient, and enough room is left for the driver to put his head out of the window.

The head lamp beam is good, though rather more length of beam in the anti-dazzle position would have been useful at times. The horn note is a little "thin" for a car of this character. A good view is given by the mirror, there is a convenient rear-window blind control, the windscreen can be opened, and a sliding roof of satisfactory area is provided. The instruments are in two main dials, easily read and well illuminated at night. As is the Lanchester-Daimler practice, instead of an oil pressure gauge a warning lamp is fitted, but there is an engine thermometer. The speedometer proved to be 1.1 m.p.h. fast at 30, increasing to 3.2 at 40, 4.8 at 50, and 6.3 at 60, and showed a highest reading of 77 during maximum speed timing.

There is a useful size of luggage locker, and a portable hydraulic jack attaches conveniently to brackets at front and rear. The bonnet opens normally from the sides, and a neat, well-finished and generally accessible engine is disclosed. The oil filler is particularly well situated. This engine starts readily and does not require much use of the mixture control before settling down to steady pulling from cold. The admirable and rare feature of a reserve petrol tap is provided, and to mention the fact that it is housed in the spare-wheel locker is not to detract from its practical value.

Over-bonnet vision is good, immediately in front as well as to the near side, where the wing lamp can just be seen—the wing itself by leaning over. The off-side wing is seen well. The windscreen is deep and wide, and its pillars are not seriously thick.

F14

The AUTOCAR ROAD TESTS

No. 1,317.—14 h.p. Lanchester Roadrider De Luxe Saloon

ONE senses a long-developed process of mechanical refinement built into the Lanchester Fourteen. It is no ordinary car of its size, following a set plan, but a vehicle of character alike in its road behaviour as in its appearance and appointing. Mechanical quietness and smoothness it exhibits in an outstanding degree, and these qualities extend throughout the chassis.

The six-cylinder overhead-valve engine is barely audible at any speed, and seems to "lose itself" at 45 to 50 m.p.h., a rate which, not unduly wasteful of petrol, at the same time enables the ground to be covered very satisfactorily in the uncongested road conditions of the moment. The whole effect of a silky engine matches admirably with the qualities of the preselector gear box and fluid flywheel transmission, and the combination results in a car that is very easily handled in a restful manner.

Also, this Lanchester has the happy knack of making a stranger feel quickly at home in it, the driving position being well arranged and the controls being reached naturally. There is at all times a strong impression of travelling in a car of quality.

It lends itself to a leisurely method of handling which is likely to be economical, and also can put forth a quite spirited acceleration performance, helped at the lower speeds by the rapid gear changing that can be made if desired. The smooth and effortless engine is apt to render the performance deceptive, but it is noticed over familiar journeys that decidedly good times are achieved.

Although it is well to-day, if the most is to be made of the available petrol, that maximum speeds should not be employed, and also that the circumstances of these tests by *The Autocar* should conform with prevailing conditions of use, it is worthy of note in connection with the normal use of this car that speeds of 50 to 55 m.p.h. are reached readily, and that it continues to travel with outstanding ease at the higher rates.

The special property of the fluid flywheel is to allow "zero speed" on any gear with the engine ticking over, but not driving the car even though gear is engaged. As soon as the throttle pedal is depressed the car moves away again. Traffic driving is greatly facilitated, top and third sufficing for almost all conditions except actual starting from rest, and control resolving itself into a matter largely of brake and throttle pedals only.

There is no easier or more certain method of changing gear than with the preselector box, for all that is necessary, of course, is to move the finger lever mounted on the steering

Width and depth of windscreen shown by the Visibility Chart are very satisfactory, and the bonnet does not intrude awkwardly into near-side vision. The screen pillars tend to thickness. The left-hand wing lamp can just be seen, and the right-hand wing is well in view. Forward vision is good, due to the radiator and bonnet not being unduly high. (Right) The Lanchester is clean in general outline, and of well-balanced appearance.

ERW 308

B 11

"The Autocar" Road Tests

column to the required gear position on its quadrant, and press down the transmission pedal. The gears of this Lanchester are notably quiet.

Smooth short-distance manœuvring is obtained through the medium of the fluid fly-wheel. The transmission pedal should not be used as a clutch pedal for moving to and fro when entering or leaving a garage, for instance, but be employed only to engage gear—first or reverse as required—and a smooth result is then obtained, with the car under precise control.

The engine power is such that a good range of top-gear climbing ability is provided. As to steeper gradients, second gear took the car over the 1 in 6½ hill frequently employed in these Road Tests. A useful feature to-day is a setting lever on the instrument board for advance and retard of the spark, allowing adjustment to be made while running according to the quality of the fuel. A good degree of advance could be maintained on Pool petrol without excessive pinking, and when this engine does pink it is in a subdued fashion.

Excellent suspension goes with the other pleasing qualities to render this machine a restful, indeed a luxurious, form of progression. The front wheels are independently sprung by a large coil spring at each side. The "ride" is level, corners can be taken fast if desired without swaying or any feeling of insecurity, and there is a definite suggestion of the wheels remaining firmly on the road in spite of changes in the quality of the road surface.

General stability is first rate, and the accuracy of control contributed to materially by the nature of the suspension is well supported by steering that is light but positive, even though it is fairly low geared, needing rather more than 3½ turns of the wheel from lock to lock. No road-wheel tremors, let alone shocks, are given back through the steering wheel, and a light finger hold is enough to control the car.

Safe power with a reserve for all occasions is afforded by the Bendix braking system. The light pedal pressure that slows the car smoothly in the ordinary way, as apart from emergency requirements, is in keeping with the general tenor of the machine. The hand-brake lever is of push-and-pull type, moving horizontally, being out of the way yet easy to reach. The absence of an ordinary gear lever makes it possible for the driver to use either door conveniently.

The seats give firm support, being shaped to the back, and having just the right resilience for comfort on a long journey. The steering wheel is telescopically adjustable, and thus can be placed to individual taste. Its angle makes for a confident driving position.

Two big dials combine all the instruments, which are clear to read. The speedometer was only 0.8 m.p.h. fast at 30, rising to 5.1 m.p.h. at 50. A highest reading of 75 was reached during the timing of maximum speed, for which purpose a run of less than a mile was available from a standing start.

For ventilation purposes in bad weather louvres are provided over the door windows; the sliding roof is of large area. In the back seat an atmosphere of spaciousness is produced, coupled, as in front, with a restful but supporting style of upholstery. At the centre of the squab is a folding arm-rest. The interior finish is very well done, an initial effect of tastefulness being increased by the use made of polished hardwood for the instrument board and door cappings. The rear window blind is easily operated, and the driving mirror gives a comprehensive view behind.

The luggage compartment is of the kind that at once suggests really useful space. The spare wheel and wheel-changing tools are in a separate compartment below, and here also is that rare but now doubly appreciated fitting, a reserve petrol tap.

A normal two-piece bonnet, hinged down the centre, discloses a neat, well-finished and accessibly arranged engine on which one auxiliary does not appear to get in the way of another. Really convenient jacking brackets are provided at front and rear, and the jack is a portable hydraulic type, easily operated from a standing position.

Instant starting is obtained, and without prolonged use of the mixture control for the S.U. carburettor the car gets under way satisfactorily from cold. Temperature is quickly shown on the instrument board thermometer.

As is the Lanchester-Daimler practice, there is no actual oil-pressure gauge, a green warning light being provided to indicate any unduly low pressure. A decidedly useful driving light was provided through the Lucas approved head lamp mask, tried during the test on both the near and the off side, with superior results on this particular car in the former position.

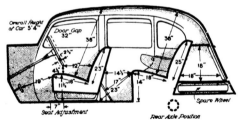

Seating dimensions are measured with cushions and squabs uncompressed.

DATA FOR THE DRIVER (Wartime Test on Pool Petrol) 19-1-40

14 H.P. LANCHESTER ROADRIDER DE LUXE SALOON.

PRICE, with four-door six-light saloon body, £375. Tax, £17 10s.
RATING : 14.06 h.p. six cylinders, o.h.v., 61.47 × 101.6 mm., 1,800 c.c.
WEIGHT, without passengers, 28 cwt. 1 qr. 4 lb. LB. PER C.C : 1.75.
TYRE SIZE : 5.75 × 16in. on bolt-on perforated pressed-steel wheels.
LIGHTING SET : 12-volt. Automatic voltage control.
TANK CAPACITY : 12 gallons ; approx. fuel consumption 22-25 m.p.g.
TURNING CIRCLE : (L. and R.) : 42ft. 6in. GROUND CLEARANCE : 5½in.

Overall gear ratios	ACCELERATION			SPEED	m.p.h.
	From steady m.p.h. of			Mean maximum timed speed over ¼ mile	65 69
	10 to 30	20 to 40	30 to 50		
5.25 to 1	14.9 sec.	15.2 sec.	16.6 sec.	Best timed speed over ¼ mile	67.16
7.74 to 1	10.8 sec.	11.2 sec.	14.3 sec.		
11.55 to 1	8.8 sec.	—	—	Speeds attainable on indirect gears (normal and maximum) :—	
20.16 to 1	—	—	—	1st ... 15—19	
From rest to 30 m.p.h. through gears			10.7 sec.	2nd ... 27—33	
To 50 m.p.h. through gears	24.5 sec.			3rd ... 43—50	

BRAKE TEST : Mean stopping distance from 30 m.p.h. (dry concrete), 30ft.
WEATHER : Cold ; showers ; wind fresh, S.E. Barometer : 29.70in.

Performance figures for acceleration and maximum speed are the means of several runs in opposite directions, with two up.

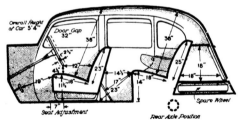

B12

LANCHESTER CARS
FROM 1946 TO 1956

Both before and after the war, several large Daimler-based Lanchesters were produced to special order. (This one was built on the 27 h.p. chassis in the late 1940s for the Royal House of Nawanagar which had been buying Lanchesters for many years, for the use of "Ranji" the famous cricketer.)

Lanchester 10 with Briggs all-steel body, which was conceived before the war and commenced production in 1946. It was replaced in 1949-50 by the coachbuilt Barker-bodied car illustrated below

The last Lanchester was the 1½-litre Sprite of 1956, which incorporated the Hobbs automatic gearbox. On the left is one of the three prototypes. Ten production models (right) were also built.

One of two 2.4-litre Lanchester Dauphin (Hooper) prototypes of 1953.

Lanchester 14 (later called the Leda) introduced in 1951. The bodywork of this car was adapted for the Daimler Conquest.

Convertible coupé version of the Lanchester 14.

Autocar ROAD TESTS

No. 1375
LANCHESTER
TEN SALOON

In general appearance the Lanchester is trim and traditional, though the radiator grille has the modern touch and the bonnet is of the current one-piece type, as fitted, incidentally, in a slightly different form on Daimler cars for many years.

DATA FOR THE DRIVER

LANCHESTER TEN

PRICE, with four-door six-light saloon body, £725, plus £202 2s 9d British purchase tax. Total (in Great Britain), £927 2s 9d.

RATING : 10 h.p., 4 cylinders, overhead valves, 63.5 × 101.6 mm, 1287 c.c.

BRAKE HORSE-POWER : 40 at 4,200 r.p.m. **COMPRESSION RATIO** : 7.1 to 1.

WEIGHT: 22 cwt 3qr 10lb (2,558 lb). **LB. per C.C.** : 1.99. **B.H.P. per TON**: 35.03.

TYRE SIZE : 5.25 × 16in on bolt-on steel disc wheels. **LIGHTING SET** : 12-volt.

TANK CAPACITY : 8 gallons ; approximate fuel consumption range, 25-30 m.p.g.

TURNING CIRCLE : 35ft (L and R). **MINIMUM GROUND CLEARANCE** : 6in.

MAIN DIMENSIONS : Wheelbase, 8ft 3in. Track, 4ft 0in (front and rear). Overall length, 13ft 2½in ; width, 4ft 10in ; height, 5ft 2½in.

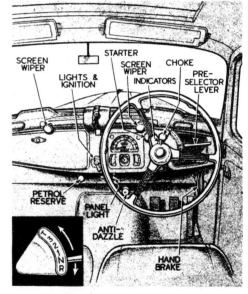

ACCELERATION			
Overall gear ratios	*From steady m.p.h. of*		
	10 to 30	20 to 40	30 to 50
5.125 to 1	15.4 sec	16.4 sec	20.3 sec
7.72 to 1	10.3 sec	11.5 sec	17.0 sec
11.95 to 1	8.0 sec	—	—
22.00 to 1	—	—	—

From rest through gears to :—		sec
30 m.p.h.	.. .. ..	9.6
50 m.p.h.	.. .. ..	25.9
60 m.p.h.	.. .. ..	44.7

Steering wheel movement from lock to lock : 2¾ turns.

Speedometer correction by Electric Speedometer :—			
Car Speedometer	Electric Speedometer	Car Speedometer	Electric Speedometer
10 =	11	50 =	49.25
20 =	22	60 =	57
30 =	32	70 =	65.25
40 =	41.5		

Speeds attainable on gears (by Electric Speedometer)		M.p.h. (normal and max.)
1st	.. .. ..	12—19
2nd	.. .. ..	24—35
3rd	.. .. ..	44—53
Top	.. .. ..	68—69

WEATHER : Damp patches, mild ; wind negligible.

Acceleration figures are the means of several runs in opposite directions.

Described in " The Autocar " of September 27, 1946.

IN the class that used to be called 10 h.p. this Lanchester has important features which are outstanding among small cars and one or two, notably the Daimler fluid flywheel with pre-selector gear box, which are unique. It is high in price for its size, but it sets out to give exceptional refinement and a number of unseen qualities which make for lasting worth, such as, for instance, a three-bearing crankshaft, full-flow pressure filter in the engine lubrication system, and, perhaps even more importantly, hardened steel liners forming the cylinder bores. Length of life of a car without expensive replacements can be verified only under prolonged actual ownership, but as to the former aim, general refinement, it can certainly be said that the Lanchester Ten succeeds.

It is produced in association with the Daimler, and with the design knowledge behind it that applies to that famous marque, and broadly it may be regarded as being a junior Daimler, although preserving a separate identity. This Ten, when it appeared soon after the war, displayed a then quite advanced appearance and was unusual among the smaller cars in having independent front suspension, the system being by coil springs, in principle as on the Daimlers. In the meantime marked changes in styling and the adoption of i.f.s. have ceased to be exceptional among the smaller cars as well as the larger, but the Lanchester still stands out in offering the fluid flywheel and pre-selector gear box, bodywork and equipment of high quality, and an o.h.v. four-cylinder engine which is decidedly efficient for its size without losing mechanical refinement even when pressed hard.

For anti-dazzle purposes a pass light is used, transfer from the head lamps being by a foot-operated switch. Above the windscreen is the neat aerial for the radio fitted as an extra (£46 12s 9d); this can be turned vertically from inside the car.

Bumper over-riders are noticed in this view, also the sockets beneath the step boards, one for the front wheel and one for the rear wheel, to which a conveniently operated pillar jack is applied. The petrol filler cap in the left-hand wing is of captive type to prevent loss.

"THE AUTOCAR" ROAD TESTS   .   .   .   .   .   continued

A run which was made in 1946 in one of the earlier examples of this post-war model has been remembered keenly for the way in which the car covered lengthy journeys at a good average, partly through hilly country, in a high degree of comfort for all the occupants, and for its rather remarkable stability. The present car, now subjected to the comprehensive Road Test, has confirmed those impressions of some two and a half years ago.

In general style the car is attractive, with an interior and seating of above average appeal even at first sight. It runs with a soothing quietness and smoothness and an almost indefinable feeling of being "well within itself" at ordinary speeds up to about 50 m.p.h., and it has a complete flexibility and a top gear ability equalled by no current small car, by reason of the special properties conferred by the fluid flywheel transmission. It also proves on a journey to have another side to its character in that it can be driven as fast as it will go without protest, feeling under complete control and being able to make a distinctly good average on a normal give-and-take main road.

It readily puts in 40-41 miles in the hour, and driven with the definite purpose of hurrying over a route well known to the driver concerned, and with favourable traffic and weather conditions, it covered 45 miles in one hour and 88 miles in two hours, including a quick stop for petrol. Reasons for such useful point-to-point abilities are found not in particularly quick acceleration or an exceptional maximum speed for the size of car, but in the engine's willingness to keep going at practically its limit, and certainly to remain mechanically pleasant at around 60 m.p.h.

Additionally the Lanchester rides very comfortably, the suspension allowing the speed to be maintained virtually without reference to minor surface deteriorations, and also allowing the car to be taken fast round the multitude of bends that are a feature of a journey on British roads, even main roads. Lateral stability is decidedly above the average associated with the smaller cars even nowadays. Thus it makes quite an appeal to a driver who likes to get the best out of a car, and who finds satisfaction in the stability already indicated and in the quality of the performance. The engine develops 40 b.h.p., yet such pinking as arises even on the present quality of British petrol is of a subdued nature. In performance and general behaviour this is a car to please the owner who sets economy of running costs, comfort, accuracy of control and safety of handling very high on his list of requirements. It is a handy size of car for parking in towns and for driving in traffic and narrow roads, and the steering lock is noticeably good for turning round and on exceptionally sharp corners.

Steering and Brakes

The steering is entirely satisfactory for both normal and fast driving, being firm, accurate, free from road shocks, with a nice degree of caster action, and neither disconcertingly light nor tiresomely heavy for low speed turning and manœuvring. In short it is a moderately geared steering which gives confidence. The brakes are Girling mechanically operated. They require firm pedal pressure for maximum results, when they slow the car safely from speed, and also they act with real decisiveness if called on for an emergency stop at the lower speeds.

As an entirely different style of motoring from that suggested by averages of over 40 miles in the hour the Lanchester can admirably meet the requirements of the more leisurely and perhaps less experienced driver. Once the advantages afforded by the gear box and transmission have been fully exploited—and to do so is not difficult—it is realized that control in traffic is almost wholly a matter of the throttle and brake pedals alone, not even the hand brake being required in holding the car temporarily on an up gradient in traffic. The car can be brought down to zero speed on any gear without stalling the engine, which

An inviting-looking and roomy interior, with cloth upholstery of very good quality. The door openings are strikingly wide and the doors remain of their own accord at these convenient positions. Other points are the simple form of height adjustment for the separate driving seat, the deep arm rest at the centre of the rear seat, in addition to elbow rests, the flat floor at each side of the propeller-shaft tunnel, and the absence of obstructive controls at the centre of the driving compartment, the pre-selector gear lever being on the steering column and the pull-and-push hand brake lever beneath the facia board. Hinged handles on the doors make it convenient to close the doors from inside.

Showing the decidedly useful size of the luggage compartment and the lid forming a platform level with the floor of the locker. Spare wheel and tools are in an entirely separate compartment beneath. The larger items, including a foot-operated tyre pump, are carried in a canvas bag.

has an exceptionally regular, slow tickover, and without the driver having to think of a clutch pedal, and it will accelerate away simply on opening the throttle. This is possible even on top gear, though, of course, more normally and more briskly on third or second gears.

The principle of the pre-selector gear box is well known, but may be reiterated briefly, namely, that to change between any two gears is a matter only of moving the pre-selector lever and depressing the gear-changing pedal, which occupies the position of the normal clutch pedal but is not used as such. The car having been smoothly started from rest on second gear there is rather surprisingly little need for subsequent gear changing in average country, except that, the gears being so easily engaged, third can be used fairly frequently for additional acceleration or for holding the speed up a gradient. Second gear sufficed to maintain a speed of 20 m.p.h. up a hill of 1 in 6½ maximum gradient and for rounding a sharp corner at the summit.

At first the driving position seems to place the driver rather high and a trifle awkwardly as regard leg position, but there is the excellent and still far from commonly found provision of a simple type of adjustment for the height of the seat, which is separate from the passenger seat, in addition to the normal fore and aft movement. After a certain amount of experiment with the adjustments a comfortable, confident position is obtainable and the support given by the back rest is good, it being shaped to encircle the shoulders; the left foot finds a comfortable place, and the treadle throttle does not involve an awkward ankle angle. The spring-spoked steering wheel has a comfortably shaped rim.

Easy to Get In and Out

Advantages as regards ease of getting in and out by either door, of which much is now made in connection with modern steering column gear levers, belong to the Lanchester, which has had a steering column gear lever for many years. The driver is in fact encouraged to use the door remote from the driving seat, as this is the one fitted with a key. Driving vision is satisfactory, with a good view of the road over a quite short sloping bonnet. The left-side wing is not seen, however.

Features which many owners still call for, and with every justification as regards the majority of them, are included in the shape of a sliding roof, an opening windscreen and a rear window blind, the last mentioned having a convenient control. Wide sun vizors almost meet at the centre and give very adequate protection against sun glare. Among modern amenities, provision is made for the fitting as an extra (£15 6s 8d) of a Clayton interior heater, in conjunction with which there are ducts to the windscreen for de-misting and de-icing. This equipment was fitted to the car tested and proved very effective, with a quiet-running fan for circulation of the warmed air.

There is good leg room at both front and rear and an air of luxury about the upholstery which suggests the bigger and more expensive style of car. Detail fittings have been well thought out. A standard fitting is a reserve petrol control, now all too rare whatever the size of car and virtually unknown among current small cars. It comprises a pull-out control instantly reached from the driving seat and releases the last 1¼ gallons in the tank. There are a lockable compartment in the left-hand side of the facia board and an open cubby hole at the other side.

The instrument lighting is subdued, a good point but

a little overdone as regards reading the speedometer and mileage recorders at night. In Daimler-Lanchester fashion an oil pressure gauge is replaced by a green tell-tale light and an ammeter by a red light. An engine thermometer is fitted and remained very steady at 170 deg F (approximately 77 deg C). Twin wind-tone horns give a quite powerful but pleasing note, and the head lamp beam is excellent. The car could be driven straight off from cold with the choke control in an intermediate position termed "fast idle," at which it can be set as distinct from the full-rich position for a cold start. Incidentally the starter switch, of pull-out pattern, could be more conveniently located. There is a very useful size of luggage compartment.

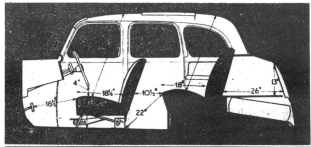

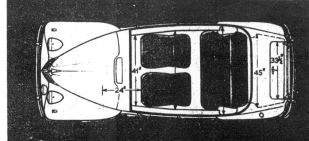

Measurements in these scale body diagrams are taken with the driving seat at the central position of fore and aft adjustment.

The one-piece bonnet is released from the front of the car and it is spring balanced to remain up without use of a strut. It discloses a neatly and accessibly arranged engine and auxiliaries, including a conveniently placed oil filler and dipstick. The ignition distributor and sparking plugs are protected by an easily removable moulded cover. The oil-bath air cleaner is fitted to export cars; home market cars have an ordinary air silencer. Evidence of detail care is seen in the adjustable rubber "buttons" on to which the bonnet closes at the front.

The**Motor** Road Test No. 1/46

Make: Lanchester.   **Type:** 10 h.p.   **Makers:** Lanchester Motor Co. Ltd., Coventry.

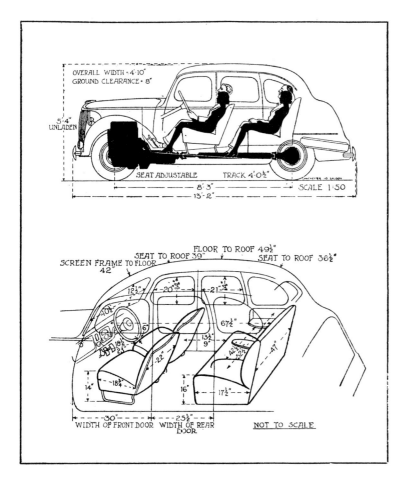

OVERALL WIDTH · 4'10"
GROUND CLEARANCE · 8"
5'4" UNLADEN
SEAT ADJUSTABLE   TRACK 4'0½"
8'3" —— SCALE 1:50
13'2"

FLOOR TO ROOF 49½"
SEAT TO ROOF 39"   SEAT TO ROOF 36½"
SCREEN FRAME TO FLOOR 42"
67½"
WIDTH OF FRONT DOOR 30"   WIDTH OF REAR DOOR 25½"   NOT TO SCALE

Test Conditions

Dry, moderate wind. British Pool Petrol and synthetic rubber tyres.

Test Data

ACCELERATION TIMES on Two Upper Ratios:

	Top	3rd
10–30 m.p.h.	15.3 secs.	9.6 secs.
20–40 m.p.h.	15.7 secs.	10.5 secs.
30–50 m.p.h.	18.3 secs.	14.3 secs.
40–60 m.p.h.	27.7 secs.	—

ACCELERATION TIMES: Through Gears

0–30 m.p.h.	7 secs
0–40 m.p.h.	12.5 secs.
0–50 m.p.h.	22.0 secs.
0–60 m.p.h.	36.8 secs.
Std. ¼ mile ..	24.1 secs.

MAXIMUM SPEED: Flying ¼ mile

Mean 6 opp. runs ..	68.0 m.p.h.
Best time equals ..	70.3 m.p.h

BRAKES at 30 m.p.h. :
0.75 g. (=40 ft. stopping distance) with 200 lb. pedal pressure.
0.55 g. (=54.5 ft. stopping distance) with 100 lb. pedal pressure.
0.33 g. (=90 ft. stopping distance) with 50 lb. pedal pressure.

FUEL CONSUMPTION
Overall consumption for 203 miles, 6 gallons, equals 33.8 m.p.g.
25.3 miles on measured gallon at 41 m.p.h. cross-country average.
34.5 m.p.g. at constant 30 m.p.h.
34.5 m.p.g. at constant 40 m.p.h.
28.5 m.p.g. at constant 50 m.p.h.
22 m.p.g. at constant 60 m.p.h.

HILL CLIMBING
Max. top-gear speed on 1 in 20 .. .. 44 m.p.h.

STEERING
Left-hand lock ..	..	35 ft.
Right-hand lock ..	..	36 ft.

2¼ turns of steering wheel, lock to lock.

In Brief

Price £595, Tax £166 0s. 7d.=£761 0s. 7d.

Tax	£12 10s. 0d.
Road weight unladen	23½ cwt.
Laden weight as tested ..	26 cwt.
Consumption	33.8 m.p.g.
Speed	68.0 m.p.h. (mean both ways) 55 m.p.h. 3rd. 35 m.p.h. 2nd.
Acceleration ..	10-30 on top 15.3 secs. 0-50 thro' gears 22 secs.
Gradients ..	1 in 15½ max. on top. 1 in 9½ max. on 3rd. 1 in 6¼ max. on 2nd.
Gearing ..	13.3 m.p.h. on top at 1,000 r.p.m., 56.2 m.p.h at 2,500 ft. per min. piston speed

Specification

Cubic capacity .. .	1,287 c.c.
Cylinders	Four
Valve position .. .	Overhead
Bore	63.5 mm.
Stroke	101.6 mm.
Comp. ratio	7.4
Max. power	40 b.h.p.
at	4,200 r.p.m.
H.P.: Sq. in. piston area	2.04
H.P. per ton unladen ..	34.0
Piston Area per ton ..	16.7 sq. in.
Ft./min. piston speed at max. h.p.	2,800
Carburetter	Zenith downdraught
Ignition	Lucas coil
Plugs: Make and type	Lodge CB, 14 mm.
Fuel pump	A.C. mechanical
Oil filter	Tecalemit full-flow
Clutch	Daimler open-circuit fluid flywheel with preselective epicyclic gearbox
1st gear	21.40 : 1
2nd gear	11.65 : 1
3rd gear..	7.55 : 1
Top gear	5.00 : 1
Reverse..	31.15 : 1
Prop. shaft	Hardy Spicer, open
Final drive	Spiral bevel
Brakes	Girling mechanical 2 LS. front
Drums	9 ins. dia.
Friction lining area ..	116 sq. ins.
Car wt. per sq. in. ..	22.7 lb.
Steering gear	Bishop cam
Tyre size	5.25 × 16

Fully described in " The Motor," December 12, 1945.

Maintenance

Fuel tank : 8 gallons, including 1¼ gallons reserve. **Sump :** 1 Imp. gallon S.A.E. 30. **Gearbox :** 4 pints S.A.E. 30. **Fluid flywheel :** 5½ pints S.A.E. 30. **Rear axle :** 3 pints E.P. Spirax. **Radiator :** 2 gallons. **Grease points :** 18, R.B. Grease. **Spark timing :** 11 degrees B.T.D.C. (Hand micrometer adjustment provided on distributor for varying grades of fuel.) **Plug gap :** .030 in. **Contact gap :** .012 in. **Tappets :** .012 in. minimum. **Front wheel toe-in :** ⅛ in. **Castor angle :** 1 degree 30 mins., car unladen. **Damper fluid :** Luvax piston type oil ; **Tyre pressures :** 26 lb. sq. in. front, 28 lb. sq. in. rear. **Oil filter element :** Clean every 3,000 miles, change at 20,000 miles. **Lights :** Headlamp bulbs, 12 volt, 36 watt ; sidelamp bulbs, 12 volt, 6 watt ; passlamp bulbs, 12 volt, 36 watt ; Tail lamp bulbs, 12 volt, 6 watt ; stop lamp bulbs, 12 volt, 24 watt. **Trafficators :** 12 volt, 3 watt. **Warning lights :** Ignition and oil, No. C.252A (M.E.S. Cap) ; instrument panel light, 12 volt, 6 watt ; interior light, 12 volt, 6 watt.

Ref. B 13/46

^25

MOTOR CAR MANUFACTURERS
TO H.M. THE KING
THE LANCHESTER MOTOR CO.
LTD.

BY APPOINTMENT

LANCHESTER NEWS

LANCHESTER INTRODUCE NEW "FOURTEEN"

It has Everything!

★ Smoothly powerful 14 h.p. overhead valve engine developing 60 b.h.p. at 4,200 r.p.m.

★ Full flow oil filter in engine lubrication system, reducing engine wear.

★ Thermostatically controlled engine cooling by water-pump, providing rapid warming-up.

★ Zenith downdraught carburettor with accelerating pump and weakening device for part-throttle operation. Air silencer and cleaner.

★ Ignition by distributor having automatic advance and hand adjustment for varying grades of fuel.

★ Daimler fluid transmission with pre-selective gearbox, providing finger-touch control.

★ High efficiency cam-gear steering.

★ Independent front suspension by torsion bars and wishbone links, with anti-roll bar.

★ Girling hydro-mechanical brakes acting on 11″ drums.

★ Headlamps fitted into wings with separate wing lamps below.

★ Reserve petrol control.

★ Large luggage boot.

★ Curved windscreen and rear window, with excellent all-round visibility.

★ Pivoting Ventilators in front and rear windows.

★ Split bench type front seat, each half separately adjustable.

★ Rear seat with fold-down centre armrest and fixed side armrests ; unobstructed floor to rear compartment.

★ Deep upholstery in soft leather.

★ Push-button exterior door handles.

★ Lockable petrol filler cap and interior glove box.

★ Provision for built-in interior heater and radio with speaker in roof.

★ Automatic chassis lubrication operating when engine warms up.

Mr. James Leek, Managing Director, Lanchester Motor Company.

Entirely New Production Plan

BY THE MANAGING DIRECTOR

"A high-class car of medium size, styled for use anywhere and with performance suited to a very wide range of varying conditions —economically priced, economical to run and maintaining the high degree of refinement found in previous Lanchesters". T h a t briefly describes what we set out to produce in the new 'Fourteen'.

NEW FACTORY 'TAILORED' TO "FOURTEEN" PRODUCTION

Our designers were given complete freedom to exploit new developments and technique in the design of this car, unhampered by any limitations of machine or factory capacity. We aimed at and planned the production of the car in line with the layout of a new factory in our rebuilding programme.

This has allowed us to "tailor" many thousands of square feet of factory space and plant to the production of the "Fourteen". By so doing, no desirable feature or characteristic of the car has been subordinated to an existing production layout.

From the outset our plan has included the production of right-hand and left-hand drive models, with interchangeable equipment suiting the car to the home and a wide range of export markets.

MAINTAINED QUALITY

In design, we have employed all that is best in modern styling and technique ; in quality we remain t r a d i t i o n a l . Material form is being given to our plan by engineers and craftsmen on whose habitual skill and pride - of - workmanship Lanchester quality has always been based.

We are confident that the new "Fourteen" will perpetuate this high reputation, and will bring to many new friends the satisfactory ownership which we strive to ensure.

A Completely New Car

From bumper to bumper the "Fourteen" is a completely new car. It brings together all that is best in up-to-the-minute automobile design, whilst embodying all the fine attributes associated with the name Lanchester.

Sparklingly styled in the modern manner, yet with beautifully balanced proportions, this new car at once suggests swiftness and elegance without ostentation. In character it is a skilfully proportioned blend of performance, comfort and grace, equally at home in city or rugged country.

In size and interior planning, equal consideration has been given to driver and passengers. The car's slender styling and well balanced exterior belies an interior which provides roominess in every quarter.

Careful planning of seating accommodation, flat floors and upholstery in the Lanchester manner provide excellent leg room and exceptional comfort for four passengers with allowance for an additional passenger when desired.

Beneath its nymph-like appearance, the new Lanchester embodies a sturdy construction which allows full and safe exploitation of its performance capabilities.

In-built into the car are those unseen features of mechanical soundness and lasting quality that have always characterised the Lanchester. A rigid cruciform box-section frame, superb suspension and mechanical refinement in detail confer a degree of stability and road-worthiness unsurpassed in this class of car.

Ideally matched to the size and weight of the car is a completely new 14 horsepower 4-cylinder o.h.v. engine developing 60 b.h.p., mounted in special flexible rubber mountings to ensure true Lanchester smoothness.

The mechanical refinement and exceptional quality of this engine may be judged by an examination of its features which include a three-bearing crankshaft, steel-backed big end bearings, full flow oil filter and thermostatically controlled cooling system.

Special attention has been paid to fuel consumption, the carburettor being of the downdraught type with a weakening device for part-throttle operation and an accelerating pump. The distributor, with automatic advance and retard mechanism, has an over-riding hand adjustment to suit the ignition to varying grades of fuel.

The inherent smoothness afforded by an advanced form of independent front suspension by torsion bars and by mechanical refinement throughout the car is further enhanced by the employment of Daimler fluid transmission. This incorporates the fluid flywheel with pre-selective 4-speed epicyclic gearbox.

The pre-selector, placed on the steering column, provides true finger-touch control and velvet smooth gear changing with a degree of precision unmatched by other means.

Indeed this is a car in which to cruise at high speed over long distances or crawl in traffic without the slightest feeling of stress or fatigue—in which the driver will always feel at his best, no matter what the road conditions, and from which his passengers will step out fresh no matter the distance travelled.

HOW WE DESIGNED
the new
LANCHESTER
"FOURTEEN"

In the new Lanchester "Fourteen" we have had the opportunity to design a completely new car embodying all the ideas we have developed and proved during recent years. We have been able to apply well tried principles and modern technique with equal consideration, and to take advantage of the most up-to-date production methods in a completely new factory.

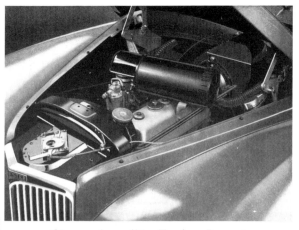

Clean, Accessible Engine Layout

Beneath the spring-balanced bonnet can be seen the neat layout of the "Fourteen" engine. The carburettor is placed high on the right, with air-cleaner and silencer above it, and the oil-filler is positioned accessibly on top of the engine. A quickly detachable radiator filler cap is used. The bonnet catch, unlocked from inside the car, locks automatically when the bonnet is lowered.

AIM : BALANCED UNITY

With full freedom of design allowed us, our aim has been to produce a well-balanced car seating four passengers in exceptional comfort, with allowance for carrying an additional passenger when need be, and with an economical engine giving all-round performance.

Styling would be modern yet graceful, and the whole must blend to maintain the traditional smooth running and distinction synonymous with the name Lanchester.

ACCENT ON MECHANICAL REFINEMENT

Performance must include the ability to cruise at high speed for long periods, provide swift acceleration through the gears and have ample power throughout the whole engine-speed range.

In all phases of design and production we would instil into the car that degree of mechanical refinement which has given so much satisfaction to owners of earlier Lanchester models.

With these considerations in mind we have produced a completely new four-cylinder o.h.v. engine of 1968 c.c. capacity, designed to meet all our performance requirements.

The compression ratio (6.7 : 1) is not too high to provide consistently good performance on varying grades of fuel, and maximum power (60 b.h.p.) is developed at the most suitable engine speed (4,200 r.p.m.) for unstressed economical and trouble-free running in the wide range of conditions for which the car is designed.

ENGINE CHARACTERISTICS TAILORED TO MODERN CONDITIONS

Maximum developed brake-horsepower cannot, however, tell the whole story. Ample power is required throughout the whole engine-speed range.

We have, therefore, given careful attention to all-round characteristics, providing a high torque to ensure rapid acceleration at all points of the engine speed range and an excellent top gear performance for maintaining high average speeds without effort.

Reliability and durability have been major considerations in the detailed mechanical design of the engine. The camshaft and crankshaft each have three bearings, and steel-backed bearings with white-metal liners are used for camshaft and big ends, affording a large bearing area and a degree of rigidity which reduces vibration and wear to a minimum.

The potential life and smooth running effected by these and other mechanical refinements are fully maintained by the use of a full-flow oil filter in the lubrication system, cleaning under pressure all the oil circulated through the bearings and on to the cylinder walls.

It is, indeed, to these details of mechanical refinement and careful construction that the Lanchester owes much of its overall soundness.

FLEXIBLE ENGINE MOUNTING

Traditional vibrationless running of the Lanchester is further promoted in the new "Fourteen" by the employment of the latest developments in flexible engine mounting.

Both at high and low revs. and under all conditions of load, the torque reactions of the engine are virtually isolated from the chassis of the car.

FUEL ECONOMY

So that the varying quality of present day fuels will not detract from the consistently good performance of the car, much attention has been given to carburation. The distributor in the coil ignition system is fitted with an automatic advance mechanism and an automatic vacuum control which takes control for part-throttle operation.

Over-riding these automatic control mechanisms, there is a vernier adjustment which can be hand set in a matter of a minute or two to suit the ignition system to varying grades of fuel.

Very real fuel economy is afforded by the carburettor used. This is of the Zenith downdraught type having a weakening devise for part-throttle operation and an accelerating pump. This arrangement permits very economical setting of the carburettor for normal running without detriment to overall performance, the accelerating pump providing momentarily rich mixture for rapid acceleration immediately the accelerator is depressed.

An effective air filter and silencer is fitted which together with the full-flow oil filter ensures maintained efficiency in the engine.

EAGER STARTING FROM COLD

The carburation system also takes into account the very desirable ability to start readily from cold. Furthermore, the warming-up period is reduced to a minimum by the engine-cooling system employed. This embodies a thermostatic control which limits water circulation to the cylinder block until the engine is warm.

In addition to convenience, this shortened warming-up period is of prime importance in that the engine is not subjected to extended periods of running on a rich mixture—thus eliminating one of the major causes of cylinder bore wear.

FLUID TRANSMISSION

Further to pursue our policy of extreme smoothness and mechanical reliability in the car, we have employed the patented Daimler fluid transmission, which has been developed and proved in Daimler and Lanchester cars since 1932. This combines the fluid flywheel with a 4-speed pre-selective gearbox.

The reasonably high top gear ratio (4.55 to 1 overall) permits economical running at high speed, yet is low enough to allow a very good overall top gear performance. The lower ratios are carefully stepped to provide fast acceleration through the gears.

STABILITY AT SPEED

Lateral and direction stability of a very high order and light, positive steering have been treated as essential requirements of the car.

To afford the maximum basic rigidity we have employed a sturdy chassis frame of box-section, cruciform braced, and have carefully arranged the distribution of the load. To this we have fitted an advanced form of independent front suspension by torsion bars, and half-elliptic springs at the rear, affording the maximum flexibility compatible with the degree of stability required.

An anti-roll bar is fitted to the front, and hydraulic telescopic shock absorbers at front and rear. This arrangement provides a very smooth flat ride and excellent road holding and cornering qualities.

Light and positive steering are attained by using in conjunction with this suspension layout a high efficiency cam gear steering mechanism (ratio 13 : 1)

In suspension and steering layout we have also allowed for the fitting of low pressure cushion tyres, and these add further to the riding quality of the car.

MAINTAINED EFFICIENCY

As important as the provision of effective suspension and steering in a car is the maintenance of the efficiency of those parts. With this in mind, we have fitted a thermal automatic chassis lubrication system which will keep all the necessary points in fully lubricated condition from a central lubricant reservoir under the bonnet. This eliminates much of the tedious and sometimes neglected work usually requiring the use of a grease gun.

POWERFUL BRAKES

The potential performance of the new car entails the provision of highly efficient brakes. We have therefore fitted a Girling hydro-mechanical system, with 11″ diameter brake drums, providing a progressive braking effect by a light pedal pressure and excellent stopping power in emergency.

BODY MATCHED TO PERFORMANCE

Throughout the design of the car, we have constantly had before us the object of blending performance and mechanical characteristics intimately with the body size and style. By so doing, we have produced in the Lanchester "Fourteen" a unity in which functional and aesthetic qualities are perfectly balanced.

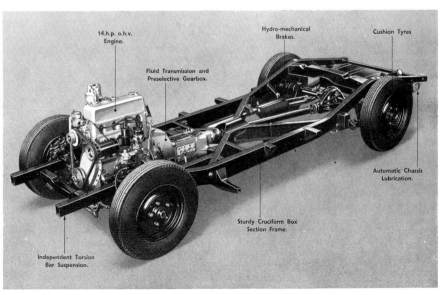

FINGER-TIP CONTROL

*Cushioned drive with Fluid Transmission**

You cannot know the joy of really effortless travel and precise control of your car until you motor with Daimler Fluid Transmission as fitted to the new Lanchester "Fourteen".

Cruising at high speed or filtering through city traffic, the 'Fourteen' driver is always at ease and at one with his car. And his passengers are no less appreciative of the silken smooth motoring made possible only by this form of transmission.

GEARCHANGING is simplicity itself, a finger-touch movement of the pre-selector lever at your convenience, then a stroke of the gearchange pedal when you require the new ratio, and you have changed gear. The change is indiscernible to your passengers, and your hands never leave the steering wheel.

WHEN temporarily halted in traffic you have no need to engage neutral—you simply remove your foot from the accelerator and apply the brake pedal ; the car comes to a standstill with gear still engaged and engine gently "ticking over" ; your left foot remains idle. To move off again, release the brake, accelerate and glide away.

TRAVELLING uphill, or when vivid acceleration is needed for overtaking, you can pre-select your lower gear well beforehand and then operate the gearchange pedal at the crucial moment ; your gearchange is the work of a split second.

DOWNHILL you have the same positive control, and in emergency any desired lower gear can be engaged in a fraction of a second, no matter what your road speed. The braking effect of the engine is the same as with other forms of transmission.

FOR intricate parking, your 'Fourteen' allows one-pedal control with a degree of precision unchallenged by other transmission systems ; with a gear engaged and your engine set at a slightly higher speed on the hand throttle, the movement of the car can be controlled solely by the brake pedal, allowing the driver to "inch" into position if desired.

IN ALL these circumstances the motion of the engine is conveyed to the roadwheels solely through the oil in the fluid flywheel, providing a cushioned effect which renders the "Fourteen's" transmission as smooth as silk and inherently foolproof.

Fluid transmission, pioneered and developed in Daimler motor cars since 1932, is licensed under Daimler and Vulcan Sinclair patents.

The cushioned drive afforded by the fluid flywheel stands unchallenged as the smoothest, most foolproof and most easily handled form of transmission available to-day.

Carefree Driving

When you step into the invitingly comfortable driver's seat of the "Fourteen" you will find it quickly adjustable to give that position which is "just right" for your stature and driving style—no cramped or encumbered feeling, no unnatural position of hands and feet and no sense of being lost in coachwork built for appearance's sake.

You will find yourself immediately at one with the car, comfortably supported in a relaxed attitude, the steering wheel lying ready in your hands, the pre-selector gear-change lever immediately responsive to a finger-touch without your hands leaving the wheel, and your feet restfully poised at the controls.

Before you, the curved windscreen provides a very wide, unrestricted field of view and below that the neatly arranged instrument panel tells its story at a glance.

The headlamps dipper switch is convenient to your left foot, the handbrake accessibility to hand, and at the top of the steering column a windtone horn and trafficator switch. At the top of the dash a small yellow light gives immediate notice when a traffic indicator is in use.

TESTED DRIVING POSITION

This Lanchester "Fourteen" driving position has been thoroughly tested by selected drivers of all sizes and driving styles, and tailored to suit them all.

The front seat is of the bench-type split centrally into two, with each half separately adjustable for distance allowing individual comfort for driver

Each half of the centrally divided bench-type front seat is quickly adjustable for individual comfort and driving position.

and front seat passenger. The deep upholstery is designed to provide support for the tall and short driver alike.

In this position you will be prepared to drive for very long periods in relaxed comfort and always in full control of the car. In the fluid transmission and pre-selector gearbox you will have a precision of control which will allow you to make full use of the smooth power of the "Fourteen" without fuss or hesitation.

You can quickly reach a high cruising speed through the gears, or, if so minded, accelerate gently from zero to high speed in top gear.

Whatever your mood, the surging power of the Lanchester "Fourteen" will be at your instant call, to use as you will, and to spirit away the miles with effortless ease.

At the lights . . .
. . . or when temporarily halted, you have no need to disengage gear. Just remove your foot from the accelerator and apply the footbrake. To move off again, accelerate and away you go.

Downhill . . .
. . . You have positive control. In emergency you can engage any required lower gear without hesitation. The braking effect of the engine is at your immediate call.

Uphill . . .
. . . Or when vivid acceleration is required for overtaking, you can pre-select your next lower gear in advance and engage it smoothly at the crucial moment by a stroke of the gear-engaging pedal.

Parking . . .
. . . You can have one-pedal control for "inching" into position by speeding up the engine on the hand throttle and engaging gear ; your movement is then controlled solely by the brake pedal.

Inter-axle seating, with superbly comfortable riding, flat floors, spacious leg room and exceptional stability on the road is afforded by careful design and balance of chassis, engine and transmission.

Luxury Roadriding
INTER-AXLE SEATING WITH SPACIOUS LEG ROOM

High-speed cruising with exceptional stability and passenger comfort is made possible in the Lanchester "Fourteen" by a number of developments which affect the basic design of the car. In producing this completely new car, Lanchester engineers have been able to exploit these developments to the full.

The positioning of the seats in relation to the chassis is so arranged as to allow maximum comfort and convenience for the passengers and spacious luggage accommodation whilst giving full consideration to the length of wheelbase, rigidity of the chassis and weight distribution in order to afford directional and lateral stability in keeping with the power and performance of the engine.

CONSTANT STABILITY

By mounting the engine well forward and employing a sturdy cruciform box-section chassis frame, both front and rear seats have been mounted well within the wheelbase, yet allow spacious leg-room and comfort for the tallest of passengers. Being placed within the wheelbase, the seating provides maximum freedom from roadshock and reduces to a minimum the effects of varied loading due to the presence or absence of rear passengers.

The spaciousness and comfort afforded passengers is further enhanced by the employment of a rearward sloping engine mounting and hypoid bevel rear axle which allow unobstructed floors in front and rear compartments.

Further, the position of the engine allows a forward position for the door pillars, thereby affording space for wide doors for easy entry to the car.

At the rear, the layout provides spacious unobstructed room for a very large luggage boot without disturbing the flowing lines of the bodywork.

HIGH AVERAGE SPEEDS

In conjunction with these factors of design, full consideration has been given to the weight to power ratio of the complete car, so that the whole is well matched to its 14 h.p. engine. The stability and roadriding qualities of the car thereby allow full use to be made of the power available, in order to provide sparkling performance and the maintenance of high average speeds in full safety and comfort.

Added to this, the quiet running qualities of the Lanchester form a perfectly proportioned design for smooth, fast and untiring motoring.

Independent front suspension by torsion bars, with torsional stabilising bar.

SUPERB SUSPENSION
Automatically Lubricated

Extremely comfortable flat riding throughout the speed range and over widely varying road surfaces is afforded by the suspension system employed in the new "Fourteen". The independent front suspension is of the latest torsion bar and wishbone type, providing the maximum flexibility compatible with the excellent stability and roadholding qualities of the car. Stability is further maintained by the use of a torsional anti-roll bar at the front.

Rear suspension is by half-elliptic road springs, and hydraulic telescopic type shock absorbers are fitted at front and rear. These shock absorbers considerably reduce "build-up" and the progressive hardening effect experienced when travelling over repititive bumps such as on cobble stones or pavé.

The complete suspension system is included in the parts lubricated by the automatic chassis lubrication system fitted to the car, so that the springs and suspension parts are maintained in fully lubricated condition, thus eliminating any variation in functioning.

The design also makes possible the use of extreme low pressure wide-rimmed tyres which afford considerable dampening of vibration and roadshocks normally transmitted to the axles.

POWERFUL BRAKES

Powerful Girling hydro-mechanical brakes on the new Lanchester provide effective control under all conditions of speed. They are designed to afford efficient braking from a light pedal pressure, giving a progressive braking effect for gradual slowing down, and a vivid arresting effect in emergency.

Brakes operate hydraulically on large 11 inch drums on the front wheels, as seen above, and mechanically at the rear. Connections from the automatic chassis lubrication system to parts of the steering gear can also be seen.

The footbrake operates on all four wheels, being connected to the rear wheels by mechanical means and to the front wheels by a hydraulic system. The handbrake, of the pistol grip type mounted conveniently on the dash, operates by mechanical means on the rear wheels only.

11 INCH DRUMS

The brake shoes act on eleven inch diameter drums on all wheels providing a very large frictional area and large cooling surface which eliminates rapid brake fade during high-speed travel, and ensures dependability in emergency.

Simple brake adjustment is provided on all wheels.

101

ROOMY COMFORT

THOUGHTFUL PLANNING throughout the Lanchester "Fourteen" endows the car with a degree of spaciousness, passenger comfort and refinement that is equalled only in larger, highly priced saloons.

In the rear compartment exceptional comfort is provided for two passengers or occasionally three, by a deeply upholstered seat with fixed side armrests and fold-down centre armrest.

FLAT FLOOR

The floor is flat, and provides ample unobstructed leg room for the tallest of passengers. A central rooflight is fitted and deep leather pockets are fitted to the back of the front seat.

At the front, the seat is of the bench type split centrally into two and upholstered to provide comfortable support for driving. Each half of the seat is separately adjustable for distance.

It will carry two extremely comfortably, or occasionally three passengers when adjusted as one seat. Side pockets are provided in the front doors, and a lockable glove box in the nearside of the dash; a convenient cubby hole is provided at the driver's side of the dash.

WIDE DOORS

The doors to front and rear are of a width allowing easy entry to the seats and are hinged at their forward edges. Push-button type handles are fitted to the exterior of the doors, with handles of the normal pivot type on the inside.

Roll-down windows and pivoting ventilator windows are fitted at front and rear, and with the large curved rear window and curved windscreen provide excellent all round passenger and driver vision.

Upholstery and furnishing throughout is in the Lanchester manner, with deep soft leather seating, high grade carpeting with felt underlays, high quality headcloth and tasteful fittings finished in chromium. Dashboard and door fillets are in polished grained walnut.

EFFECTIVE AIR-CONDITIONING
Ventilators Front and Rear

Agreeable ventilation under normal conditions is effectively supplied in the "Fourteen" by the arrangement of roll-down door windows and pivoting quarter ventilators provided at both front and rear.

The ventilators are fitted at the forward edge of the front windows and in the rear compartment side windows. Pivoted outwards, they draw out the air from the interior of the car, providing draughtless ventilation.

An air inlet, controlled from the dash, is fitted to the exterior of the car above the scuttle. When opened, this allows air to be drawn in and delivered below the dash.

Provision is made for fitting to the car a built-in heater and ventilating fan incorporating the air inlet in the scuttle. The heater unit is built into the scuttle below the bonnet and is connected to the engine cooling system.

Without taking up any interior space this system provides heating and air conditioning to meet a variety of requirements, and is controlled from the air inlet control and a heater control on the dash.

By means of this system fresh air drawn through the inlet can be circulated unheated, through the car; alternatively warmed air can be similarly circulated; or a small amount of air drawn through the heater can be circulated for rapid warming up.

The outlet from the heater is so arranged that the air is forced downwards and along the floor of the car, providing ventilation or heating at both front and rear.

Built-in demisters, blowing warm air into the inside of the windscreen are also arranged for connection to the

Provision is made for a neatly built-in interior heater under the bonnet.

heater system when fitted. These are controlled by a separate control on the dash.

PROVISION FOR RADIO

Provision is made in the car for radio to be fitted, with controls on the dash and speaker built-in to the roof.

Quarter-ventilators in both front and rear windows can be simply adjusted to draw out air from the interior of the car and provide very effective draughtless ventilation. Below is shown the air circulation obtainable by use of the interior heater.

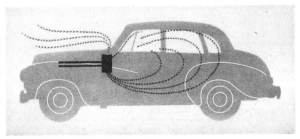

SPACIOUS LUGGAGE BOOT

All the room needed for full touring luggage is available in the exceptionally spacious luggage boot on the "Fourteen".

The space above the luggage shelf is 38 inches in depth, with central width of 4 feet and a clear central height of 16 inches.

Below the luggage shelf the spare wheel is accessibly placed, whilst a recess at the forward edge provides convenient stowage for the comprehensive tool kit, with foot pump and jack, supplied with the car.

Protection from Theft

LATEST FITTINGS

Push-Button Door Locks

Positive door locks of the latest push-button type are employed on the exterior of the doors, providing simple yet safe door opening by pressure on a button embodied in the door handle.

Normal type door handles are used in the interior. Three doors lock from inside and an exterior lock is provided on the nearside front door.

These handles and other fittings, including window edging, bumpers, wheel hubs, filler cap, dual windscreen wipers, lamp rims, ashtrays, and interior metal fittings are all heavily chromium plated.

Risk of theft is minimised by provision of locks on the petrol filler cap, luggage boot and interior glove box.

NEAT ELECTRICAL LAYOUT AND EFFICIENT LIGHTING

The neatly arranged electrical equipment in the "Fourteen" includes long-range headlamps fitted into the wings and separate side lamps, also fitted into the wings below.

In these positions they harmonize with the lines of the car and are very easily cleaned. Dip and switch headlamp control is operated from a foot switch, and a small blue light on the dash indicates when the lights are on full beam.

Combined tail and stop lights are built into each rear wing. Rear number plate illumination is by separate central lamp.

A dependable 12 volt, voltage controlled electrical system is employed. Other equipment operated by the system includes dual windscreen wipers controlled by a single pull-switch, a windtone horn, and trafficators with a small yellow light on the dash indicating when they are in use.

Convenient Jacking System

A very convenient jacking system is supplied, in which a neat folding bipod jack fits into jacking positions for each wheel and is operated very easily from a standing position.

A light rotary movement of the handle quickly raises the wheel from the ground, making wheel-changing a simple and speedy operation.

Connections from the automatic chassis lubrication system to the rear suspension.

AUTOMATIC CHASSIS LUBRICATION

Most of the periodic work usually entailing the use of the grease gun is carried out automatically in the "Fourteen" by an automatic chassis lubrication system.

This system ensures maintained lubrication of all points on the chassis except the propellor shaft and water pump. Spring shackle pins and all points of the steering linkage are maintained in fully lubricated condition, ensuring unvaried performance and long life.

All that is required of the owner is a simple periodic replenishment of a lubricant reservoir situated under the bonnet.

The system operates by means of an expansion chamber mounted adjacent to the exhaust manifold, with valves drawing lubricant from the reservoir and supplying it to the lubrication points. Each time the engine is started and warmed up a supply of lubricant is forced through the distributing pipes and into the lubrication points. Meter valves apportion the lubricant to the various points.

EASILY RAISED BONNET

The bonnet is counterbalanced by springs and can be raised with the minimum of effort, remaining in the open position with the use of struts or other form of support. The bonnet catch is operated by a pull-knob in the front compartment for opening, and closes automatically when the bonnet is lowered.

GENERAL SPECIFICATION

Lanchester "Fourteen"

ENGINE.
4-cylinder, o.h.v., bore 3 ins., stroke 4¼ ins., capacity 1968 c.c.; compression ratio 6.7 to 1 ; maximum b.h.p. 60 at 4,200 r.p.m. Statically and dynamically balanced three-bearing crankshaft ; big ends fitted with steel-backed white-metal liners ; three-bearing camshaft with steel-backed white-metal liners. Lubrication by submerged gear-type pump ; Tecalemit full-flow oil filter with safety by-pass ; pressure relief valve.
Cooling by water pump ; thermostatic temperature control.
Zenith downdraught carburettor with weakening device and accelerating pump, A.C. mechanical petrol pump with hand priming lever.
Lucas 12 volt coil ignition ; distributor has automatic advance and vacuum control, with over riding vernier hand adjustment for varying grades of fuel. Lodge CB 14 3-point sparking plugs.

TRANSMISSION.
Fluid transmission with fluid flywheel and pre-selective 4-speed epicyclic gearbox.
Overall gear ratios : 1st 14.95, 2nd 8.83, 3rd 6.21, Top 4.55 to 1 ; reverse 18.2 to 1.
Hardy Spicer open propeller shaft with needle roller universal joint. Hypoid bevel rear axle.

STEERING.
High efficiency cam gear ; ratio 13 to 1 ; 17 ins. diameter spring spoked steering wheel.

SUSPENSION.
Independent front by torsion bars ; half-elliptic rear ; torsional stabilising bar at front ; Girling hydraulic telescopic shock absorbers front and rear.

BRAKES.
Girling hydro-mechanical on 11 ins. diameter drums ; frictional lining area 148 sq. ins.

FRAME.
Box-section, cruciform braced.

CHASSIS LUBRICATION.
Thermal automatic chassis lubrication system.

WHEELS AND TYRES.
Disc-type bolt on wheels ; 6.4 × 15 cushion tyres.

ELECTRICAL.
12 volt system, voltage controlled ; battery under front seat. Headlamps in front wings, with separate wing lamps below ; dip and switch control by foot switch ; combined tail and stop lamps in each rear wing ; central rear number plate lamp.
Wind tone horn, dual windscreen wipers and trafficators.

INSTRUMENTS.
Speedometer, petrol gauge, ammeter, water temperature gauge, oil and ignition warning lamps, reserve petrol control.

FUEL TANK.
Capacity 15 gallons with reserve operated from dash.

GENERAL.
"Bevelift" mechanical jacking system. Dimensions of car : Wheelbase 8 ft. 8 ins. Track 4 ft 4 ins ; Overall Length 14 ft 7 ins ; Width 5 ft 5 ins ; Height 5 ft 2 ins ; Ground Clearance 6 ins. Turning Circle 33 ft 3 ins.

STOP PRESS

WIDE RANGE OF COLOURS.

The following wide range of colour styles is available for the "Fourteen". In each case the paintwork treatment includes a gold line.

BLACK with Brown, Red or Green leather.

BLUE with Blue leather.

GREY with Blue or Red leather.

DARK GREEN with Green leather.

LIGHT GREEN with Beige leather with Green piping.

MAROON with Red leather.

FAWN with Green leather with Biege piping.

PRICE

Lanchester "Fourteen"
£895 plus £249-7-3
purchase tax

Published by The Lanchester Motor Company Ltd., Coventry, and printed in England by Edwards The Printers Ltd., at Coventry

Publication No. 601/2240

*A*THLETIC in line and performance, tranquil and well-mannered in traffic, this thoroughly weatherproof drop head coupé with power-operated hood and windows brings all the fine features of the new Lanchester "Fourteen" chassis to those who on occasion prefer the freedom of an open car. It is a roomy two-door four-seater with a realistically large luggage boot at the rear. The hood has a smart intermediate de ville position, and at a touch of a button folds away neatly into a compartment behind the rear seat. Power operated door windows and rotating quarter lights provide ventilation and protection to suit all conditions. In its soft leather upholstery and superb interior finish, the car embodies all the refinements of the Lanchester saloon.

SPECIFICATION

ENGINE. 4-cylinder, o.h.v., bore 3in., stroke 4¼in., capacity 1968 c.c.; compression ratio 6.7 to 1; maximum b.h.p. 60 at 4,200 r.p.m. Statically and dynamically balanced three-bearing crankshaft; big ends fitted with steel-backed white metal liners; three bearing camshaft with steel-backed white metal liners. Lubrication by submerged gear-type pump; Tecalemit full-flow oil filter with safety by-pass; pressure relief valve. Engine flexibly mounted, isolating torque reactions. Cooling by water pump; thermostatic temperature control.
Zenith downdraught carburettor with economy device and accelerating pump; air silencer (oil bath air cleaner fitted to export cars); A.C. mechanical petrol pump with hand priming lever.
Lucas 12-volt coil ignition; distributor has automatic advance and vacuum control, with over-riding hand adjustment for varying grades of fuel.

TRANSMISSION. Fluid transmission with fluid flywheel and pre-selective 4-speed epicyclic gearbox; selector on steering column. Overall gear ratios: 1st 17.47, 2nd 10.55, 3rd 6.71, Top 4.55 to 1; reverse 23.7 to 1. Hardy Spicer open propeller shaft with needle roller universal joint. Hypoid bevel rear axle.

STEERING. Right-hand or left-hand drive; high efficiency cam gear; ratio 18 to 1; 17in. diameter spring spoked steering wheel.

SUSPENSION. Independent front by laminated torsion bars; half-elliptic rear; torsional stabilising bar at front; Girling hydraulic telescopic shock absorbers front and rear.

BRAKES. Girling hydro-mechanical on 11in. diameter drums; frictional lining area 148 sq. in.

FRAME. Box section, cruciform braced.

CHASSIS LUBRICATION. Thermal automatic chassis lubrication system delivering to lubrication points whenever engine warms up.

WHEELS AND TYRES. Disc-type bolt on wheels; 6.7 x 15 low pressure cushion tyres. Spare wheel and tyre.

AIR CONDITIONING. Built-in heater delivering warm or cool fresh air to interior; demister ducts deliver to windscreen.

ELECTRICAL. 12-volt system, voltage controlled; battery under rear seat. Headlamps in front wings, with separate wing lamps below; dip and switch control; combined tail and stop lamps, reversing light; central rear number plate lamp; wind-tone horns, dual windscreen wipers and self-cancelling trafficators with internal indicator light on dash.

INSTRUMENTS. Speedometer, petrol gauge, ammeter, water temperature gauge, oil and ignition warning lamps, reserve petrol control.

FUEL TANK. Capacity 15 gallons with reserve operated from dash.

JACKS. "Bevelift" mechanical jacking system with two easily accessible positions on each side of the chassis.

BODY. Two-door drophead coupe of pressed steel construction with rear luggage boot. Power-operated hood folding into compartment behind rear seat. Power-operated door windows and rotating quarter lights. Front seats separately adjustable and with hinged backs providing easy access to rear seat. Seats upholstered in leather, with high grade toning carpets and felt underlays. Pressed steel instrument board and fillets in walnut grained finish; lockable glove box and cubby hole in dash; provision for radio; full width pockets in doors; twin sun visors. Separate spare wheel compartment below luggage boot.

DIMENSIONS. Wheelbase 8ft. 8in.; Track 4ft. 4in.; Overall length 14ft. 7in.; Height 5ft. 2in.; Width 5ft. 5½in.; Ground clearance 7in.; Turning circle 33ft. 6in.

*Daimler Fluid Transmission is licensed under Vulcan Sinclair and Daimler patents.

COLOURS AND UPHOLSTERY

The Lanchester drophead coupe is beautifully finished in a choice of the following colour schemes. In each case the exterior finish includes gold line treatment : Black with

Red, Green or Beige leather ; Bronze with Green leather ; Light Green with Beige leather ; Light Blue with Red leather.

CONDITIONS OF SALE

THE LANCHESTER MOTOR COMPANY LIMITED · COVENTRY · ENGLAND

PUBLICATION No. 901/204

Convertible" LANCHESTER

The mechanical refinement of the Lanchester "Fourteen" chassis, with its smoothly powerful 2-litre engine, independent front suspension by laminated torsion bars, fluid transmission with preselector gear change, Girling hydro-mechanical brakes and automatic chassis lubrication, places this new coupe in a class of its own as a medium-sized "tourer for smooth fast travel. Its agile performance, untroubled demeanour at high cruising speeds and utter reliability will inspire the driver with that quiet confidence which only a high class car can give.

The new Drop Head Coupé by LANCHESTER

Lovely to look at – delightful to drive

Swift modern body styling...thoughtful interior planning for roomy comfort...high speed cruising with exceptional stability...new developments in engineering design...every feature adds up to the superb achievement of the Lanchester Fourteen. It's a car you will enjoy—built in the famous Lanchester tradition.

Independent front suspension. Hydraulic telescopic shock absorbers. Complete suspension system included in the fully automatic chassis lubrication system

the lively...likeable

Lanchester
Fourteen

BY APPOINTMENT
Motor Car Manufacturers
To H M King George VI THE LANCHESTER MOTOR CO. LTD. COVENTRY

THE NEW LANCHESTER "FOURTEEN"